D1732838

Post-Revolutionary Iran

Published in cooperation with
the Center for Iranian Research and Analysis

Post-Revolutionary Iran

EDITED BY
Hooshang Amirahmadi
and Manoucher Parvin

Westview Press
BOULDER & LONDON

Westview Special Studies on the Middle East

Published in 1988 in the United States of America by Westview Press, Inc.; Frederick A. Praeger, Publisher; 5500 Central Avenue, Boulder, Colorado 80301

Library of Congress Cataloging-in-Publication Data
Post-revolutionary Iran/edited by Hooshang Amirahmadi and Manoucher Parvin.
p. cm.—(Westview special studies on the Middle East)
Includes index.
ISBN 0-8133-7227-5
1. Iran—History—1979- . 2. Iran—Economic conditions—1945- .
I. Amirahmadi, Hooshang, 1947- . II. Parvin, Manoucher.
III. Series.
DS318.8.P68 1988
955′.054—dc19 87-31700
CIP

Printed and bound in the United States of America

The paper used in this publication meets the requirements of the American National Standard for Permanence of Paper for Printed Library Materials Z39.48-1984.

10 9 8 7 6 5 4 3 2 1

Contents

PART THREE
SOCIOECONOMIC TRANSFORMATIONS AND POLICIES

PART FOUR
CONCLUSIONS

Acknowledgments

Most of the chapters in this book extensively utilize sources in native Persian language on post-revolutionary Iran. In some cases, the research is based on on-site observations. More than half of the chapters were originally presented at the 1985 conference of the Center for Iranian Research and Analysis (CIRA) held at Rutgers, The State University of New Jersey, and organized by Hooshang Amirahmadi. Others were written specifically for this volume.

The editors wish to thank those who helped in the publication of this book: Professors Donald Krueckeberg, Robert Beauregard, and Gregory Rose for reviewing certain chapters; Barbara Ellington, Christine Arden, and Paul Sprachman for reading the entire manuscript; Sonia Hamberg, Brenda Leonard, and Phyllis Blackhurst for administrative assistance; Lea Leadbeater, Samy Amer, and Zahra Beheshti for technical help; and Rahmat Tavakol, Manijeh Saba, Mahvash Saba, Sabine Malbranche, and Farhad Atash for assisting in the organization of the 1985 CIRA conference. The editors also greatly appreciate the assistance of Lynn Coffey-Edelman, who patiently typed the entire manuscript and helped in the final packaging of the book for publication.

Hooshang Amirahmadi acknowledges the financial and administrative support of the Rutgers International Programs for the 1985 CIRA conference. In this connection, special thanks are due to Dr. C. S. Whitaker, Henriette Cohen, and Connie Burke. The financial support of the Rutgers Research and Sponsored Programs in the publication of this book is also gratefully acknowledged. Manoucher Parvin acknowledges the Faculty Improvement Leave granted by the University of Akron.

The editors are also grateful to the members of CIRA for material and intellectual support of the Center's publications. CIRA is an independent, nonprofit, educational organization dedicated to generating, promoting, and publicizing scholarly research on Iran. The views expressed in the chapters that follow are those of the authors and do not reflect the views of the editors, of CIRA itself, or of those acknowledged for their help and support, including Rutgers, The State University of New Jersey.

Hooshang Amirahmadi
Manoucher Parvin

1

Introduction: From Ideology to Pragmatic Policy in Post-Revolutionary Iran

Hooshang Amirahmadi

Few revolutions have shocked the world with such intensity and created so many imponderable questions as the Iranian Revolution of 1979. The rapid speed at which the Revolution took place and its predominantly Islamic character still remain sources of mystery even to well-educated students of Iran. Equally obscure are the multiple roots of the Revolution and its largely spontaneous, but well-orchestrated, mass character. Although a growing literature has shed light on many aspects of these and other similar questions, our knowledge of the state and society in post-revolutionary Iran and the probable future direction of the Islamic Republic in matters of domestic transformations and international relations remains largely inadequate.

Aside from the scarcity of information, the major factors contributing to this problem include the conflicting policies and practices of the Islamic government and their diverse interpretations by scholars and political analysts. Although the inconsistencies in government policies are rooted in factional politics, the ongoing war with Iraq, and the unsettled state of the Revolution, disagreements among observers of Iran arise largely from ideological differences. Consequently, a generally accepted analysis of post-revolutionary Iran has not yet emerged.

The primary purpose of this book is to analyze transformations in the ideological, political, and socioeconomic structures of post-revolutionary Iran and to discuss government policies in order to shed light on the nature and direction of the state and society in the Islamic Republic. Clearly, the complexity of the issues discussed in this book as well as the ideological differences among the authors prevent a definite conclusion from emerging. In addition, the analyses are constrained by inadequate information about the inner workings of the Islamic Republic and about the many causal-consequential networks affecting post-revolutionary Iran.

Nevertheless, the chapters, most of which were written by young scholars with fresh insights and some of which are based on recent on-site research, present interesting, even controversial, conclusions. Three major themes recur throughout the chapters: (1) the enormous changes in the material and intellectual aspects of life in post-revolutionary Iran when compared to pre-revolutionary times; (2) the severe domestic and foreign-policy problems requiring immediate solutions; and (3) the gradual shift of the Islamic state from its initial ideological commitments to more pragmatic policies.

Among the many implications of these and other findings, one is crucial: The state must balance pragmatism and its initial revolutionary promises in order to maintain its stability. This may prove difficult, though not impossible, given the resource constraints, the war, the lack of a unified front for attacking the enormous socioeconomic and political problems, conflict with imperialism, and dependency on the world market. Various chapters also indicate why these and other factors are increasingly forcing the Islamic Republic to abandon its initial ideals and accept technocratic solutions to domestic and international problems.

Part One focuses on politics and ideology; the chapters in the second part provide the link between ideology and practice that is the focus of the third part. Although a single explanatory framework has not been imposed, most of the authors have adopted a critical method in an attempt to analyze carefully the successes and failures of various policies and practices. In addition, the authors have assessed the national and global factors that are influencing the behavior of the Islamic Republic and, where appropriate, the consequences that have followed.

Chapter 2, by Hamid Dabashi, concentrates on the specific conditions that led to the transformation (by the 1950s) from Islam as a religion to Islam as a largely secular ideology. The factor most responsible for this transformation was the breakdown of the balance between politics and ethics in Muslim communities, largely as a result of Western penetration. The writings of Jalal Al-i Ahmad, 'Ali Shari'ati, and Murtada Mutahhari as the chief architects of the "Islamic Ideology" in Iran are analyzed to reveal the roots of the new ideology. Although Ayatollah Khomeini was not a contributor to the "Islamic Ideology," the concept has been institutionalized by the Islamic Republic along with *Husayniyah Irshad* and the *Mujahidiyn-e Khalq*. Dabashi concludes by assessing the perils and promises of this new ideology, arguing that the novelty is torn by inherent contradictions between faith and ideology. While the transformation of Islam into an ideology has been noted by others as well, Dabashi's argument is uniquely revealing; it also provides a good account of "Islamic Ideology" up to and through the Revolution.

Ideological transformation was by no means a unique experience of Islam, as indicated in Chapter 3 by Val Moghadam, who focuses on the ideology and practices of the Iranian Left. Specifically, she offers a historical/critical analysis of the Left's acceptance and application of dependency theory—that is, of Third Worldism as an ideological/practical guide, particularly during and after the Revolution of 1979. A major consequence was the subordination of democratic and socialist aims to anti-imperialist politics. Moghadam concludes that this strategy, coupled with inappropriate tactics and other unfavorable factors, led to the defeat of the Left. Among other causes, she lists the Left's lack of theoretical preparedness to deal with complex revolutionary issues, the Shah's repression, uneven socioeconomic development in Iran, the Left's failure to advance an alternative to the Islamic Republic's populism, and the lack of unity among the many small Left groups.

Despite the Left's relative neglect of democracy as an important political demand, different sectors of the society continued to struggle for its realization. In Chapter 4, Assef Bayat examines the relationship between labor movements, democracy, and politics in post-revolutionary Iran. He argues that, through the organization of Workers' Councils, or *Shurahs*, the Iranian workers were able to provide conditions conducive to the growth of a workplace democracy, which had been completely absent under the Shah. Yet, owing to internal contradictions arising from the conflict between the short- and long-term interests of the councils on the one hand and the state's repression on the other, the *Shurahs* did not survive long enough either to become institutionalized or to create economic democracy. As a result of this failure, the *Shurahs* were further unable to influence the consolidation of political democracy in the country. Bayat concludes that grass-roots organizations are essential for the democratization of Iranian society.

The politics of the Islamic Republic are further examined in Chapter 5 by Nader Entessar, who focuses on the role of the armed forces in pre- and post-revolutionary Iran, including the Islamic Revolutionary Guards Corps (IRGC). The Imperial Army, he asserts, played two major functions, both of which delegitimized it in the eyes of an absolute majority of Iranians: to secure the Shah's authoritarian rule, and to safeguard the Gulf region for the United States. Coupled with lack of leadership within its ranks and its dependency on the United States, the Imperial Army's illegitimacy led to its speedy disintegration during the revolution. The Islamic Republic, argues Entessar, quickly moved to transform the Iranian armed forces from a dependent military to a citizen army by purging high-ranking Imperial officers and by recruiting from the religious population. In the process, the new armed forces became Islamicized and politicized to a degree unprecedented in the contemporary history of Iran. Entessar details these developments along with his discussion of the creation of the IRGC as a countervailing force. He concludes that the Islamic Republic has been successful in creating a remarkably able and efficient armed forces capable of containing both internal uprisings and external challenges to the Republic.

The part of the book devoted to politics and ideology ends with Chapter 6 by Annabelle Sreberny-Mohammadi and Ali Mohammadi, who move us from domestic to international politics. The authors examine a number of political cartoons from issues of *Imam* magazine throughout the period 1980–1984 to indicate both the Islamic Republic's image of the outside world and its foreign policy. The magazine is published by the embassy of the Islamic Republic in London and is aimed at a foreign audience. It is designed to neutralize what the Republic considers the "news imperialism" of the Zionist-dominated mass-media machinery of the West. The cartoons are as offensive as they are defensive and reactive. According to the authors, they illustrate the nonaligned foreign policy of the Islamic Republic and its bipolarized image of a world dominated by superpowers. The United States and Zionism are closely identified with one another and are portrayed as the most vicious of all earthly satanic forces. To the educated Western audience, argue Sreberny-Mohammadi and Mohammadi, most of the cartoons appear one-sided, negative, and conspiracy based; in addition, they fail to convey a meaningful understanding of international events and relations. On the contrary, their real effect is to cut off crosscultural communication.

The second part of the book, which is concerned with the implementation of Islamic ideology, links the first part on politics and ideology to the third part on policies, international relations, and socioeconomic transformations. In Chapter 7, Sohrab Behdad examines the factional politics surrounding national-development planning in the context of an Islamic economic model and gives an outline of the processes that led to the formulation of the First Islamic Plan. He argues that, while such an economic system is compatible with the working of capitalism, the Iranian conception of it originated with Islamic radicals and tends to be populist in its orientation. This tendency, however, is vehemently opposed by many Grand Ayatollahs who fear that national-development planning might lead to an impermissible extension of the state into the private sector. In the face of growing socioeconomic problems, the war, and the declining oil revenues, the two tendencies have resulted in a pragmatic solution that prescribes a mixed planned economy and belittles Islamic economics. Behdad asserts, however, that as the convergence is far from complete, little planning might be expected for some years to come.

Chapter 8, by Hooshang Amirahmadi, further investigates the unsettled state of debate on a development strategy in the Islamic Republic. After documenting the extent and type of war damage, Amirahmadi evaluates the reconstruction strategy and activities of the government. His analysis reveals the existence of extensive human, material, physical, and financial damage and, in so doing, underscores the need for an immediate and comprehensive reconstruction plan. Amirahmadi argues that the reconstruction activities of the Islamic government focus primarily on private housing and infrastructure, lack clear direction, and are largely unplanned. These inadequacies are rooted mainly in the war itself and in disunity of perspective among Islamic policy-makers regarding a suitable development and reconstruction strategy. The two dominant and opposite ideological tendencies are identified as "Islamic traditionalist" and "Islamic modernist." Whereas the first advocates large-scale government intervention and planning, the second emphasizes the role of the individual and comes close to the position of nineteenth-century liberalism. Nevertheless, in the face of growing problems of various types and magnitudes, the two ideological positions are converging in the direction of the more pragmatic/technocratic tendency.[1] Amirahmadi advances a number of critical ideas to be incorporated into a self-reliant reconstruction strategy; he concludes, however, that so long as the war continues, recent attempts to formulate a suitable unified strategy, even if successful, would not improve the quality of reconstruction activities in the Islamic Republic of Iran.

In the third part, the contributors focus on the policies, socioeconomic transformations, and international relations of the Islamic Republic, themes introduced in previous chapters. In Chapter 9, Akbar Aghajanian presents an overview of social and legal changes in the Islamic Republic and examines the consequences of such changes, along with the impact of the war with Iraq, on population dynamics in Iran. His analysis reveals an increase in divorce, a decline in actual age of marriage, an upsurge in polygamy cases, and an increasing birth rate. The combined effect of these trends has been a high rate of population growth. If the current official ban on family planning continues, the population growth rate will lead to an even larger labor force and a sharper reduction in family income. In the face of declining oil revenues and a faltering war economy, the consequences of these trends might prove devastating.[2]

The themes of change and policy are also the focus of Chapter 10, by Manoucher Parvin and Majid Taghavi. The authors offer a broad comparison of land reform programs (LRPs) under both the monarchy and the Islamic Republic, and discuss their impact on production and productivity in agriculture. The Shah's LRPs, they maintain, aimed at the extension of dependent capitalism into rural areas and at its expansion in urban centers through large-scale industrialization. As a consequence, subsistence agriculture was undermined, and tillers became wage earners in urban industries. In the early years of the Islamic Republic, all attempts to reform land tenure were branded as non-Islamic and were blocked by the Council of Guardians. The indecisiveness in this area prevented the state from achieving its goal of agricultural self-sufficiency. Since 1985, however, a number of LRPs have been enacted in the Islamic Republic to correct such deficiencies as low productivity and ownership disputes, which are crippling agriculture in the country.

In Chapter 11, Michael Renner points out the international factors influencing domestic policies and changes. Specifically, he investigates the major determinants of the Islamic Republic's oil policies and indicates the nature and extent of its dependency on the world market. Among the issues discussed are the goals of the 1979 Revolution, certain aspects of macroeconomics including foreign trade and balance of payments, the war with Iraq, the structural changes in the world oil market, and the Islamic Republic's relations with OPEC and Saudi Arabia. Renner concludes that because the Islamic Republic has failed both to stimulate nonoil exports and to diversify the economy, it continues to depend on oil and, hence, on the world economy. This dependency has been exacerbated by the war with Iraq and the collapse of world oil prices beginning in 1986. Under pressure from these and other factors (including the growing domestic problems), the Islamic Republic has gradually developed a more pragmatic oil policy.

In Chapter 12, Mehrdad Valibeigi sheds additional light on the international relations of the Islamic Republic. The author gives an overview of the trade relations between Iran and the United States, and discusses the impact of the hostage crisis and the subsequent freezing of Iranian assets by the Carter administration. He argues that the financial strains caused by the Iran-Iraq war and the technical dependency of Iran's industries and military on U.S. markets are major factors compelling the Islamic Republic to continue trading with the United States despite apparent hostilities between the two countries. The United States, he maintains, has encouraged such relations because of its strategic interests in the region, and because it continues to consider Iran a regional power as well as an anti-Soviet state. The recent Irangate controversy is a vivid illustration of Valibeigi's conclusion that the mutual desire for continued economic relations will persist.

In the concluding chapter, Hooshang Amirahmadi extends the analyses of the book by bringing the many disparate facts and ideas about the Iranian Revolution, as well as the middle-class revolutions elsewhere in the Third World, into a single comprehensive/comparative framework. In attempting to explore the causal-consequential networks responsible for the roots of these revolutions and their characters, perils, promises, achievements, shortcomings, and constraints, he crosses disciplinary and ideological boundaries and identifies a host of national and international factors. He also insists that, for a deeper understanding, we must think about and research post-revolution Iran in comparative terms, along empirical/historical lines, and in the context of the contradictions between imperialism and the Third World revolutions. He concludes that, given the present international arrangements and domestic politics in the Third World, the middle class revolutions have no real chance to realize their utopia in the form of a middle class post-revolutionary society.

In sum, post-revolutionary Iran has undergone significant socioeconomic, political, and ideological transformations with legal, material, intellectual, and institutional consequences. Many pre-revolutionary organizations, ways of life and of thinking, productive factors, and human relations have changed; some, in fact, have been totally eradicated and replaced by wholly new ones. Although the government has taken an active role in reshaping the society and the state in an Islamic image, its policies have been limited by such national and international factors as the dynamics of the Revolution itself, the war, the politics of opposition, the leadership's inability to formulate a coherent development strategy, and imperialistic interventions. In most cases, the desired policies had to be relinquished or adapted only after significant modifications. Post-revolutionary Iran is thus neither a wholly Islamic community nor a society with predominantly secular values. Rather, it is a blend of the two.

The constraints, in combination with the factional infighting, have also resulted in conflicting pronouncements and policies on the part of the state.

As a result, prediction of the state's future direction has become most difficult, if not impossible. However, a number of developments at the national and international levels indicate that the Islamic government is moving away from its initial ideological commitments toward a more pragmatic "quick fix" approach to the enormous problems of the country. Irangate and the current crisis in management-type state budgeting are two consequences of the new directions being taken. A reasonable answer to the question of whether this pragmatism will be reversed or consolidated has to await two important developments in the Islamic Republic: termination of the war, and the resolution of factional politics. The enormous energy and intelligence that a lasting peace would generate could put a temporary end to ideological disputes and strengthen the position of the technocratic elements within the government. In the meantime, however, the Islamic Republic must continue its struggle against the tension between ideology and pragmatism.

Notes

1. Factionalism within the Central Council of the Islamic Republican party (CCIRP) was the main reason for its eventual dissolution. The action is intended to mitigate factional infighting and to facilitate the state's pragmatic direction.

2. Since this chapter was written, the 1986 national census has been completed. Although details have not yet been made public, preliminary results indicate an annual population growth rate of 3.57 percent per year over the 1976–1986 period, with poorer regions growing at even higher rates. In 1986, about 78 percent of the country's population of 48,181,463 were six years and over; and, of these, only 28.5 percent were employed and 62 percent were illiterate.

PART ONE

Politics and Ideology

2

"Islamic Ideology": The Perils and Promises of a Neologism

Hamid Dabashi

There is, however, another religion and that is ideology.

—'Ali Shari'ati

Introduction

The Islamic Revolution in Iran is the most recent institutional expression of that massive transformative movement through which Islam has been redefined from a universal religion to a political ideology with universal claims. The key expression that captures this metamorphosis is *Islamic ideology*. To be sure, this ideology, in all its political and revolutionary dimensions, is not a uniquely Iranian or Shi'ite phenomenon. The conceptual and semantic roots of the metamorphosis are already present in the work of such architects of the revolutionary pan-Islamism as Jamal al-Din al-Afghani (1838–1897), Muhammad 'Abduh (1849–1905), Rashid Rida (1865–1935), and Abd al-Hakim Khalifah. The latter even published a book entitled *Islamic Ideology*.[1]

The primary and most articulate proponent of this concept in Persian (*ideologi-i Islami*) was 'Ali Shari'ati (1933–1977). The Iranian roots of the concept in modern history, however, go back to Jalal Al-i Ahmad (1923–1969). Murtada Mutahhari (1920–1979), too, found the concept quite useful and sought to elaborate it further. The terms has also been widely used in the literature of Mujahidin-i Khalq organization. But the official usage has been nowhere more widespread than in the organs of the Islamic Republic of Iran itself. In fact, among both the established revolutionary forces and those opposing the Islamic Republic, the term *Islamic ideology* has been so widely used that no one stops to question its conceptual legitimacy.

The massive redefinition of Islam from a religion promising other-worldly salvation to an ideology harboring this-worldly utopia is perhaps the single most important feature of Muslim collective consciousness in modern times. The following is an attempt to examine the specific mechanism and dynamism of this revolutionary transformation of a basically metaphysical discourse into a patently political semantic. The term *Islamic ideology* represents a revolution in both Islamic thought and action, and is undoubtedly a neologism. It does not exist in any classical Islamic text or context. The term has been widely circulated only since the turn of the century. Most recently, it was applied to the ideological foundation of the Islamic Revolution in Iran.

A few conceptual clarifications are necessary at the outset. *Islam* and all its derivatives refer to the body of doctrinal beliefs that emanates from the Quran and its ancillary human counterpart, the prophetic (and, for the Shi'ites, the Imamite) traditions. This doctrinal apparatus constitutes the foundations of both the Islamic culture and civilization. As such, Islam postulates an atemporal frame of metahistorical reference. Human experience in the Islamic context begins in pre-eternity (*azal*) and leads to post-eternity (*abad*). *Ideology* and all its derivatives refer to a set of interrelated conceptions and notions of political commitment and mobilizations that seek to (1) provide an interpretation of the existing relations of power and (2) chart the course of actions to alter them. At this conceptual level, then, the term *ideology* also encompasses *utopia*, defined by Karl Mannheim[2] as an intellectual commitment to negate and alter existing conditions.

In its revolutionary posture, as during the 1979 Revolution, the *Islamic ideology* was utopian. It emerged not as the dominant ideology of the dominant class but as the utopian aspiration of a revolutionary movement. Through this ideology, contemporary realities were seen as indications of an inevitable cataclysm. The *Islamic* aspect of this ideology was construed in patently religious symbols that were employed in its constructions of "reality." But in the course of the revolutionary movement, and as the Islamic aspect of the uprising gradually assumed an upper hand, the utopian design of a better future became the ideological posture of an existing condition.

Roots of the Neologism

The term *Islamic ideology* conceals more of its conceptual origin than it reveals of its political agenda. In its concealment, the term embodies the most integral self-contradiction animating the cultural revolution that Islam is now experiencing. The political agenda it reveals shall extend beyond one specific revolutionary event, such as the 1979 episode in Iran.

Though conceptually a neologism, the Islamic ideology is the end result of forces that have been operative at least since the turn of the century. A massive and multivariate exposure to what Marshall Hodgson called "the great Western transmutation" brought to the Muslims' collective consciousness selective elements from the Western ideological experience, in contradistinction to the equally selective reminiscences from their own past.

The Islamic ideology was created partly in response to the accusation that Islam itself, being "the opium of the masses" as well as a "false consciousness," systematized the dominant ideas.[3] In Iran the Islamic view of Marxism has superseded the Marxist understanding of Islam. Ironically, the "ruling intellectual force"[4] of pre-revolutionary Iran was not the prerogative of "the ruling material forces of society."[5] Quite to the contrary, it came from the most unproductive force of society: the alienated intelligentsia. The Islamic ideology was in fact (or at least in part) an Islamic response, however convoluted, to the dominant secular ideas of pre-revolutionary Iran.

The age of the Islamic ideology is predicated on a long process of disruption of the balance between the Islamic stipulations of ethics and politics. This process is a universal one, but for Islam it has been the result of a combination of external factors and internal tendencies. A widespread political subjugation to alien forces, a vast hegemonic ascendancy of diverse ideological outbursts from the European age of revolution, and a bewildered Muslim intellectual elite in search of some sense of revolutionary identity are among the constituent forces that have precipitated the transformation of the Islamic culture, following that of the West.

The disintegration of the balance between Islamic piety and Muslim communal life was the most important outcome of this transmutation. Being a Muslim increasingly became a matter of private piety. Historically valid social and political institutions began to lose their foundations of legitimacy. New and more powerful doctrines of institutional legitimation began to restructure the Islamic culture and character.

Islamic ethics and politics became bifurcated, and Muslims became secluded in their private pieties. The newly created political and economic problems persisted and intensified. At this point, the spirit of Islamic politics, segregated from its ethical counterbalance, assumed specific doctrinal ends that were of alien origin. The Islamic encounter with the West, particularly with its ancillary exaltation of European ideological movements, introduced political concerns that were peculiarly occidental and of no immediate relevance to Muslim societies. Such alien conceptions and concerns as church-state relations, the class struggle, capitalism, socialism, imperialism, dialectic materialism, liberalism, democracy, nationalism, equality, parliamentarianism, and colonialism abruptly imposed themselves on the bewildered and passive-aggressive mind of the Muslim intelligentsia. These concerns, thus implanted in Islamic soil, could not but engender two concomitant ideological movements: (1) the extension of European political doctrines that best articulated the above concerns in Islamic societies and, hence, constituted the origin of similar conceptions and concerns in the Muslim world; or (2) the enunciation of a mixture of such alien conceptions and concerns with patently Islamic symbols as those articulated by al-Afghani, 'Abduh, Rida, and Shari'ati.

Although these two ideological movements in the Islamic world were almost concomitant, the former—the patently "secular" ideologies—proved to be less successful than the latter. The political and tactical failures of the secular ideologies ultimately lent further legitimacy to ideological movements in Islamic disguise. The most obvious and immediate diagnosis of this failure of secular ideologies concerns their inability to engender and validate enough legitimating common symbols among their purported constituencies to move and mobilize those constituencies toward a set of fabricated goals. But those ideological movements that dressed up the political concerns of the patently Western origin with the traditional symbolics of the Islamic posture proved to be infinitely more successful. It is within this latter disposition that the Islamic ideology found its proper context. In order to legitimate its attempted appropriation of power, the mixture of Western political concerns and common Islamic symbols created its own doctrinal basis: the Islamic ideology.

Thus, the Islamic ideology is the logical, and perhaps inevitable, outcome of (1) a deep and pervasive segregation of Islamic ethics and politics; (2) the creation and continuity of an independent and unbalanced Islamic body politic; (3) a superimposition of Western ideological concerns on a susceptible and autonomous Islamic body politic; and, finally, (4) the need for this combination of Islamic political and Western ideological concerns to formulate a doctrinal legitimacy.

Architects of the Islamic Ideology in Iran

The doctrinal and political legitimacy of the Islamic Revolution in Iran was based on at least three organically different, yet organizationally interrelated, planes: (1) patently secular ideologies, (2) the Islamic ideology, and (3) the *welayat-i faqih* (the guardianship of jurisconsult). The last element, primarily an articulation of Ayatollah Khomeini (b. 1902), is based on some essential tendencies in Shi'ite juridical history. (The specific nature and organization of this doctrinal force is a separate question and cannot be dealt with here.) The first element, the secular ideologies, is equally important and should be carefully examined. But our main concern here is with the major components of the Islamic ideology.

One of the principal figures who articulated the shift from the secular to the Islamic symbolic context is Jalal Al-i Ahmad, who began his political activity as a deeply religious man. His religious devotion had a lasting effect on his entire life, particularly on his early political consciousness. From this background he became attracted to two major secular, and patently anticlerical, movements: nationalism and socialism. The first attraction was reflected both in Al-i Ahmad's interest in the ideas of Ahmad Kasravi (d. 1946) and in his deeply nationalist orientation. Nationalism, however, proved to be only a stepping-stone (perhaps with some lasting effect) to the next phase of Al-i Ahmad's political engagement—namely, socialism, which was institutionalized in the Tudeh party, under the ideological banner of which Al-i Ahmad pursued his political concerns. Al-i Ahmad's disenchantment with the Tudeh party, whether merely ideological in nature or based on a deeper metaphysical reorientation, paved the way to his last position on matters of politics. *Gharb-Zadigi* ("Westoxication"), a product of this period, was the most articulate formulation of the Islamic ideology short of coining this conceptual category.[6]

Having deeply experienced the fundamental problems of Western secular ideologies in mobilizing a Muslim nation for political purposes, Al-i Ahmad tried to demonstrate how the same political ends could be formulated and achieved by utilizing the Islamic sources of revolutionary symbols. He recognized that the primary task of a revolutionary ideology was to communicate its political concerns to its constituency. Toward that end, the most important element is the orchestration of a set of common symbols (i.e., indications of collective mythologies), that encompass the messenger, the message, and those who are addressed. Socialism, perhaps even more than nationalism, drew on symbols that were plainly European (or, more precisely, eighteenth- and nineteenth-century French) in origin: class struggle, proletariat, bourgeoisie, capitalism, and so on. For Muslims, however, these were alien ideological categories, incapable of striking a chord in the minds and souls of their recipients. But if rebellion was the purpose, there was a more immediately accessible channel of communication: the Shi'ite collective memory. In this connection, the supreme symbols of suffering, injustice, perseverance, rebellion, and the final establishment of the "peace of the rightly guided," constituted the marrow of public piety. Here was a vast ocean of indigenous collective symbols, neglected almost to the point of nullity, and the secular ideologues had been importing nearly meaningless slogans.

Gharb-Zadigi represents a turning point in Iranian political culture. Though primarily a scathing attack against the westernization of Iranian culture, the book also has a hidden agenda: a return to common (i.e., Islamic) thought. It begins with a diagnosis of a "disease" called "Westoxication" and concludes with references to Albert Camus's *The Plague*, Eugene Ionesco's *Rhinoceros*, and Ingmar Bergman's *The Seventh Seal*; yet the very last words are from the Quran (LIV:1) "The hour drew nigh and the moon was rent in twain."

In a revealing misreading of Ingmar Bergman's film, in which the central figure of "death" is confused with "Satan," Al-i Ahmad sees himself (along with Albert Camus, Eugene Ionesco, and Ingmar Bergman) as a visionary of the coming apocalypse. the sign of the apocalypse, in Al-i Ahmad's reading, was "the machine." Rejecting the imported Western symbols which could best be described as identified with the "machine," he put forth his argument for a complete reversal of the common "Islamic" frame of reference and, hence, for his concluding return to the Quran. But this return was intended for a specific purpose—politics. As "Westoxication" was a by-product of political hegemony, its rejection was the manifesto of a political program—the Islamic ideology.

Al-i Ahmad, however, remained deeply influenced by his years as an active member of the Tudeh party. This influence resulted in a rather cursory familiarity with, and thus utilization of, Shi'ite symbols. *Gharb-Zadigi*, after *Khasi dar Miqat* ("Lost in the Crowd"), perhaps the most religiously charged book written by Al-i Ahmad, is poorly informed by religious sources. Whether consciously or unconsciously, Al-i Ahmad either suppressed his religious knowledge or was insufficiently informed. Having been deeply moved by the

Tudeh party (i.e., by the institutional expression of the most blatantly secular movement of his time), he probably could not utilize all that was at his disposal from Islam to bid for the Islamic ideology.

That task remained for 'Ali Shari'ati, the most articulate proponent of the Islamic ideology. Shari'ati's formulation is a comprehensive one that, among other things, sought to equate specific Quranic terms with "ideology." *Al-millah*, the Quranic term for "people" or "nation," came closest in meaning to "ideology," he believed; it expressed the same "common school of all prophets."[7] "The Book" (i.e., the Quran) could also be taken for the Islamic ideology.[8] But equally applicable are the highest symbols of authority in Islam: faith (*al-din*), prophethood (*nubuwwah*), and messengership (*risalah*).[9]

Shari'ati wished to distinguish between *maktab* ("school") and ideology. The former refers to the school of philosophy articulated by al-Farabi or Ibn Sina,[10] but the latter encompasses a doctrinal movement. "Muhammad establishes an ideology," claimed Shari'ati.[11] This ideology, if propagated, would bring forth revolutionary figures such as 'Ali, Husayn, and Abu Dhar.[12] Here, *maktab* engages the mind, whereas ideology directs the action.[13]

Through a series of dichotomous statements comparing and contrasting "science and philosophy" with "ideology," Shari'ati articulated what he meant by the Islamic ideology: Philosophy and science are concerned with "phenomenology," whereas ideology evaluates what is right and what is wrong. Philosophy and science do not advance further than "understanding"; ideology "leads." Philosophy and science justify "the values"; ideology annihilates and creates values. Philosophy and science "describe and discover you"; ideology "creates you." Philosophy and science bring forth philosophers and scientists; ideology brings froth "revolutionary intellectuals."[14]

After contrasting the active ideology with the passive knowledge, Shari'ati articulated a series of conceptual categories that constitute the "common language" (*zaban-i mushtarak*) of Islam and ideology: "Armed struggle" is *jihad*; "the people" are *nas*; collective ownership is divine ownership; "leadership" is *imamah*; the demeaning life of the bourgeoisie is this-worldliness; and "the government of the people" is *ijma'*.[15]

Through a dual metamorphosis of conceptual and existential identity, socialist ideology for Shari'ati became ideology *par excellence*, and Islam became the supreme ideology. Thus, Islam is socialism, and both converge in ideology—or, more precisely, in the Islamic ideology.

Shari'ati's ideological semantic, which is almost exclusively revolutionary Marxist in nature, encompasses message, commitment, responsibility, armed struggle, the masses, the elimination of classes, man as the god over nature, elimination of private ownership, collective ownership, alienation, the low bourgeois life, economics as the foundation of ethics and spirituality, and classless society.[16] Each of these ideological categories, according to Shari'ati, have their precise equivalent in Islam.[17] Thus Islam is an ideology; it is the semblance of Marxist ideology. Muslim intellectuals need not adopt the alien doctrine of an atheist orientation, which creates the discomfort of misplaced piety.

The Islamic ideology is both revolutionary *and* Islamic. This existential conjunction closely articulates the collective therapy of "getting even with the hegemonic West," on both the material and the intellectual fronts. Materially, the quasi-colonial rule of the native dictator—"the puppet of imperialism"—will be challenged and overcome, thus reflecting a rebellious rejection of the economically and politically domineering West. Intellectually, a metamorphosis of Islam into the most "scientifically based" ideology would rob the occident of its crowning achievement in its age of enlightenment. Just as Marx turned Hegel's dialectics upside down and called them materialist dialectics, so Shari'ati turned Islam upside down and called it the Islamic ideology.

Whereas Al-i Ahmad envisioned the Islamic ideology as a rebellion against the West and Shari'ati articulated it in comprehensive political terms, Mutahhari tried to extend it to the very heart of Islamic jurisprudence and philosophy so as to give it an intellectual legitimacy. Nothing less than the Shari'ah, Mutahhari argued, was the Islamic ideology.[18]

Mutahhari's definition of ideology reflects his attempt to mobilize public pieties:

> What will give unity, direction, and shared aspirations to the man of today, and *a fortiori* to the man of tomorrow, what will serve as his touchstone of good and evil, of musts and must nots, is an elective conscious, inspirational philosophy of life armed with logic—in other words, a comprehensive, perfect ideology.[19]

A comprehensive and perfect ideology—namely, the Islamic ideology—is thus the only prelude to a total and perfect society. Mutahhari posited the totalitarian adoption of this ideology (i.e., the intellectual imagining of the utopia to come) in direct response to the other one, which was secular and imported: Marxism. His dual purpose was to attack and impede all intellectual manifestations of the total secular ideology, and to propagate the total Islamic ideology. His *'Ilal-i Girayish bi Maddigari* ("The Causes of Attraction to Materialism")[20] as well as his substantive notations to 'Allamah Sayyid Muhammad Hussayn Tabataba'i's *Usul-i Falsafah wa Rawish-i Realism* ("The Principles of Philosophy and the Realistic Method") were directed specifically against the total secular ideology at both its political (Marxist) and philosophical (materialist) levels.[21] The formulation of the total Islamic ideology was concomitant with Mutahhari's rejection of any mode of secular ideology.

Mutahhari's main objective was to give the Islamic ideology a philosophical (i.e., rational) grounding; but it is in precisely this respect that he differed from Shari'ati. By classifying human actions as "pleasure-oriented" and "goal-oriented," Mutahhari argued that insufficiency of reason directs the course of human conduct.[22] Ideology, he maintained, is the suprarational legitimacy of "a comprehensive, harmonious, and concrete design whose central object is to perfect man and secure universal happiness."[23] This grand design is ideology. But there are two types of ideologies:

> human and corporate: human ideologies are addressed to the human species, not to some special nationality, race or class, and have for their motive the salvation of the whole human . . . species. Corporate ideologies (on the other hand) are addressed to a certain group, class or stratum and have for their motive the liberation, or the hegemony, of that group.[24] . . . Beyond all doubt, Islamic ideology is human and arises from the primordial nature of man.[25]

By directing the Islamic ideology to reflect on three subjects that are Quranically stipulated as "useful and fruitful to reflection upon"[26] (i.e., "the nature," "the history," and "the inner being of man"),[27] Mutahhari gave the doctrine its most elaborate philosophical and theological groundings.[28]

By addressing, and further legitimating, the neologism of the Islamic ideology in a juridical and philosophical language, Mutahhari, who was significantly more erudite than either Shari'ati or Al-i Ahmad in his understanding of the traditional Islamic sciences, engineered the intellectual foundation of the concept into the very germane conceptual apparatus of Islamic thought. His was by far the most elaborate doctrinal systematization of the Islamic ideology. Yet, he would probably never had used the term if Shari'ati had not demonstrated its political potential, or if Al-i Ahmad had not provided for its logistic necessity.

Islamic Ideology Institutionalized

The conceptual elaboration and institutional propagation of the Islamic ideology were influenced by a number of ad hoc organizations. *Anjuman-i Mahanih-yi Dini* ("Monthly Religious Society"), a short-lived institution led by Mutahhari, was perhaps one of the most influential of these organizations.[29] From 1960 to 1963, the society actively expounded its ideas through its organ, *Guftar-i Mah*. Other principal figures associated with the Islamic Revolution, such as Muhammad Ibrahim Ayati and Sayyid Muhammad Beheshti, were also active in this organization.

Perhaps the most successful institutional expression of the Islamic ideology was the Husayniyah Irshad. A key individual in this organization was 'Ali Shari'ati. Established in 1965, Husayniyah Irshad was the institutional extension and elaboration of the Monthly Religious Society. Although the organization ostensibly revolved around *Husayniyah* (in that it was devoted to the commemoration of Husayn, the martyred third Imam of the Shi'ites), the adjective *Irshad* ("guidance") reflected its propagandistic purpose.

As one of the primary architects of Husayniyah Irshad, Mutahhari clearly articulated the purpose of this organization:

> The Husayniyah Irshad . . . knows its task to be to introduce *Islamic ideology* (to the youth) such as it is. This institution deems it sufficient to unveil the beautiful face of the beloved martyr of Islam (Imam Husayn) in order to transform the love-seekers into restless lovers.[30]

In addition to these two ad hoc organizations, mosques (the established institutions of public sermons for religious ceremonies, especially in the three months of Muharram, Safar, and Ramadan) gave momentum to the revolutionary appeal of the Islamic ideology. The prestige and fame of the organizers of these institutions encouraged the religious community to respond favorably to the call for an Islamic ideology. The intellectual dimensions of this ideology were elaborated in other institutional settings, including the department of theology at Tehran University (where Mutahhari taught) and the Madrasah-yi Fayziyyah (theological school) at Qum. Mutahhari also held extensive dialogues with Western-educated professors and students from Tehran University at his residence in Tehran.[31]

The most militant organization to proclaim successfully the institutional legitimacy of the Islamic ideology was the guerrilla movement of the Mujahidiyn-i Khalq organization. Its militancy demonstrated the most essential component of the Islamic ideology—physical force. This force took the form of massive mobilization, along with the legitimate (i.e., considered to be legitimate) use of violence.

From the ideal to the real, the Islamic Republic and the Islamic Republic party are the highest institutional achievements of the Islamic ideology. Indeed, the former is the Islamic ideology incarnate, wherein the perils and promises of the neologism have assumed concrete and dogmatic expressions. In its passage from mobilization to establishment, the Islamic ideology now faces the paradox implicit in its very inception. The dialectic of contradictions that animated the Islamic ideology engenders, as perhaps it must, the newest phase of its self-denial.

Concluding Remarks

Faith and ideology, one sacred and the other secular, are associated with completely separate sets of symbols, which are organized in such a way as to move their constituencies to active obedience. Indeed, the two sets of symbols are essentially contradictory. The legitimating symbols of both the organization of society and the specific direction of social action, faith, and ideology are founded on a revelatory language and a rationalizing semantic, respectively. Faith, as a metaphysical expression of authority, is revealed; ideology, as a politicizing doctrine of rebellion, is rationally derived. If faith, as Marx argued, is a superstructural ideologization of the existing material conditions, then ideology, in its utopian or revolutionary form, is indoctrination by some remote abstraction that necessitates a complete reversal of the status quo. Labeling faith as the "conservative or reactionary ideology" and the diverse doctrines of rebellion as elements of the "revolutionary progressive ideology" does not alter this dichotomy. This manifesto can perhaps move and mobilize, but it fails to separate the two claims to total obedience. The dual claims draw on their respective motifs of command and obedience—two separate sets of motifs that, in essence, are contradictory and mutually exclusive.

The contradiction between faith and ideology is at the root of the current Muslim predicament; the *Islamic ideology* is its symptom. The two claims to truth defy each other, and the attempt to strike a balance between them shall always be subject to a centrifugal disintegration. The defiance of ideology in sanctioning the exclusive claim of Islam to truth is reciprocated by the resistance of *Islam* against being metamorphosed into a false consciousness.

As the faith of a triumphant culture, Islam cannot bear to be denigrated to a state of intellectual or political nullity. The Islamic ideology is *ressentiment* expressed positively: Islam is the best ideology. Islamic triumphalism, one last victory over the "great Satan" at all costs, is *ressentiment* expressed negationally. Both the Islamic ideology and triumphalism are bifocal expressions of one condition: The West is mightier than Islam. In this equation, "the West" usually contracts the sacred into the secular, whereas "Islam" does precisely the opposite. The West is thus, in the Muslim collective consciousness, the mighty technology of a world without God, and Islam is the besieged and superseded explication of a metaphysical claim to truth.

The tense dichotomy of Islam and the West encompasses yet another duality that is equally significant in shaping the political posture of the Islamic ideology. Exposed to Western imperial power, Muslim society tolerated the alien hegemony of a superpower whose strength was beyond its comprehension. When it tried to expel the alien force through its own secular ideologies, the tormented Muslim collective consciousness plunged even more deeply into the unknown Western world. Fear of the unknown, doubly intensified through compelling material and ideological forces, became intolerable. Relapse into the familiar is always the nearest way out. The messianic movements of the Mahdi in Sudan and the Bab in Iran, as well as the puritanical reversal of the Wahabi movement, are examples of this cultural reformulation of the familiar. But a confrontation between the foreign and new, on the one hand, and a metamorphosis of the old and familiar, on the other, was logically possible as well. The Islamic ideology was the realization of this possibility.

The Islamic ideology, as an extension that remains always distant from Islam itself, is the last vestige of an exhausted and tormented order of sacred symbols. This order, in its present form, extends the pale shadows of a forgotten truth to its outer limits. On these limits, the incessant rationalism of this order places a strong foot forward and proclaims: "Here I stand." The commanding presence of that forgotten truth, however, once animated the material expression of a vast civilization and a thriving culture; now it can only haunt the dreams of a disillusioned mass. That the belated age of ideology has caught up with Islam is no accident, nor it is a chronological discrepancy. Al-Afghani, "the Islamic revivalist," had wished for it quite early in the modern Islamic history: "I cannot keep from hoping that Muhammadan society will succeed someday in breaking its bonds and marching resolutely in the path of civilization after the manner of Western society."[32] That manner has materialized now, almost completely; it is not, nor could it be, a replica of the original model. Distorted and fragmented pictures, almost unrecognizable semblances, of socialism, nationalism, or parliamentarianism are matched by the revolutionary claims and promises of the Islamic ideology. The synergetic coefficiency of the *Islamic* and the *ideology* has been tested in a successful revolution; its endurance as a cultural motif is a different matter.

But for now the Islamic ideology is prototypically doing for Islam what liberation theology has done for the West; both entail a sort of collective therapy. The therapy rests on the paradox best captured by Soren Kierkegaard, the individual dialectician: "They have changed Christianity and have made it too much of a *consolation*, and forgotten that it is a *demand* upon man."

Notes

1. A. H. Khalifah, *Islamic Ideology* (Lahore, 1953).
2. K. Mannheim, *Ideology and Utopia: An Introduction to the Sociology of Knowledge* (New York, 1936), p. 40.
3. K. Marx and F. Engels, *German Ideology* (New York: International Publishers, 1965), p. 61.
4. Ibid.
5. Ibid.
6. Jalal Al-i Ahmad, *Gharb-Zadigi* [Westoxication] (Tehran, 1341 [1962]).
7. 'Ali Shari'ati, *Shi'ah* [Shi'ism] (Tehran: Husayniyah-i Irshad, 1357 [1978]), p. 91.
8. Ibid.
9. Ibid.
10. Ibid.
11. Ibid.
12. Ibid.
13. Ibid.
14. Ibid., pp. 93–94.
15. Ibid, pp. 95–97.
16. Ibid.
17. Ibid.
18. M. Mutahhari, *Fundamentals of Islamic Thought* (Berkeley, Calif.: Mizan Press, 1982), p. 51.
19. Ibid.
20. M. Mutahhari, *'Ilal-i Girayish bi Maddigari* [The Causes of Attraction to Materialism] (Qum, 1357 [1978]).
21. A.S.M.H. Tabataba'i, *Usul-i Falsafah wa Rawish-i Realism* [The Principles of Philosophy and the Realistic Method] (Qum, 1332 [1953]).
22. Mutahhari, *Fundamentals*, pp. 46–50.
23. Ibid., p. 50.
24. Ibid., p. 52.
25. Ibid., p. 53; emphasis added.
26. Ibid., p. 60.
27. Ibid., pp. 60–61.
28. See the first chapter in Mutahhari's *Fundamentals* for a comprehensive treatment of Islam as a philosophically based ideology.
29. S. Akhavi, *Religion and Politics in Contemporary Iran: Clergy-State Relations in the Pahlavi Period* (Albany, N.Y.: State University of New York Press, 1980), pp. 118–119.

30. Ibid., p. 144; emphasis added.

31. M. Mutahhari, *Sharh-i Manzumah*, vol. 1 [Commentary on Mulla Hadi Sabziwari's Philosophical Compendium] (Tehran: Sadra, 1360 [1981]), p. 6.

32. J. J. Donahue and J. L. Esposito, eds., *Islam in Transition: Muslim Perspective* (Oxford: Oxford University Press, 1982), pp. 16–17.

3

The Left and Revolution in Iran: A Critical Analysis

Val Moghadam

Introduction

The emergence of the Islamic Republic in 1979 and the subsequent repression of the Left have created an ideological and practical crisis for the socialist movement of Iran today. The objective of this chapter is to show how and why secular leftist groups were eliminated from the competition for power.

The term *Left* is used to denote all those who (1) defined themselves as such and (2) came into opposition to the Pahlavi state, and, later, the Islamic Republic using Marxist, neo-Marxist, and socialist concepts and categories. Hence, this discussion of the Left includes the Tudeh party and the Mojahedin but not the National Front, a liberal/social democratic grouping. Specifically, this chapter includes the following: the Fedaii, the Tudeh party, the Mojahedin, Peykar, Hezb-e Ranjbaran, the Ashraf Dehghani group, the Organization of Communist Unity, Fourth International (Trotskyist) organizations such as the Hezb-e Kargaran-e Sossialisti (Socialist Workers' party), and smaller socialist groups such as Rah-e Kargar and Rah-e Fedaii. The term *new revolutionary movement* refers to the guerrilla organizations that arose around 1970, whereas the term *militant Left* is used to distinguish the anti-regime Left from the pro-regime Left.

Since the attack on and subsequent fragmentation of the Iranian Left, much soul-searching has taken place, along with reevaluations and criticisms of organizations, their politics, leaderships, and lines. A survey of the Left literature in exile reveals that much of the post-facto discussions about the Left are either dismal exercises in apologia or remarkably ahistorical condemnations. For example, the Tudeh party continues to defend its past policies and has not offered a self-critique of its support for the Islamic state. Rather, it ignores the question while deciding that the Islamic state is no longer deserving of the party's support.[1] At the same time, there has been much discussion in Iranian Left circles about the political bankruptcy and "betrayals" of the various Left organizations and/or their leading cadres.[2] There is a tendency, for example, to reject outright the *entire* history of the Tudeh party and the Mojahedin. The question arises as to how best to approach the question of Left theory and practice (or praxis) in the Iranian Revolution and the Islamic Republic.

It is important, first, to recognize that Left history and more recent Left praxis have had both positive and negative trends. Second, it is possible to evaluate the problems and prospects of the Iranian Left without falling into either pitfalls or structuralism/historical determinism or subjectivism. Third, it is necessary to analyze both the opportunities for and constraints faced by the Left forces in the revolutionary conjuncture and in the immediate transitional period. The experience of the Left in Iran is incomprehensible outside the context of overall economic, political, and ideological conditions, including the history and development of leftist political activity, the structure of production and distribution in Iran, and the resulting class forces and social relations. A proper reconstruction of the Left's historical role must consider a combination of "objective" and "subjective" factors: the contributions the Left has made, its mistakes, and the imperatives and constraints it has confronted. To look solely at objective factors—whereby the Left is seen as the victim of structural processes, cultural imperatives, traditional values, and so on—is not enough, as this perspective negates the roles of human agency, class struggle, and political practice. Conversely, to condemn the Left for not doing what it was in fact politically, organizationally, ideologically, and militarily incapable of doing is an ahistorical, subjective, and voluntarist approach to complex social processes.

This chapter employs an alternative approach that encompasses both the strengths and the weaknesses of the Left. But beyond an identification of such elements as the contributions and mistakes of the Left, the chapter demonstrates and critically assesses the underlying theoretical, political, and practical framework within which the entire Left has operated, notwithstanding the tactical differences among groups. The framework—anti-imperialism and dependent capitalism—resulted in a Third Worldist praxis that blurred the distinction between the socialist and nationalist projects.

Capitalist Development and Anti-Imperialist Politics

Third Worldism

Third Worldism refers to an analytical perspective that arose in the late 1950s and found currency in the 1960s and 1970s as an alternative to the Marxist orthodoxy. It focused on the liberation movements then developing in Latin America, Asia, and Africa (e.g., Algeria, Cuba, Guinea-Bissau) and rejected the old gradualist sequence of three successive stages: (1) industrialization, (2) formation of the working class, and (3) proletarian revolution.[3] Among the writers and activists associated with the Third Worldist perspective are Regis Debray, Ernesto "Che" Guevara, Samir Amin, Andre Gunder Frank,

Paul Sweezy, Leo Huberman, and Harry Magdoff—all of whom had a great deal of influence not only on thinkers and activists throughout the Third World but on movements in the advanced capitalist countries as well.[4] The writings of the Chinese leader Mao Tse-tung were also highly influential. These authors argue that the problems of the Third World were caused by imperialist penetration, and that the other side of the coin of First World development was Third World underdevelopment. They also argue that "dependent capitalism" was a "distorted" form of development caused by neocolonialism. The idea that within a capitalist context there are no prospects for Third World development became known as the "blockage theory." The solution to the perpetuation of Third World underdevelopment and exploitation by imperialism, then, was a "delinking" from the imperialist system through liberation movements and popular revolutions.

Chaliand describes this theoretical process as the replacement, in the 1960s, of the "dogma of Soviet Marxism" with the "new dogma of Third Worldism."[5] At the root of Third Worldism was the conviction that a revolutionary model could be exported to other countries. In a similar vein, Morosini writes:

> The belief in exportability assumed an absolute interchangeability of models, independent of differing levels of socioeconomic development (underdeveloped countries of the Third World, developed countries of the West), independent of differing levels of the spread of democratic institutions, independent of cultural contexts (the Christian West, the Arab-Islamic and Confucian East, traditional African culture, etc.), and independent of national specificity. The password was "One, two . . . a hundred Vietnams," where Vietnam was generalized to a single meaning: armed struggle against imperialism.[6]

One of the earliest critiques of Third Worldist orthodoxy came from the late Bill Warren. In his controversial challenge to the prevailing Left wisdom on the adverse effects of imperialism on national economies, he pointed out that capitalism both exploits and develops:

> Empirical observations suggest that the prospects for successful capitalist development . . . of a significant number of major underdeveloped countries are quite good; . . . that the period since the Second World War has been marked by a substantial upsurge in capitalist social relations and productive forces (especially industrialization) in the Third World, . . . that the imperialist countries' policies and their overall impact on the Third World actually favor its industrialization; and that the ties of dependence . . . have been and are being markedly loosened. . . . None of this is meant to imply that imperialism has ceased to exist. . . . What we wish to indicate are elements of change.[7]

In Iran, the rise of the "new revolutionary movement" in 1970—of guerrilla organizations and political-military groups, and of the strategy of armed struggle—echoed an earlier development in Latin America, where guerrilla groups broke from the orthodox communist parties in the wake of the success of the Cuban Revolution. The year 1970 saw the rise of the

Organization of the Iranian People's Fedaii Guerrillas, an avowedly Marxist-Leninist group, followed by the formation of the Organization of the People's Mojahedin, which combined Marxist concepts with an Islamic ideology.[8] The discourse was very similar to revolutionary discourse (Third Worldism) in Latin America, Africa, and elsewhere in Asia: It was the discourse of anti-imperialism, dependent capitalism, neocolonialism, and armed struggle.

Uneven Development and the Evolution of Third Worldism in Iran

During the 1960s and 1970s, the Pahlavi state embarked upon an ambitious capitalist development program that combined agrarian reform and rapid industrialization. This program was crystallized in the so-called White Revolution, which was put to a plebescite in January 1963. In its initial stage, the agrarian reform offered land redistribution. The beneficiaries were those peasants who had been sharecroppers (*saheb-nasaq*). The reform thus transformed some of the peasantry into landholders. Indeed, the dominant form of rural production came to be small-scale farming. In the later stages of agrarian reform, the small farmers were neglected and large capitalist enterprises were promoted.[9] Some of the landholding peasants consequently migrated to the cities in search of a better livelihood. Those peasants who did not receive any land in the agrarian reform became rural and urban wage laborers.

At the same time, the regime was using the tremendous oil revenues at its disposal to finance industrialization. The policy of import-substitution supported domestic producers and resulted in the rapid expansion of the manufacturing sector. An urban, industrial labor force was thus created. State policy came to favor large-scale, capital-intensive industry and eventually discriminated against small-scale manufacturers. Neglect of the countryside displaced thousands of peasants, who were increasingly drawn to the urban areas in search of services and work. Meanwhile, a high birth rate led to the expansion of rural and urban populations. Both "push" and "pull" factors contributed to the massive rural-urban migration during the 1960s and 1970s, as well as to the creation of a pool of immiserated semiproletarians.[10]

The Pahlavi state was a developing capitalist state. As part of its project to facilitate the conditions for accumulation, it sought to take control over previously autonomous commercial, financial, and industrial operations, much of which were "traditional," small- and medium-scale, and concentrated in and around the bazaar. The expansion of big capital, both private and state, in concert with foreign investment also increasingly encroached upon the markets of smaller domestic producers and merchants.[11] At the same time, the Shah's autocratic rule, his military adventures in the Gulf as the regional gendarme of the United States, and the conspicuous consumption of the upper class created enormous resentment among many Iranians. Opposition to the regime came to focus on its ties to U.S. imperialism, on the dominance of the "comprador bourgeoisie," and on the consumer culture that capitalist development had created.

The main Left organizations of the pre-revolutionary period—the Tudeh party, the Fedaii, and the Mojahedin, all of which were underground but active—described the Shah's regime in similar language. The discourse included the concepts of "U.S. imperialism," "dependent capitalism," and "comprador class." Opposition to the Shah's regime, however, was not limited to the Left but came also from the religious forces, which likewise focused on "dependence," "consumer culture," and ties to U.S. imperialism. The Left thus converged with the religious forces in its reasons for opposing the Shah—that is, in reaction to his economic policies (which they defined as pro-imperialist and antinational), his political program (which, again, was pro-imperialist as well as dictatorial), and his cultural creations, such as consumerism and "Westoxication."[12]

A revealing source of the Left analysis of Iranian political economy is a book by Fedaii founder and theorist, Bizhan Jazani.[13] The chapter titles reveal the problems: "the development and rule of the comprador bourgeoisie," "increasing foreign exploitation in a neo-colonialist form," and "the formation of the minority consumer society." Perhaps the most original piece in the book, one that considers the specificities of the Iranian political economy, is the chapter on monarchic dictatorship. The chapter entitled "the revolutionary forces in Iran" describes "the people" as "the working classes, the peasants, the petty-bourgeoisie and the national bourgeoisie." Jazani explains further that the clergy (excluding its "upper crust" and leadership) is located within the petty-bourgeoisie.

The Fedaii, of course, was not the only Left organization submerged in the anti-imperialist, dependency paradigm. The entire Iranian Left—and this includes the Tudeh party (the CP), the Maoists, the Trotskyists, and the independent Communists—spoke a similar language even when they were criticizing each other. The influence of dependency theory on the minds and practices of the Iranian Left is readily discerned from a reading of Left literature. Various Iranian Left groups drew from the works of Frantz Fanon, Mao Tse-tung, and Latin American *dependistas*. Iranian society was variously described as "neo-colonialist," "semi-feudal, semi- colonialist," or thoroughly capitalist. Many Iranian revolutionaries who called themselves Marxists—such as the Revolutionary Organization (which broke away from the Tudeh party, became thoroughly Marxist, and later formed the Ranjbaran party in post-revolutionary Iran)—took to Third Worldism to such a degree that they applied the national-liberation model to Iran rather than give priority to social revolution.[14] Such an analysis and strategy naturally called for the unity of "the people" against the regime within one large anti-imperialist front—industrial workers, urban poor, radical students, the Left, the national bourgeoisie, and the clergy.

The word *melli*—meaning "national"—figured prominently in Left discourse. The Maoist Peykar's primary objections to the Shah's regime was that the system of dependent capitalism tied to imperialism had precluded the formation of *melli* and independent industries, and argued that oil revenues should be used to build a domestic capital goods sector rather than encourage the proliferation of consumer goods. Another Maoist group, Ranjbaran, sought an independent, "national" Iran aligned to neither the United States nor the USSR, wherein a primary objective would be the creation of "national technology." Bizhan Jazani had written on the "national democratic revolution" and the establishment of a "national" political rule. In situations of Left agitation in factories, the focus was on severing economic ties with imperialism, defeating imperialist domination, and establishing an independent "national economy." For the Tudeh party, the fundamental question was the possibility of a national democratic revolution based on anti-imperialism and severed ties of dependency.

There was considerable confusion over the Shah's land-reform program and its outcome. Some writers conceded that some capitalist development had occurred in the countryside and that it had resulted in the further differentiation of the peasantry.[15] Others, who were especially prolific after the Revolution, referred to the land reform as "fictitious" and a "sham," demanded "genuine land reform," and raised the slogan "land to the tiller." These writers also emphasized the exploitative role of agribusinesses. But there were two problems with this analysis and approach, both of which worked to the Left's disadvantage. First, some land distribution did occur under the Shah's land-reform program, although it had not been generalized, had not extended land deeds to all the peasantry, and had exempted commercialized, mechanized, and profitable farms and orchards from redistribution. These farms and orchards (in addition to certain large capitalist farms), however, constituted a very small part of rural production. As mentioned above, the dominant form of agricultural production by the end of the 1970s was small farming. Second, this analysis was echoed by elements within the Islamic ruling circles and, indeed, came to be associated with them. In this context, "land to the tiller" was not the appropriate demand, as some Left writings later conceded.[16] Rather, the Left ought to have called for greater support for the peasantry/small farming class toward increased prosperity and productivity.

Such were the questions that dominated Left discourse: independence versus dependence, national versus "comprador" development, "the people" versus imperialism and its internal base. The problem with the analysis was twofold: (1) It did not take into consideration the *developmental* effects of the Pahlavi state's capitalist project, and (2) it echoed the criticism advanced by the religious forces. The Left's discourse blurred the distinction between the religious project and the Left alternative, thereby ultimately undermining the Left's position and bolstering the Islamic forces.

The Left's Lack of Preparedness and Unity

Like the New Left in Europe and the United States, the Iranian Left was not unified but composed of small groups, organizations, and parties. For the most part, these groups were young, inexperienced, and unable to carry out open political activity due to the state's repression. When the anti-Shah struggle broke out, the Left opposition was therefore not in a position as secure as that of the religious opposition (whose members had a nationwide network of mosques and bazaars) as a hegemonic ideology. The Left was unprepared for the opportunities afforded by the disintegration of the Shah's regime. Because of the sustained and systematic repression of the Left opposition by the Pahlavi regime during the 1960s and 1970s, none of the Left groups was in a position either to play a leadership role in the mass movement or to define or influence the discourse and strategy of the anti-Shah struggle. The Fedaii and Mojahedin, in particular, were at a decided disadvantage: Their organizations, formed in the early 1970s, had been hounded and nearly decimated by 1977. Unlike the Tudeh party—founded in 1941 and in possession of both a longer history and greater resources—the Fedaii and Mojahedin entered the political arena in 1978 without years of experience, development, and preparation for the events ahead. The Fedaii had the further disadvantage of being a Communist organization in a country characterized by religious (Islamic) fervor and extremely uneven socioeconomic development. Thus the Left as a whole was catapulted into the 1978–1979 Revolution without having been able to develop strong links with and bases among key social forces, such as urban industrial workers or the semiproletariat. Under these circumstances, the clergy–bazaar–urban poor alliance dominated the discourse of the Revolution and influenced its outcome.[17]

Matters were not helped by the problems within the Left, either. The various Left forces were unwilling or unable to coalesce and unite, and no single Left organization was large enough, strong enough, or influential enough to present a viable program that would appeal to different social groups and provide an alternative to clerics and their collaborator-rivals, the "liberal bourgeoisie." From the beginning, the Tudeh party wanted simply to find a niche for itself within the new political rule. To do this, it quickly aligned itself with the clerics. The Mojahedin, whose Left politics were combined with Islamic ideology, tried to accommodate the religious fervor of the Islamic masses while also demarcating themselves from the ruling clerics. This proved to be a contradictory and self-defeating task. The Mojahedin were essentially replicates of the radical wing of the Islamic Republican party (IRP) and, as such, were becoming increasingly redundant and irrelevant. When the Shah's regime fell, various Left groups offered quite disparate analyses and positions on the Revolution and the new regime. For the most part, Left groups avoided any serious criticism of the ayatollahs holding political power. Of the large Left organizations, only the Fedaii expressed reservations, doubts, and criticisms of the new regime at the beginning. Moreover, these were often wrong-headed. The combined factors—uneven development, the Shah's repression, the deficiencies of dependency theory, and anti-imperialist politics, and the lack of unity and preparedness on the part of the Left organizations—resulted in a weak Left opposition, missed opportunities (especially during the pivotal year 1979), and, finally, defeat and crisis.

The Left and the Islamic Republic

After the February 1979 Revolution, which toppled the Shah/Bakhtiar regime and installed the Provisional Government of Mehdi Bazargan under the leadership of Ayatollah Khomeini, the Left was faced with the difficulty of coming to grips with the new regime and formulating a policy of coexistence or confrontation. Most Left organizations chose to extend either qualified support or total defense of the new political authority. Only two organizations were absolutely opposed to the new leadership from the outset: the Maoist Peykar and the group led by former Fedaii guerrilla, Ashraf Dehqani. Their opposition was based on the notion that the new regime was still a capitalist, comprador regime that would and could do nothing to sever the ties of dependency on and relations with U.S. imperialism. Peykar was particularly opposed to any alternative to a *people's democratic* republic and was staunchly against the idea of an *Islamic* republic. It was also very critical of those Left organizations that toyed with "populist" and "revisionist" notions of "sovereignty of the people."[18] Because Peykar did not expect anything better of either the Mojahedin (whom it did not even consider to be on the left) or the Tudeh party (which came to support the new order quite enthusiastically), it reserved most of its criticisms for and debates with the Fedaii. For example, in an article in its weekly newspaper entitled "The Fedaii and the Question of State Power: A Review of the Revisionist Theory of the Division of the State into a Good and a Bad Part," Peykar ridiculed the characterization of the new regime as "petty-bourgeois," calling it a "capitalist government" serving the interests of "comprador capitalists."[19]

At this time (1979 to early 1980), the political differences within the Left centered on the democratization of the new political order (toward which the Fedaii, Tudeh party, Ranjbaran, Trotskyist groups, and Mojahedin were inclined at this time) versus total rejection of the new regime (the position taken by Peykar and Ashraf Dehqani). The Left group demanding democracy justified supporting the new regime because it was presumably constituted by the petty-bourgeoisie, whereas the Left group rejecting the new regime characterized it as thoroughly capitalist and bourgeois. Still, even though Peykar was adamantly opposed to the Islamic regime from its inception, the organization did make a distinction between the two ruling factions, based on their respective attitude toward imperialism. For example, in an article entitled "The Heightening Anti-Imperialist Struggle of the Masses and the Resignation of Bazargan," Peykar referred to Bazargan's government as "traitorous" and as having a "direct link with imperialism." In contrast, he said, "the clerical faction in power and the Revolutionary Council (even though it has clearly proved its counter-revolutionary role in these nine months) does not have a *direct* interest in ensuring U.S. imperialist rule in Iran. . . ."[20]

In contrast to Peykar's unequivocal opposition to the new regime, the Fedaii had difficulty formulating a "line" on the new regime, and offered differing and contradictory analyses and positions in their weekly newspaper

Kar (Labor). For example, the Fedaii first called the Provisional Government of Mehdi Bazargan "legitimate" and "national," contrasting Bazargan's respect for democratic freedoms to the "reactionary fundamentalists."[21] Shortly afterward, however, the Fedaii denounced members of Bazargan's cabinet as "comprador," criticized Bazargan for opposing executions of the Shah's ministers, and counterposed the "liberal bourgeoisie" to the "anti-imperialist Khomeini."[22] An article in *Kar* on the disputes in Khorramshahr (a port city in the southern province of Khuzestan with an ethnically Arab population), entitled "The Role of Imperialism and Reaction in the Bloody Events of Khorramshahr," blamed the National Front for the "conspiracy."[23] Compared to the invective directed at the "liberals," the government and the National Front, the criticism of the IRP, the Revolutionary Council, and the Imam Committees was very mild. There was no direct criticism of Ayatollah Khomeini or of the power he wielded.

The most serious problem confronting the Fedaii was their inability to reach internal consensus on the nature of the Revolution, the character of the new ruling circles (the Provisional Government and the Revolutionary Council), the nature of the petty-bourgeoisie, and so on. This inability was reflected in the ambiguities and zig-zags discerned in *Kar*. As stated above, the initial Fedaii warnings about Islamic fanaticism gave way to a dogmatic stance against the "liberal bourgeoisie," based on the dubious notion that the petty-bourgeoisie, as a social stratum, is "close to the working class." Finally, the Fedaii, during 1979, decided to uphold the "genuine anti-imperialism" of the radical wing of the regime, ignoring its profoundly anti-democratic character. This position derived from their conception of Iranian capitalism. The equation was as follows: Iranian capitalism equals Shah plus big industrialists, agribusinesses and transnational corporations. Everyone else—peasants, proletarians, petty bourgeois, clerics, bazaaris, urban poor, and so on—were "popular masses," oppressed and exploited by foreign capital, U.S. imperialism, and its local "puppet" in particular. Considering the earlier criticism of the "minority consumer culture" created by imperialism and dependent capitalism, it is no wonder that very few in the Fedaii (or, for that matter, in the Left as a whole) realized that the *kulturkampf* being waged by the Islamic forces—which many in the Left explained as an understandable and "popular" reaction to "Westoxication"—would eventually engulf them, too.

Another Left organization, the Organization of Communist Unity (OCU), generally considered more theoretically advanced, was also caught up in the problem of whether the new order was thoroughly capitalist (and therefore indefensible) or petty-bourgeois (and consequently redeemable). In an article in its newspaper, *Raha'i*, entitled "Class Rule: Iran One Year after the Uprising," the OCU distinguished between "regime" and "state," calling the state capitalist though Islamic: "We believe the present state in Iran cannot and does not differ fundamentally from the state of two or even ten years ago."[24] The OCU sought to counter the "revisionist" (i.e., Tudeh party) line about the noncapitalist and petty-bourgeois character of the clergy, but it overstated their case. It could hardly characterize the Islamic regime's economic policies—such as the ban on interest and the bias against transnational corporations and big private capital investment—as reflecting "capitalist laws of accumulation." The OCU also overlooked the absence of consensus on a "capitalist program" within the regime—a situation that has persisted to this day. At any rate, the OCU's analysis of the Islamic regime was inadequate, for the fundamental problem with the regime was not that it was capitalist, but that it was incapable of organizing a viable and just political economy based on democratic rights and on the socio-economic needs of the population.

However, if the OCU could not offer an adequate explanation of the situation, *Rahai's* critique of its comrades elsewhere on the Left spectrum was insightful and worth quoting at length:

> [T]he significant part of Iran's Left, instead of drawing the petty-bourgeoisie toward itself, has in fact moved toward the petty-bourgeoisie and thus contributed to its strength and illusions. [The article then points out that the Mojahedin had directed their energies toward supporting Bani-Sadr.] . . . Unfortunately, the main part of the Left in Iran is living for the moment, acting day by day and pragmatically. It lacks a correct practice. If the situation stays the same, the Left will not be able to present an alternative. In future developments, even perhaps in the next political revolution, the Left will remain a supporter of this or that force instead of being a possibility itself.[25]

Secular leftists were not unaware of the enormity of either the problems they faced or their own inadequacies. They hardly found time to seriously consider these problems and inadequacies as they were faced with daily events and developments that required their immediate attention, such as the U.S. hostage crisis, the Iraqi invasion, the growing contention within the regime between liberals and fundamentalists, and the deepening social and political crisis that culminated, in June 1981, in a mini–civil war. Addressing this dilemma, the Fedaii wrote in March 1981:

> Due to the rapidity of daily events, we do not have sufficient time for periods of rigorous theoretical work and all-round ideological struggle to come up with thorough answers to each and every question. Today while a pile of undone tasks weighs on our shoulders and every day new events face us, we are forced to find, in a short time, concrete, clear, and explicit answers. Postponing these tasks until after a long period of theoretical work and ideological struggle is equivalent to inaction, to falling behind the mass movement and being metamorphosed into an appendage of petty-bourgeois crusaders.[26]

By early 1981 the Marxist Left had become dismayed by the Mojahedin, who were exhibiting blatant disregard for a united Left front and an interest only in promoting their own organization and influence, with a view toward seizing state power. Particularly galling was their alliance with President Bani-Sadr, whose contention with his erstwhile clerical partners was growing daily. The OCU rightly called this alliance the Mojahedin's choice of the

Right over the Left. The Iranian Left learned about the pact with Bani-Sadr and the formation of the National Resistance Council (NRC) through leaflets and newspapers. No one from the Mojahedin consulted with them on its establishment, although, as the OCU caustically remarked, the door was Left "half open" for them if they wished to join in a "government for the reconstruction of the Islamic Republic." The OCU then continued: "No doubt, some will still enter and only then will they realize that they must sit on the floor, by the door, as second-class citizens—their presence merely contributing to the legitimacy of the assembly and nothing more."[27]

The Mojahedin had difficulties not just with the secular Left but also with Khomeini's people. Early on, they had been quite respectful and conciliatory. As late as 1981 they were praising Khomeini, although by now they were strongly critical of the IRP and openly supportive of Bani-Sadr. However, their reinterpretation of Islamic law led Khomeini to denounce them first as "eclectics" and later as *monafeghin* (hypocrites). Their ideology, which combined neo-Marxist concepts (such as imperialism and dependent capitalism) with a modernized version of Islam, was criticized by Ayatollah Khomeini as un-Islamic—a very serious attack, coming from the charismatic leader of the Revolution and the ultimate interpreter of Islam.

Leftists today believe that the most serious analytical and political mistake of Left organizations in 1979 was their inability or unwillingness to fully comprehend the significance of, and to unequivocally support, democratic rights. The Fedaii, for example, did distribute leaflets, and *Kar* carried articles protesting the attacks on freedom of the press, women's rights, and other personal and civil liberties. But the organization did not make democratic rights a priority issue: It did not organize and mobilize people around this issue, nor did it unite with a left-liberal group, the National Democratic Front, which *was* making democracy its main concern throughout 1979. Instead, the Fedaii concentrated on the anti-imperialist struggle, adopting its own, dependency-informed conception of what constituted imperialism, capitalism, and anti-imperialism. The struggle for socialism and democratic rights was placed on the back burner. The Fedaii directed all their efforts toward preventing an "imperialist counterrevolution," which in fact was not on the agenda, while ignoring the danger of the IRP's creeping dictatorship.

An example of how the Left's emphasis on combating imperialism led it to neglect democratic-socialist tasks is its approach toward the issue of women's rights in early 1979. Its attitude toward women also exemplifies the serious consequences of the total rejection of capitalist reforms. All of the rights obtained by or granted to women during the Pahlavi era were dismissed as a "sham," an "imposition," or a "bourgeois conspiracy." They were not considered important rights and freedoms that had to be defended and furthered. There was thus no significant opposition from the Left as a whole to the new Islamic regime's abrogation of the Shah's Family Protection Law and the return to retrograde Islamic precepts concerning divorce and child custody. Nor did the Left offer more than superficial and formal criticism of the law on *hejab* (requiring women to wear Islamic dress in public). Even women writers on the Left took the contradictory position of rejecting the Pahlavi reforms (thus echoing the clerics' position) *and* protesting Khomeinist attempts to turn back the clock on women's social, economic, and political progress. The National Union of Women, organized by Fedaii women, was more involved with political questions (concerning the character of the regime and the promotion of the Fedaii organization) than with issues of direct and immediate relevance to Iranian women of various class and cultural backgrounds. The Left's approach toward women is indicative of its considerable misjudgment, miscalculation, and confusion over the issues.

Why was the question of democracy so bereft of content for the Left? In order to understand the Left's approach to democratic rights, we will find it useful to examine a Fedaii document. In a two-part series entitled "The Principal Tasks of Marxist-Leninists at the Present Stage of the Development of the Communist Movement in Iran," published in the fall of 1978, the Fedaii revealed vague formulations and theoretical deficiencies. The pamphlet was ostensibly written in an attempt to define the Fedaii's socialist and democratic tasks in the context of a mass, anti-imperialist revolutionary struggle. However, it never really defined "socialist" and "democratic"; rather, it equated these terms with "working class movement" and "liberation movement," respectively. The Fedaii's notion of democracy derived from the two-stage model of revolution whereby the first stage constituted a mass, popular, democratic, anti-imperialist revolution, and the second stage consisted of a socialist, working-class, proletarian revolution. Small wonder, then, that the issue of democracy was later neglected: The concept of "democracy" was equated with a stage of revolution (and the less important one at that) and not with the inalienable rights of citizens. Moreover, "democracy" was looked at with some contempt. An article in *Kar* entitled "Iran: Can Democracy Last Long?" attacked bourgeois democracy as entailing freedom only for the capitalist.[28]

The Tudeh party was the main proponent both of the theory of the noncapitalist road of development and of the role of the petty bourgeoisie in the national democratic revolution.[29] However, it wasted much time by concentrating on philosophical issues such as the nature of matter, the role of the individual in history, and the relationship between base and superstructure. The Tudeh party was also the leading proponent of the idea of "progressive clergy"—an idea that the party first introduced and then popularized. The party's leader, Nurredin Kianuri, described the "sustained struggle" in Iran as proceeding on four main fronts: (1) against various external plots, against the political, economic, and military pressures of world imperialism headed by the United States, and against regional reaction; (2) against the intrigues of domestic counterrevolutionaries who would like to carry out a coup, and against political terrorism; (3) against the "economic terrorism" of the big capitalists and landowners and for social justice; and (4) for guaranteed civil rights and freedoms.[30] Kianuri's priorities are interesting, as was his deflection of criticism of the regime by externalizing the contradictions and pointing to U.S. imperialism. Elsewhere in the article,

Kianuri writes of U.S. imperialism as the "main instigator of the Iranian-Iraqi war."

By underscoring the anti-imperialist nature of the clergy, the Left helped in its legitimation. Had the Left groups instead underscored the democratic-socialist project (pertaining to the personal and civil rights of citizens, the socialization of production, and workers' control), they would have revealed the regime's Achilles' heel (i.e., its anti-democratic, anti-socialist stance) while simultaneously demarcating themselves from the regime by offering an alternative that even the regime's radical wing could not and would not adopt.

It should be acknowledged that, notwithstanding the difficult ideological climate and their own serious mistakes, sections of the Left did contribute to some of the achievements of the Revolution. The Fedaii, for example, directed much of their attention to working-class struggles and to the minority nationalities' right to autonomy. Along with the Mojahedin and several smaller Left groups in 1979 and 1980 (and in contrast to the Tudeh party), the Fedaii were active in workers' councils in Tehran and in other large urban areas. They also supported the struggle for autonomy in Kurdestan and the progressive movement in Turkaman Sahra, which included peasants' councils and a resurgence of ethnic cultural activity.[31] However, these efforts were undermined by the internal crisis of the Fedaii. The contradictions, inconsistencies, and disagreements that had wracked the organization since early 1979 finally came to a head and resulted in the split of June 1980. The organization was divided into a "Majority" and a "Minority" group. The beginning of the end of the Iranian Left as a whole occurred at this time. The split had a devastating effect on four movements upon which the Left, and notably the Fedaii, had considerable influence: the workers' councils, the students' councils, the Kurdish struggle for autonomy, and the National Union of Women. Each of these movements split and eventually disintegrated (with the exception of the Kurdish struggle). The split was inevitable, perhaps, given the irreconcilability of the two completely opposing views on the regime. In any case, it greatly weakened the revolutionary Left.

Following the split there now emerged a Fedaii-Majority, which followed the Tudeh party in supporting the regime's "anti-imperialist" and "progressive" character, and a Fedaii-Minority, the more radical organization, which opposed the regime as reactionary. But while the Fedaii-Minority's opposition to the regime was now unequivocal, its analysis and strategy remained unsatisfactory. It opposed the regime for being a *capitalist* regime and a *bourgeois state*. Its rationale was that the initial coalition between the middle-capitalists and the petty-bourgeoisie had been resolved in favor of the former, and that the regime was now engaged both in the reconstruction of the capitalist structures and institutions inherited from the old regime and in the suppression of the new organs that had emerged during the revolution.[32] It followed from this that the anti-regime movement would unite the petty-bourgeoisie, working class, and peasantry against the capitalist state. A faction within the Minority, called the Tendency for Socialist

Revolution, disputed this line of reasoning and called for a fundamental reassessment of the political position, socioeconomic objectives, tactics, and strategy of the Left in general and of the Fedaii-Minority in particular. In place of what it saw as "populist strategy," it advocated "turning to the factories." Instead of the two-stage revolution, it proposed democratic socialism.[33] The Tendency criticized what it regarded as the lack of democracy within the ranks of the organization, as well as a "religious" approach toward women and sexuality shared by all Left groups notwithstanding the emancipatory declarations being made regarding women. The Tendency also denounced the Tudeh party's "treason" and the adventurism and anti-democratic practices of the Mojahedin. But all of this protest eventually became moot. If the Left was unprepared and disunited in 1978–1979, and greatly weakened with the Fedaii split in 1980, its days were certainly numbered when the IRP, with the support of Khomeini, turned on President Bani-Sadr and the Mojahedin in 1981. The regime ferreted out the Left organizations and their partisans one by one until even the conciliatory Tudeh party was suppressed in May 1983.

Conclusion

Following the defeat of the Liberals and the Left in the mini–civil war that began in June 1981, three important developments within the Left could be discerned: (1) the secular Left's disenchantment with the Mojahedin; (2) the shattering of illusions about the Islamic regime; and (3) the self-consciousness, self-criticism, and eventual disarray among the Left. The last development led to splits between the militant Left and the pro-regime Left, to the dismantling of several organizations, to the exile of certain political leaders, and to further fragmentation of the Left opposition. The Tendency for Socialist Revolution later split into various journal collectives, located in the United States and Western Europe, and is now part of what is known as the "New Left," which rejects the past organizational and political practices of the Left.

Socialists have frequently been deceived by anti-imperialist rhetoric into supporting very reactionary regimes. In an essay entitled "Reflections on the Iranian Revolution," James Petras states that the primary lesson of the Iranian Revolution, particularly for socialists, concerns the nature of imperialism, its impact on Third World social formations, and the resultant nature and orientation of the various strands of "anti-imperialist" movements. The complexity of anti-imperialist forces and the profound historical experiences that divide them raise the issue of the proper relation (if any) that should exist between them. A related point is the importance of recognizing the capacity of precapitalist classes to utilize their political and ideological power to compensate for eroding economic power when threatened by modern economies. Required is an analysis of their capacity to adapt to the demands of capitalism and to co-opt modern classes.[34] Left experience in Iran also calls into question the validity of the tactics and strategies of armed struggle and the absence of a revolutionary ideology that is also *modernizing*—one that, while exalting national identity, could also "prune the socially and culturally conservative elements out of the national tradition and free the energies of the greatest number of people."[35] Finally, the Iranian Revolution underscores the importance of the democratic-socialist project rather than the subsumption of diverse interests, needs, and aspirations under the rubric of nationalism and anti-imperialism.

Much of the Left failed to recognize the expansive and developmental nature of the Shah's dictatorship (which is *not* the same as saying that the role of imperialism was politically or socially progressive, given the authoritarian and repressive context within which this economic development took place). By simply defining the Shah's regime by its reactionary political and social character, the Left was unable to come to grips with the dual character of the opposition. As Petras writes,

> Their superficial understanding of imperialism precluded a recognition of the heterogeneity of the social formation. Insufficient attention was given to the fact that the apparent *convergence* of classes in the anti-shah movement was a temporary phenomenon which attenuated the very diverse interests, demands, and aspirations within the coalition.[36]

In particular, parts of the Left failed to discern the retrograde project of the merchants, clerics, and petty producers; failed to recognize the dangers of theocracy; and failed to direct its energies toward a democratic-socialist goal.

The Left's experience in the Iranian Revolution and with the Islamic Republic has led it to call into question past practices and theories, assumptions, and aims. One of its current preoccupations is the importance of the struggle for democratic rights. It is now recognized that the absence of a democratic tradition in Iran was a major impediment to Left progress, and that the Left's own authoritarian and dogmatic tendencies derived from this absence. Thus the need to establish a democratic tradition is now widely accepted as the primary task.

Third Worldism, the dependency problematic, and dogmatism are being targeted in journals and meetings. The tendency toward "statism"—expressed both in demands for nationalization and in the goal of seizing state power—is being questioned and discarded by some in favor of the Gramscian concept of ideological hegemony and "war of movement." The predisposition to models has been questioned, too. The conclusion now generally accepted is that there can be no replication of national experiences elsewhere, that Iran can reproduce neither the Soviet, the Chinese, nor the Cuban model. (The desirability of these particular models is a separate matter.) Debates now focus on the meaning of revolution, of socialism, of democracy, and of the agents of social change in Iran. Clearly, some of those forces previously considered "friends" are no longer considered so. In general, old sacred cows are being demolished, and new ideas entertained, resulting in a broader conception of socialism, an appreciation of democratic rights, and a criticism of authoritarianism and centralism. The positive, reverse side of the defeat of the Left has been its auto-critique, skepticism, and new-found liberality. But it is too soon to tell where all this might lead. What is more likely than a revitalization of past Left groups is the gradual formation of a reconstituted Left movement with a very different theoretical and political orientation.

Notes

1. Ali Khavari, "Anti-Communism on the Rampage in Iran," *World Marxist Review*, August 1985. The author is the current first secretary of the Tudeh party, having replaced Nurredin Kianuri, who has been in prison since 1983.

2. What follows is a partial listing of Left journals published in the United States and Europe that are taking up questions of socialism, democracy, and feminism; most of them have had articles sharply critical of Left praxis in the recent past: *Aksariyat* (organ of the Fedaii-Majority abroad); *Alef Ba* ("ABC"), Paris; *Andisheh va Enghelab* ("Thought and Revolution"), Washington, D.C.; *Dowlat va Enghelab* ("State and Revolution"), London; *Jahan* ("World"), New York; *Kommunist* (organ of the Communist party of Iran, [re]formed in 1981 and currently active in Kurdestan); *Ketab-e Jome'ha*, Paris; *Koumaleh* (organ of the Koumaleh, a Kurdish-based Communist organization); *Nameh-e Mardom* (Tudeh party); *Nazm-e Novin* ("The New Order"), New York and Washington, D.C.; *Nimeh-ye Digar* ("The Other Half"), London; *Raha'i* (organ of the OCU); *Rah-e Kargar* (organ of the Organization of the Revolutionary Workers of Iran); *Sossialism va Enghelab* ("Socialism and Revolution"), Paris; *Women in Struggle* (a periodical published by women supporters of the Fedaii), Chicago; and *Zaman-e Now* ("New Times"), Paris.

3. Giuseppe Morosini, "The European Left and the Third World," *Contemporary Marxism*, no. 2, 1981.

4. See, for example, Regis Debray, *Revolution in Revolution? Armed Struggle and Political Struggle* (New York: Grove Press, 1967); Ernesto "Che" Guevara, *Che Guevara on Revolution: A Documentary Overview*, edited by Jay Mallin (Coral Gables, Fla.: University of Miami Press, 1969); Samir Amin, *L'Accumulation a l'echelle mondiale* (Paris: Editions Anthropos, 1970); Andre Gunder Frank, *Capitalism and Underdevelopment in Latin America* (New York: Monthly Review Press).

5. Gerard Chaliand, "D'un mythe à l'autre," *Le Tiers Monde et la gauche* (Paris: Seuil, 1979).

6. Morosini, op. cit., p. 70.

7. Bill Warren, "Imperialism and Capitalist Industrialization," *New Left Review*, no. 81, September/October 1973.

8. For an elaboration of the rise of these guerrilla organizations, see Fred Halliday, *Iran: Dictatorship and Development* (New York: Penguin, 1979). It should be stated that the new revolutionary movement did make a contribution to the popular discourse, and that the guerrillas' heroism contributed to the organizations' popularity following the Revolution.

9. Ahmad Ashraf, "Peasants, Land and Revolution," *Agrarian and Peasant Questions* (Special Issue of *Ketab-e Agah*) (Tehran: Agah Publishers, 1982) [in Persian].

10. Ibid. According to the International Labor Office, *Employment and Income Policies for Iran* (Geneva: ILO, 1973), some 400,000 peasants migrated to the cities in the 1960s.

11. See Robert Looney, *Economic Origins of the Iranian Revolution* (New York: Praeger Publishers, 1982); see also Nikki Keddie, *Roots of Revolution* (New Haven, Conn.: Yale University Press, 1981).

12. "Westoxication" is a translation of "Gharbzadegi," from an essay of the same name by the late writer Jalal Al-e Ahmad. For an elaboration of this phenomenon, see Brad Hanson, "The 'Westoxication' of Iran: Depictions and Reactions of Behrangi, Al-e Ahmad, and Shari'ati," *International Journal of Middle East Studies*, vol. 15, no. 1, 1983, pp. 1–23. Al-e Ahmad has not been popular with Iranian Marxists, who view his critique as "traditionalist." The late Amir Parviz Pouyan, a Fedaii theoretician, called his analysis "social- feudalist."

13. Bizhan Jazani, *A Socio-Economic Analysis of a Dependent Capitalist State* (Tehran, 1973) [in Persian].

14. An English-language source for Iranian Maoist analysis is *Review of Iranian Political Economy and History* (RIPEH), now discontinued.

15. See Jazani, op. cit.; see also Organization of Iranian People's Fedaii Guerrillas, *Land Reform and Its Direct Effects in Iran* (London: Iran Committee, 1972).

16. For example, see the journal *Nazm-e Novin*, no. 5, 1985 [in Persian], for a critique of past Left perspectives on the agrarian/peasant question.

17. For a discussion of the clergy-Bazaar-urban poor alliance during the Revolution, see Keddie, op. cit.

18. *Peykar*, no. 47, March 19, 1980. It might be worth noting that Peykar had its origins within the Mojahedin. It once constituted the Marxist wing of the organization. At one point in the mid-1970s it carried out an internal "coup" in an attempt to transform the organization into a Marxist-Leninist organization. The coup included execution of an opponent from the Islamic wing. This action ultimately failed, and the Marxist-Mojahedin were expelled, later forming Peykar. The action was severely criticized by the Fedaii, who considered it unprincipled and damaging to the revolutionary movement.

19. Ibid.

20. *Peykar*, no. 30, November 1979.

21. *Kar*, no. 2, March 1979.

22. *Peykar*, no. 47, March 19, 1980.

23. *Kar*, no. 12, May 24, 1979.

24. *Rahai*, no. 22, February 1980.

25. Ibid.

26. *Kar*, no. 87, March 1981.

27. *Rahai*, no. 100, August 25, 1981. Among those who joined Bani-Sadr and the Mojahedin in the NRC were a number of well-known Left intellectuals, scholars, and activists, in addition to the Kurdish Democratic party of Iran (KDPI), and the National Democratic Front. For a short time (between 1981 and 1984), the NRC appeared to be a promising alternative to the Islamic Republic. However, things began to fall apart. Bani- Sadr Left because Massoud Rajavi, the Mojahedin's leader, had met with the Iraqi foreign minister. The KDPI quit, complaining of the Mojahedin's self-promotion at the expense of the NRC. The Left intellectuals broke ranks, suddenly suspicious of a program calling for a "Democratic Islamic Republic." As of 1985, the NRC has been for all practical purposes the Mojahedin organization, and to its many critics the its practices appear cult-like. The Iranian secular Left is now totally divorced from the Mojahedin and neither has any dealings with the other.

28. *Kar*, no. 14, 1979.

29. For a discussion of noncapitalist development, see *World Marxist Review*, vol. 25, no. 3, March 1982. The article entitled "Developing Countries: State Power

and Pattern Alternatives," by S. Mitra, G. Mirsky, and E. Pahad, contains an interesting discussion of how the state power is itself an arena of class struggle; it also details the possibilities that the struggle within the State holds for Communists in the bureaucracy. But it ends on an anachronistic note, more suitable to 1962 than 1982: "In the newly-free nations, the struggle for the progressive restructuring of society is the continuation and development, under new conditions, of the anti-imperialist national liberation revolution. This is a struggle to consolidate and consummate the great historic process of the total social liberation of the colonial slaves of yesteryear" (p. 52).

30. Nurredin Kianuri, "The Arduous Path of the Iranian Revolution," *World Marxist Review*, vol. 26, no. 2, March 1983.

31. Shahrzad Azad [V. Moghadam], "Workers and Peasants Councils in Iran," *Monthly Review*, vol. 32, October 1980.

32. Fedaii-Minority, "Why We Decided to Reveal the Ideological Struggle," *Kar*, no. 100, 1982 [in Persian].

33. Fedaii-Minority, *Balance–Sheet and Prospects*, Tehran, 1982 [in Persian]. See also the first four issues of *Nazm-e Novin* (the Tendency's journal), which were published in Tehran. The fourth issue (March 1981) is devoted to the critique of populism in Left theory and practice.

34. James Petras, "Reflections on the Iranian Revolution," *Capitalist and Socialist Crises in the Late Twentieth Century* (New York: Rowman and Allanheld, 1983).

35. Quoted in Morosini, op. cit., p. 70.

36. Petras, op. cit.

4

Labor and Democracy in Post-Revolutionary Iran

Assef Bayat

Introduction

In a given capitalist social formation, the political democracy in broad economics is determined, I propose, by two fundamental factors: the degree of capitalist development and the extent of class struggle. Specifically, the more hegemonic capital is, the more likely it is that the state would take a democratic political form. The reason is that an advanced capital has the capability to accommodate the anti-capitalist and democratic struggles of the working class and other democratic forces. On the other hand, where a weak capital operates, as in the backward capitalist countries of the Third World, the state tends to assume a despotic character. Yet, it does not follow that the backward capitalist societies are doomed to be dominated by despotism. The balance of forces in the political arena may change and be maintained in favor of democracy if the subordinated classes are able to resist the undemocratic policies of the state and if they set limits upon the arbitrary functions of the state by organizing in such mass institutions as labor unions, professional societies, and associations of women, students, and the intelligentsia. Historically, the labor movement has played a major role in bringing about a democratic balance among the social forces.[1]

In a market economy, the relationship between the labor movement and democracy occurs in one of two forms. The first type, "immediate relations," refers to a situation in which labor is assumed to be a powerful economic institution united in a single national organ and capable of imposing its political demands upon the state through changing the balance of forces in society in favor of democratic processes and practices. Historical evidence in Europe suggests that "formal," or "bourgeois," democracy developed as a result of the continued anti-capitalist struggles of organized labor.[2] Similarly,

The author would like to thank the editors for their comments and suggestions on earlier drafts of this chapter.

in Bolivia (a backward capitalist country), a very strong labor movement has, since the 1952 Revolution, forced the return to periodic representative governments following each military coup.[3]

The second type, "mediated relation," refers to the labor movement–democracy relationship in which labor seeks to implement a strategy of "economic democracy" through a transformation of the authoritarian division of labor in the workplace. Such a strategy, if sustained, can provide conditions for extending and consolidating democratic institutions and traditions that may lead to political democracy. Because this strategy presupposes the institutionalization of accountability, criticism, and direct involvement, it would tend to lead to a new conception of power relations. The institution of economic democracy, then, requires, for its reproduction, a certain degree of democratization at the level of the state institutions and political decision-making. The Yugoslav self-management system, for instance, is certainly a crucial factor in determining the relatively democratic character of the state in that country in comparison to the other Eastern European countries.

In this chapter, I will discuss the relationship between the labor movement and democracy in Iran after the Revolution. Both "immediate" and "mediated" aspects are considered. By the "labor movement" in revolutionary Iran, I mean largely the "workers' councils" or *Shurahs*. The latter were an organizational manifestation of the strong desire on the part of the working classes in both industry and the service sectors to exert control over production and the administration of production.[4]

In referring to "democracy" in a capitalist social formation, I point to both the "macro" level (e.g., as political democracy) and the "micro" level (perceived as grassroots democracy). The former concept broadly defines a political system in which the state's policies are determined by the citizens of the given country through a mechanism of representation. To make such a system reality, certain types of political freedoms (e.g., freedom of expression, assembly, and political organization) have to be presupposed. Democracy at the "micro" level refers to the way in which the policies of certain economic and social institutions (e.g., industry, educational systems, and neighborhoods) are determined from below by direct involvement of the people.

Labor Struggles, 1978–1982

In the course of the revolutionary upheavals in Iran that led to the downfall of the monarchy in February 1979, labor struggles mounted and developed in two successive stages. The first stage, October 1978 to February 1979, was characterized by a wave of mass strikes, and the second stage, from February 1979 to July 1982, by the emergence and development of the labor council movement.

Mass Strikes, 1978–1979

Following massive street demonstrations in the urban centers and the oil strike in October 1978, workers' strikes spread rapidly throughout offices and industry, in both the state and the private sectors.[5] By January 1979 the entire urban working class, including white-collar and blue-collar workers, had put down their tools. The strike movement culminated in the general strike during the Bakhtiar government. Both wage earners and small-business people helped to halt all major economic activities.

The strikes by the industrial working class had already begun as early as May 1978. Initially, the demands of the strikers were overwhelmingly economic. They changed gradually into political demands, however (although some retained their economic form), directed not to limited and immediate economic objectives but to long-term political goals. In particular, the strikers aimed at dismantling the political order by inflicting economic wounds on the regime. By October 1978, some 45 percent of the demands of the strikers were political, reaching 80 percent in November and 100 percent in February.[6] Although the industrial working class as an *organized* force entered the political scene later than the urban masses, the workers as *individuals* had already been present in the street demonstrations. It was not until October that the industrial working class, alongside the state employees, started to organize concerted strike actions by creating strike committees in the industrial workplace.

For the most part, the strike committees were led by militant workers with three distinct backgrounds: experienced secular trade unionists, worker activists linked to anti-monarchy religious circles, and militant workers with leftist tendencies. The organization of the strike committees was largely decentralized, and their day-to-day affairs were directed neither by a national coordinating body nor by the official leadership of the revolution based in Paris. At times, the strike committees came into conflict with Ayatollah Khomeini's representatives or the religious leaders inside the country over matters concerning the handling of strike policies (e.g., the case of the committees in railway, oil, and customs). In the days immediately following the Revolution, it was these strike committees that, to some degree, provided the *institutional* bases for the organization of the council movement to which I turn below.

The Council Movement, 1979–1982

The second stage of the workers' movement was identified with the development of workers' councils after the Revolution. The councils constituted the organizational embodiment of a strong desire in the workforce to exert control over both the processes and the administration of production. They formed the workplace organizations that aimed to extend the control of labor over the organization of production, limit the authority of management, and democratize the work environment. Thus the activities of the councils transcended those of the typical labor unions or workplace syndicates, whose concerns did not usually go beyond matters of wages and conditions of work. In their day-to-day activities, the councils were concerned not only with wages and working conditions but also with matters of employment and dismissal, production, pricing, procurement, and investment.

Structurally, the workers' council is normally seen as an administrative apparatus, or as a directly elected body of workers who, as members of the "executive committee," are assigned by the assembly of employees to carry out the tasks specified in the councils' constitutions or demanded directly by the workers. To be more precise, a council should be viewed not merely as an administrative apparatus but as a totality encompassing the employees, the structure of power delegation, and control-oriented practices, and the rationale that governs the structure and practices in the workplace.

In the first six months after the Revolution, a form of "control from below" prevailed in the workplace through the mediation of the labor councils, which took part in decision-making processes or set into motion and ran the enterprises whose owners or managers had fled the country or had gone underground. The political and economic consolidation of the Islamic state gradually undermined the real power of the secular councils, and the system of one-man management from above was once again reintroduced.

Workers' councils emerged alongside other popular and grass-roots organs such as district committees, peasants' councils (in the northern provinces), employees' councils within the state administration, and councils of cadets in the air force. The factory councils, however, were more widespread and survived longer than the other organs.

Why did the councils emerge? The concept of such councils had no precedent in the historical experience of contemporary Iranian laborers. The experience of "council societies" (*Anjomanhaye Shuraii*), which emerged in some northern cities and among the urban people during the Constitutional Revolution (1905–1907), existed too long ago to be remembered by the present generation of industrial laborers.[7] Nor did the idea come from without—that is, from the political groups (left, secular, or religious). Only after the *Shurahs* had been organized by the workers themselves did the political groups propagate them and provide them with a loosely structured theoretical framework. In this connection, the Left political groups tended to wrongly conceive of the *Shurahs* as similar to the *soviets* that emerged during the Russian Revolution. The latter, unlike factory councils, were bodies that went beyond the workplace, representing not only the workers but also peasants and soldiers, and whose concern was mainly political. Relying on two *ayats* from the Quran, the ideologies of the Islamic Republic party (IRP) attempted to establish a Quranic origin for the *Shurahs*.[8] The IRP also wanted to change the notion of *Shuraism* as being exclusive to the Marxists whose ideological ideas about the councils predominated over those of other political organizations at that time.

The councils were conjunctural (i.e., time-specific) phenomena. They resulted from the consolidation of two distinct but interrelated factors. First was the conjunctural inability of Iranian capitalism to respond positively to the workers' "defensive" demands—the demands that aimed to preserve their already acquired gains. This inability of capital was related to the crisis conditions in which capitalism found itself immediately after the Revolution.

Specifically, the legitimacy of capitalist rationale and relations had come into question after the Revolution. Thus, in the aftermath of the insurrection when Khomeini ordered workers to end their strikes, the large-scale firms shut down, and industrialists and company owners connected with foreign capital either went into hiding or fled the country. Furthermore, the supply of raw materials had come to a halt, there had been no new investments since the beginning of the widespread strikes in industries, some companies had gone bankrupt, and many firms refused to continue their operations until the new state could assure them of favorable business conditions. Although the provisional government was relatively quick in declaring its support for private investments, productive capital could not be assured of political security. This situation prevails even today and has to do with the peculiar nature of the Islamic state.[9]

Under such conditions, capital was unable to respond to the ordinary defensive demands of the revolutionized labor force, including payment of delayed wages, re-employment and job security, and higher pay and benefits. Together, such demands constituted about 52 percent of the total demands made.[10] This inability of capital provided material conditions for workers to transcend their defensive demands and resort to offensive direct action: taking over plants and running them themselves, presiding over the financial activities of the companies, occupying factories, and so on. These actions were indeed instances of workers' control, in as much as they were institutionalized and regulated by the councils. The first five months after the Revolution witnessed at least 374 industrial incidents: strikes, sit-ins, protests, demonstrations, occupations, and hostage-takings. These incidents involved at least 286 large industrial units.[11]

Although a crisis in the capitalist reproduction process is necessary if workers are to adopt an offensive strategy, it is not by itself sufficient. An additional factor must be present—namely, the acquisition and development by the working classes of a new, control-oriented form of consciousness. Indeed, this new form of consciousness was the product of the revolutionary crisis. It was based upon the workers' feeling that "we have struggled to defeat the past, so we have the right to determine the future." Their new mentality was shaped by all those layers of the population who had participated actively in the Revolution. Yet each layer tended to give expression to this consciousness in its own immediate surroundings. For the industrial working class, it was manifested in the idea and practice of factory *Shurahs*.

In addition to new economic conditions and this different state of political consciousness, a third element contributed to the popularity of the *Shurahs* as an organizational concept: a power struggle within the provisional government. The "liberals" in the government opposed the formation of the councils, whereas the Islamic Republic party stepped up its support for them. The party aimed at dismissing the "liberals" as counterrevolutionary while presenting itself as a revolutionary alternative (as discussed in the last section).

The Council Movement and Democracy

To what extent did the post-revolutionary labor movement—in particular, the council organizations—contribute to the cause of democracy in Iran? The issue must be examined in terms of both its immediate implications and its mediated implications.

Immediate Implications

There is no strong evidence to suggest that the Iranian working class was involved in *direct* political struggle for preserving the democratic achievements of the Revolution beyond the workplaces (i.e., at the societal level). For instance, we lack evidence of organized opposition by the working class to government policies concerning freedom of expression, ethnic minorities, women, and so on. On the other hand, no evidence exists to indicate that the working class supported these policies either.[12] There is, however, an important exception to this generalization: The pro-IRP supporters among the working class, organized in the Islamic *Shurahs* and Islamic associations, opposed the policies of the provisional government but supported the government formed by the party.

The absence of effective democratic activities among the working class at the societal level may be inscribed by two sets of considerations: sociological/organizational and ideological/political.

Sociological/Organizational Considerations. The working-class organizations, whether councils or labor syndicates, were never combined in a nationwide institution. For the most part, they were scattered throughout the individual workplaces. Only a few attempts were made to unite the councils on an industrial or regional basis as exemplified by the Union of the Councils (UC) of the Industrial Units of the Gilan Province, the UC of the Oil Industry, the UC of the Organization of Industrial Development, the UC of West Tehran, the UC of East Tehran, and the Union of the Contract and Seasonal Workers of Abadan and Vicinity.

Except for the latter union and the UC of the Oil Industry, which were involved in political-democratic struggles in Khuzistan province, the scope and activities of the remaining unions were limited to workplace and economic issues.

The failure of the working class to unite the councils can be attributed to three factors. First, workers lacked experience of trade unionism. Political repression under the Shah had hindered independent trade-union activities. Some evidence points to the existence of underground trade-union activities among industrial labor in the early 1970s. Yet it must be stressed that the hasty pace of class formation since the 1960s set restraints on the scope of the clandestine trade unionism. To begin with, a large proportion of the industrial working class was still new to industrial work. In 1980, only 8 percent of factory workers in Tehran came from the industrial working class, which experienced an annual growth rate of 8 percent. Most of these workers (80 percent according to my survey) emerged directly from the rural areas with no experience of industrial work. Having come from the misery of village life (which entailed the loss of land, unemployment, and low income), such workers at least initially viewed factory employment in positive terms—as a means of job security and economic betterment—and thus had little motivation to organize secretly. It was only in the latter part of the 1970s that this new generation started to understand the misery of factory life and began to acquire a new identity.[13]

The second reason is related to the structure of council organization. As the councils were a form of workplace unionism, their common interests were based neither upon the common skills of, say, printers or engineers nor upon industrial classification, such as textile work or coal-mining. Third, the state would oppose any significant attempt by the workers to independently amalgamate the councils into larger organizations, such as the UC of the Organization of the Industrial Development).

Ideological/Political Considerations. Ideological and political factors played an important part in hindering the active intervention of the workers in the society-wide democratic struggles that occurred immediately after the Revolution. In this respect, two specific elements could be identified: the populist policies of the Islamic state, and their untenable political evaluation by the "traditional Left."

The populist policies of the Islamic state emanate from the unique nature of the *welayat-e faqih* ("government of the jurist"). This Islamic form of the state in Iran is characterized by its conflicts with both the working class and the bourgeoisie. (I have outlined the origin and unique nature of the Islamic state in more detail elsewhere.)[14] It suffices here to say that the populist stand of the state played an important part in confusing and dividing the working class politically. A small but active and privileged section of the working class identified its interests with those of the state. Organized in the Islamic associations and the Islamic *Shurahs*, which were initiated by the IRP inside the workplace, this group backed the policies of the regime and formed part of its social/political basis.

Not only the working class but also a large part of the traditional Left became confused by the populist, "anti-capitalist," and "pro-downtrodden" stance of the Islamic state. These leftist groups conceived of the Islamic state as representing the "interests of the petty bourgeoisie," which they described as having an "anti-imperialist" political character. Such conceptions of the state, which informed the political agitations of the left-wing groups, further confused those workers who leaned toward the Left organizations. In addition, the Left groups paid little attention to the issue of civil and democratic rights and liberties, dismissing them as "liberal bourgeois demands."

Mediated Impacts

The labor movement nevertheless contributed to the cause of democracy through the medium of the councils. This contribution was realized in the following terms:

Structure. The councils by their nature were democratic, grass-roots organs. Their executive committees were directly elected and were subject to recall, at any time, by the members. The committees were accountable to general assemblies of employees, and their members were not paid any extra salary for their positions in the committees. Almost all workers in a unit would attend the meetings in which heated debates would take place on issues concerning the running of the workplace. At crucial meetings, such as the ones concerning the conduct of management, a few officials from the Ministry of Labor or the "Imam's representatives" would also attend. The day-to-day activities of the *Shurahs*, including elections, debates in general meetings, and operation of the affairs of the enterprise, had a dramatic impact upon the way the workers conceptualized society, authority, and their social position in the society at large. Indeed, the workers were involved in a learning process. To understand the significance of this change, the reader should recall that, during the last thirty years, democratic institutions (whether state or nonstate) have been almost totally nonexistent in Iran. In family and school, in workplace and political organizations, both open and clandestine, decision making had been basically authoritarian. It was against such a background of political culture that the councils established a nascent democratic tradition and culture.

Function. As indicated above, the workers' councils were the organizational manifestations of the workers' struggle to exert control over the processes and administration of production. In other words, the workers' councils tended, in practice, to transform the authoritarian character of power relations in the workplace by altering the traditional division of labor between functions of "conception" and "execution." This division signifies a division between roles and positions involved in decision making on the one hand, and roles and positions involved in mere implementation of such decisions on the other. The struggle to alter or modify this division of labor is a fundamentally democratic act, because it reflects not simply a technical division of labor between certain employees but, rather, a social division. It points to the relations of domination and subordination of the workplace.

It must be stressed, however, that the *Shurahs* were not Soviet-type organizations, nor could they be an alternative to the Islamic state in pursuit of a socialist revolution. In broad terms, *soviets* in Russia represented the specifically *political* self-organization of the working class—a self-organization that transcended anti-capitalist struggles at the point of production and aimed at controlling the political power.[15] The *Shurahs* in Iran, which generally resembled the characteristics of the factory committees that emerged during the Russian Revolution, fought a battle to transform the despotic and authoritarian power relations that existed in the workplace. The *Shurahs* might have become a national political force if they had survived and combined into a national organization.

The factory councils appeared in five areas within the industrial arena.

1. Trade-union or economic struggles: After the revolution, trade-union organizations were absent. The workers were reluctant to set up syndicates,

principally because of their unpleasant experience with the state-run unions under the Shah and the lack of free and independent trade-union organization. Thus the *Shurahs* also had to play the role of typical labor unions in fighting for economic demands.

2. Struggles against authoritarian relations in the production and administrative enterprises: Authoritarian relations are a predominant characteristic of a factory system based upon the capitalist division of labor. In Iran, the despotic attitude of traditional management was an additional dimension in industrial relations. Thus the councils tended to struggle against these relations by attempting to alter them. The workers' general assemblies put on trial and sacked the elements responsible for maintaining such relations: directors, foremen, SAVAK agents, and so on. For this purpose, the councils formed "investigation committees" and factory tribunals to investigate cases of misconduct and corruption. These activities were undertaken, for example, in Pars Metal, Arj, Yamaha, and the Phillips companies.

3. Control over hiring and firing: Two motives were behind the workers' struggles to control this area of managerial authority. The first, the principal incentive, was related to the idea of "sovereignty of people over their own destiny," as indicated in the constitutions of the *Shurahs* prepared by the workers themselves. The second motive, the practical one, involved achieving the right to fire (e.g., the managers) and to prevent victimization of the workers.

4. Control over the financial affairs of the workplace: This concern related to the workers' determination to have access to the financial information of the companies and to monitor the flow of resources. The workers wanted to know how much was being produced, how many profits or losses there were, where the profits went, to whom the products were sold, and how much was being reinvested.

5. Management of production and administration of production: This concern pertained to the high degree of control wielded by the *Shurahs*. Control at this sphere rendered the management, appointed by the government, virtually redundant. In factories such as Earfoo, Saka, Behpoush, and the Alborz Electrical Industry, the councils declared themselves as "solely responsible for the company." That is, the workers regarded themselves as having the right to preside over distribution, finance, administration, communications, pricing, the purchase of raw materials, production, cultural affairs, and security. The case of the Phillips Company is a good example. "What do all these have to do with the workers?" I asked a council member in a modern plant. He replied:

> The reason the revolution was made at all is because we wanted to become our own masters, to determine our own destiny. . . . We didn't want a situation where one person or a few make decisions for two thousand. When we, two thousand, are working around these walls, we want to know what is going on here; what we'll achieve in the future, in what direction we are running the company, how much we could take for ourselves, how much we could contribute to government for national investment. For this reason, we never

> let management employ somebody to make decisions. This would be a repetition of the same previous mistakes to the extent that it would violate the rights of the workers, which are in fact the rights of the Iranian nation.

Wider Social and Ideological Implications. So far, I have focused on the means by which the council movement contributed to the democratization of the workplace. Now I want to discuss the third level at which the councils affected and could have had further impacts on democracy in Iran if they had survived. In striving to restructure the production process and to alter the inherited relations of subordination and hierarchy, the workers found themselves experiencing new terrains of control and power status previously in the exclusive domain of managers. As they functioned in this learning process, their perceptions of work, power, and society tended to change. Such an experience would confer on the workers a new perception of their role in society such that they would be seen not just as a subordinated and exploited people but as those with the right and ability to determine the direction of production. This change in perception, if sustained, would have been immensely significant in social terms. For it would have involved not only the workers in thinking differently about themselves and about other classes but also the rest of the civil society, notably the dominant classes, in acquiring different attitudes toward the workers. The workers would no longer have been identified as subordinate, miserable, crippled, and regrettable creatures, but as human beings with initiative and ability. This change of attitudes would also have acted against the exclusivist view that the subordinate classes neither need, deserve, nor understand democracy.

In the first six months after the Revolution, a kind of "control from below" prevailed. However, the real power of the councils began to be undermined when the provisional government started to implement its economic policies and to reestablish the one-man management system at workplaces by appointing professional managers from above. This second period began in the late summer of 1979 and lasted until July 1981. During this time, the industrial workplace became the scene of widespread struggles and tensions between various organs of power: professional management, Islamic (or *maktabi*) management, *Pasdaran* (Revolutionary Guards), Islamic Associations, independent councils (the subject of the present chapter), and the Islamic *Shurahs*. The latter were set up by the pro-IRP workers and backed firmly by the Islamic Republic party as a loyal alternative to the independent *Shurahs*. It is beyond the scope of this chapter to explain the logic behind those tensions and the changing composition of the alliances within the power struggles. It is enough to state that among these rivals the independent councils were incrementally undermined. We turn next to a discussion of the causes behind their disintegration.

Causes of the *Shurahs'* Disintegration

Political Pressure

The political factor underlying the dissolution of the councils concerns the attitudes of both the state and capital toward the *Shurahs*. Although (for the reasons mentioned earlier) the relationship between the Islamic state and the capitalists have long remained contradictory, proponents of both expressed their opposition to the workers' councils primarily because of the anti-authoritarian orientation of the councils.

Different factions in the Islamic state adopted different attitudes at different times toward the *Shurahs*. The provisional government categorically opposed their formation. Instead, it advocated the establishment of syndicates. The provisional government set up a Special Force inside the plants, composed of appointed inspectors, to report on the activities of the councils.

The populist faction of the IRP known as the "Imam's Line" aimed at creating a form of "Islamic corporatism" in order to integrate labor into the Islamic state. In general, corporatism is a form of populist strategy that attempts to integrate the tripartite forces of labor, capital, and the state in order to make them work cooperatively for the good of a "beloved nation." Cooperatism in Iran featured such additional ingredients of Islamic ideology as the corporatism of Islamic workers, *mashru* ("legitimate") capitalism, *maktabi* (literally, "Islamic") management, and the Islamic state, all of which cooperated for the common cause of the nation. By attempting to adopt such a policy, the IRP strengthened the notion of *shuraism* (albeit with an Islamic character) and employed it both in the workplace and in society at large in order to discredit the values and the elements that it considered "liberal." The policy also aimed to preempt the socialist ideas and organizations with which the idea of *shuraism* had been intertwined. The policy, in practice, also weakened the position of workers by dividing the councils into "Islamic" and "non-Islamic." The nonconformist councils were later dismantled.

The "fundamentalist" faction of the IRP, the Hojjatiyeh sect, believed that the very concept of *Shurahs* was irrelevant to Islam and should be abolished altogether. The sect argued that power in Islam emanates from above, from God through the mediation of the *imam* and in his absence through the *naib imam* (the substitute of *imam* on earth). *Shurahs* were un-Islamic because they constituted an institution of power from below. In 1981, Ahmad Tavakkoli, the then minister of labor and a follower of the Hojjatiyeh sect, prohibited the formation of the new Islamic *Shurahs* for a year. But the workers' resistance and the power struggle within the state led to his dismissal. Ayatollah Khomeini himself largely shared the view of Hojjatiyeh on the issue of the *Shurahs*, a fact that observers consider to be the main reason for the conflict that existed between him and Ayatollah Taleghani, who advocated the formation of Islamic councils.[16]

The practical implication of the policies mentioned above assumed different forms: (1) an economic blockade, through which (given its overwhelming control over the banking system, credit, loan, import-export operations, and so on) the state was able to bring such non-conformist *Shurahs* in Saka, Orkeedeh Chinee, Naz Nakh, the Esfahan Wool Industry, among others, to their knees; and (2) blatant political crackdowns by means of intimidation, framing, firing, arresting, and so on, which became common practices. This policy assumed a new momentum after the events of July 1981, when the clergy seized the state apparatus following President Bani Sadr's downfall.

The political crackdowns were devastating blows to the structure and activities of the independent councils. It would be a mistake, however, to attribute the disintegration of the councils wholly to political factors. I maintain that the internal contradictions of the councils should be considered the major factor responsible for their failure. In other words, for the reasons stated above, the *real* (versus the formal) power of the *Shurahs* would have been undermined, even in the absence of political pressure.

Internal Contradictions

The internal contradictions that led to the councils' dissolution consisted of conflict between the short-term and long-term interests of the councils. The workers who had fought so dramatically against the professional managers and the system they represented, who had put the managers on trial and dismissed them on several occasions, and who had been running the companies for months requested the state to send back these same professional managers to solve certain problems. This contradiction in the workers' behavior toward the managers reflected the dual function of the management task: "Coordination" and "control" corresponded respectively to the technical and social divisions of labor in the production process. The function of coordination is related to the technical coordination of the affairs—that is, to the maintenance of harmony, avoidance of waste and the like—which is required in all complex forms of organization. The function of control, on the other hand, is the manifestation of power relations in the production process and is historically determined and specific to authoritarian forms of organizations. The two functions can be separated only at the level of abstraction. In reality, they reproduce each other.

Now, the workers wanted to transform the existing management system. In so doing, however, they felt that they needed, in the short run, the skills of professional managers in order to maintain production. But the reinstatement of the very same managers meant, in fact, reestablishment of the same technical and social (power) relations. So the workers both wanted, and at the same time did not want, the existing management system. Thus, on the one hand, restructuring or modifying the existing system of the division of labor was essential to the survival of the councils in the long run. The consolidation of the councils therefore required new relations and a new system of management. On the other hand, their short-run survival depended on the same traditional forms of managerial competence. In short, the councils wanted the same managerial functions without the associated power relations; but this desire obviously could not be realized because in the hierarchical structure of management, each agent carries, within his or her position, a specific degree of power that is exerted objectively.

The immediate implication of this contradiction for the *Shurahs* was the general weakening of their real power and their transformation into institutions that had only formal power. From the time of the U.S. Embassy seizure in late 1979 and the government's growing concern with "rationalizing" industry, the executive power of the councils tended to change gradually from determination of the organization of work and production to consultation and cooperation with the management. The rapid demise of the independent councils started just after the political crackdown of July 1981, following which the pro-IRP Islamic *Shurahs* and the Islamic Associations dominated the workplace.[17]

Conclusion

I have attempted to explore the relationship between the labor movement and democracy in post-revolutionary Iran by assessing this relationship at two "immediate" and "mediated" (or indirect) levels of impact of labor upon the realization of democratic practices. My argument is that the workers' movement, embodied in the council organizations, contributed to the cause of democracy by establishing democratic institutions and a nascent democratic tradition at the workplace. The labor movement, however, failed to act as an effective force to maintain the *political democracy* that had been generated in the aftermath of the Revolution.

Having witnessed the "Islamic Revolution" and its outcome, we may once again find it possible to observe the establishment of democracy in Iran in the future. In that case, the question of how to maintain political democracy would certainly be the major issue, because the historical and structural factors constraining the practice of democracy will be present: weak capital, transitory classes, and a backward state. At this time, not much can be said about the way in which political democracy may be reproduced in Iran in the future. But what can be said at this stage is that democracy, whether at the societal or the local ones, cannot be maintained by the good will of the political leaders, however sincere their intentions may be. The future political system must be structured in such a way as to be able to *afford* the practice of democracy. Democracy can be maintained only through the establishment of a necessary balance among the conflicting forces in society: capital, labor, and the state in their totality.

Restriction or even abolition of market relations does not automatically lead to a democratic structure. Besides, as far as Iran is concerned, market relations are likely to remain even after another revolutionary upheaval. Thus, the creation of popular, independent, and grass-roots organizations seems essential to the generation and maintenance of that necessary balance. In this process, the experience of labor councils in industry, the service sector, state administration, and educational establishments, as well as the councils in local neighborhoods and among the ethnic minorities, would be of immense value. Among these, the grass-roots and independent labor councils can play a vital role, for they are able to contribute to the cause of democracy both directly (as unified organizations of working people) and indirectly (as democratic institutions in which employees would experiment, practice, and learn democracy in a systematic way).

Two points must be made in this regard. First, the objective feasibility and systematic operation of these mass organizations could only be the preconditions and products of a political order that will transcend class and elite rule. Second, there must also exist a clear vision of how to construct the necessary balance of social forces to maintain the political democracy. If it is true that mass and grass-roots organizations are essential for the creation of that balance and, thus, for the democratization of Iranian society in the future, then one must have a clear idea of how to reproduce the *real* power of such mass organizations (such as the factory councils). The answer to the above question lies in the future, in the process of experience, and partly in the present—specifically, in the construction of a *theory* of "power from below," at both the "micro" and the "macro" levels.

Notes

1. I have developed this view in my *Workers and Revolution in Iran: A Third World Experience of Workers' Control* (London: Zed Books, 1986), ch. 11. I am aware of the fact that other factors may intervene to determine the success or failure of a democratic structure in a given country (e.g., historical, cultural, international, or geopolitical factors). Yet I must stress that the two factors I have mentioned in the text (i.e., degree of capitalist development and the intensity of social [class] struggle) are the basic ones.

2. See E. P. Thompson, *The Making of the English Working Class* (London: Penguin, 1962); and G. Therborn, "The Rule of Capital and the Rise of Democracy," *New Left Review*, no. 103 (1977); G. Therborn, "The Travail of Latin American Democracy," *New Left Review*, nos. 113–114 (1979).

3. G. Therborn, "The Travail of Latin American Democracy," op. cit.; J. Dunkerley, *Rebellion in the Veins: Political Struggle in Bolivia, 1953–1982* (London: Verso, 1984).

4. In this chapter, I use the terms *Shurah*, *workers' council*, and *factory council* interchangeably. For further discussion of the Iranian council movement, see A. Bayat, op. cit.; A. Bayat, "Iran: Workers' Control after the Revolution," *MERIP Reports*, no. 113 (1983); V. Moghadam, "Workers' Councils in Revolutionary Iran," *Against the Current*, no. 2 (1985).

5. For a more elaborate account, see A. Bayat, *Workers and Revolution*, op. cit., ch. 6.

6. For an elaboration of the concept of "economic/political struggles," and the sources of the figures, see A. Bayat, *Workers and Revolution*, op. cit., ch. 6.

7. H. Nategh, "Anjomanhaye Shuraii dar Enghelab-i Mashroutiat," in *ALEFBA*, no. 4 (1363) [1984], Paris (in Persian); Kh. Shakeri, "Pishinehaye Jonbesh-i Anjomanein," in *Kitab-i Jomeha*, no. 5 (1364) [1985], Paris (in Persian).

8. The literal definition of *Shurah* in the *ayats* is as follows: "To conduct a work, the Moslems should consult among each other." See J. Shoar, *The Quranic Documents on Shurahs* (Tehran; 1360 [1981]) (in Persian).

9. I have discussed this matter in my working paper, "The Rationale of an Irrational Economy: Economic Management and the Islamic State of Iran," presented at the Fourth Annual Conference of the Center for Iranian Research and Analysis (CIRA) (Washington, D.C., April 1986).

10. These figures have been calculated on the basis of an analysis of reported industrial incidents recorded in leftist literature between February 1979 and February 1980.

11. The number of industrial incidents in the three years after the Revolution are as follows: 1358 (1979–1980): 366; 1359 (1980–1981): 180; 1360 (1981–1982): 82.

12. As a matter of fact, conversations with individual workers revealed that the workers were not particularly interested in such anti-democratic government policies.

13. See A. Bayat, *Workers and Revolution*, op. cit., ch. 4; A. Bayat, "Proletarianization and Culture: Tehran Factory Workers," in *ALEFBA*, no. 4 (1363)[1984] (in Persian).

14. A. Bayat, *Workers and Revolution*, op. cit., ch. 7.

15. Originally, the term *soviet* referred to two forms of workers' organizations that sprang up following the February Revolution of 1917—namely, the actual Soviet of Factory Committees (i.e., the Executive Committee of the Conference of Factory Committees held in late May 1917) and the Soviet of Deputies of Petrograd, which represented the workers, soldiers, and even the peasants. See M. Ferro, *October 1917* (London: Routledge, 1980), p. 150. It was the latter, the Soviet of Petrograd, that eventually questioned Kerensky's government.

16. Professor Ervand Abrahamian brought this observation to my attention.

17. It must be emphasized that the processes of transformation of the *Shurahs* were characterized by tensions, struggles, and a high degree of resistance.

5

The Military and Politics in the Islamic Republic of Iran

Nader Entessar

The armed forces of the Islamic Republic should be the antithesis of the Imperial Armed Forces. What is important for the new Islamic military is to become part and parcel of the larger society within which it operates—it should transform itself into a people's armed forces.

—Hujjatul Islam 'Ali Khamenei[1]

Introduction

The purpose of this chapter is twofold: (1) to explain the major causes of the demise of the Imperial Armed Forces and their replacement by new "Islamicized" regular and paramilitary forces, and (2) to examine the functions of the Islamic Armed Forces within the broader framework of the Islamic Republic's domestic and foreign postures.

Generally speaking, military institutions have played an important political role in Islamic societies; moreover, as Manfred Halpern has noted, military and political institutions have traditionally been intertwined and have performed overlapping functions in the Middle East.[2] Even in countries that have not experienced prolonged periods of direct military rule, the armed forces have constituted a major pillar of civilian regimes in the region.[3]

In twentieth-century Iran, the military has been instrumental in shaping political events and institutions. Reza Khan, the founder of the Pahlavi monarchy, was an army officer when he staged a military coup d'etat in 1921, thus paving the way for his 1925 accession to power as the king of the new dynasty. The second Pahlavi monarch, Muhammad Reza (hereafter referred to as the Shah), relied heavily on the Iranian armed forces to sustain his regime in the formative years of his rule following Reza Khan's abdication

The author is grateful to Hooshang Amirahmadi of Rutgers University and Gregory Rose of the University of Texas at Austin for their comments and criticism of an earlier draft of this paper.

and exile from the country in 1941. The Shah's reliance on the military was heightened after 1953, when he was restored to the Pahlavi throne by a U.S.-sponsored military coup that overthrew the nationalist government of Muhammad Musadeq, the prime minister.

Following the overthrow of the Shah's regime in 1979, it became imperative for the new revolutionary government to transform the Shah's military into an institution that would serve the interests and aspirations of the Islamic Republic. We must comprehend the structural and ideological transformation of the Iranian military in order to better understand the political dynamics and developments in post-revolutionary Iran.

Scholarly studies of the post-revolutionary Iranian military have been rare, primarily due to the paucity of accurate data. The exceptions are the published manuscripts by Gregory Rose and William Hickman, both of which deal primarily with the purge process in the ranks of the military personnel, albeit from different perspectives.[4] This chapter, as well, attempts to shed some light on the Iranian military and its metamorphosis since 1979.

The Fall of the Imperial Armed Forces

Prior to the Iranian Revolution of 1978–1979, most Western observers of the Iranian political scene attributed the ostensible stability of the Shah's regime to the power of the Imperial Armed Forces and their allegiance to the Pahlavi monarchy. Even as late as mid-November 1978, two months prior to the Shah's departure from Iran, Western military analysts were expressing confidence in the Imperial military's unmitigated loyalty to the Shah. As one military analyst put it: "Senior officers in top command are as solid as rocks in their support of the Shah."[5] After all, the Shah possessed the fifth largest military force in the world, with some 410,000 uniformed personnel and a budget of $7.3 billion in 1977.[6]

Furthermore, the Shah had carefully nurtured his top military officers. He took a personal interest in the well-being of these officers, particularly those in the Air Force—the Shah's favorite branch of the service. The Shah also provided relatively attractive salaries and generous fringe benefits and pension plans for the officer corps of his armed forces. He supervised their training programs and was directly responsible for all promotions above the rank of major.[7] Consequently, loyalty to the Shah, rather than military achievements on the battlefield or expertise in military strategy, became the principal criterion for field-grade and higher promotions in the Imperial Armed Forces.

Not only material incentives but also an ingenious multi-tiered command-and-control system enhanced the military's loyalty to the regime. As *The Economist* of London reported, "in about every decision-making field somebody somewhere was checking on somebody else."[8] Furthermore, in order to minimize the danger of collusion among various military command units, the Shah removed all intermediate levels of command among the three branches of the armed forces. The commanders of the Ground Forces, the

Air Force, and the Navy were allowed to maintain liaison only through the Shah's command staff via the prime minister's office. Moreover, no military troop movements were permitted without the Shah's prior knowledge and written consent.

The Shah controlled the military also by means of a three-layer intelligence network, each layer of which had overlapping duties. One layer consisted of the State Security and Intelligence Organization, which oversaw the Shah's secret police and acted as his "eyes and ears, and where necessary, his iron fist."[9] The second layer comprised the Imperial Inspectorate headed by General Hussein Fardust, the Shah's former classmate and his childhood friend.[10] The task of the Imperial Inspectorate included, among other things, watching SAVAK activities and monitoring the movements of high-level military officers. Finally, there was the J-2 Bureau, which, as a formal part of the armed forces, was charged with gathering military intelligence. The J-2 also kept a close watch on both the SAVAK and the Imperial Inspectorate. The heads of all the aforementioned intelligence organizations reported directly to the Shah and were not allowed to maintain liaison with each other without the Shah's consent. Intelligence activities were also performed by other units within the military-security complex, such as the military police, the Imperial Guard, the Gendarmerie (or rural police), and the police departments in Iranian cities.

The Shah's control over the vast network of military-intelligence organizations was secured to a great extent by what Farhad Kazemi has called "a policy of divide and rule which assigns overlapping duties for gathering of intelligence to separate organizations."[11] By the same token, the Shah endeavored to lessen the danger of a military conspiracy against his regime by periodically reshuffling or purging military officers at the top echelon and replacing them with individuals with no ambitions of their own or those who had proven their loyalty to the Pahlavi monarchy. This tactic was particularly evident in the last few months of the Shah's reign, when his regime was especially vulnerable to a military coup d'etat. When the Shah installed a military government on November 6, 1978, in the hope of quelling the revolutionary upheaval that was engulfing the country, he appointed General Gholam Reza Azhari as prime minister. General Azhari, a graduate of the U.S. Army's Staff College at Fort Leavenworth, Kansas, was 67 years old at the time of his appointment; his health was poor, and he had no political ambitions. Azhari had commanded the Imperial Guards, the 12,000-man elite force in charge of guarding the Shah's personal safety, and he had become the armed forces' chief of staff.

General Azhari may have been indecisive, but General Gholam 'Ali Oveissi, the martial law administrator in Tehran during the heyday of revolutionary activities in September–October 1978, did not lack initiative in confronting the anti-Shah masses. Nicknamed "the Butcher of Tehran" by the opposition groups for his brutal suppression of mass dissent, Oveissi had previously headed the Gendarmerie forces and was instrumental in crushing the massive uprisings of June 1963 in the holy city of Qum that led to Ayatollah

Khomeini's expulsion from Iran. In 1985, Oveissi was assassinated in Paris, where he was living in exile.

That the Shah viewed the armed forces as the major pillar of his regime is beyond doubt. The phenomenal rise in Iran's military budget from $290 million in 1963 to more than $1.9 billion in 1973 and again to $8 billion in 1978 was indicative of the Shah's determination to strengthen his regime's stability. The Shah's arms purchases from abroad in the decade of the 1970s constituted "the most rapid buildup of military power under peacetime conditions of any nation in the history of the world."[12] The Shah's orders for military hardware from the United States alone amounted to $20 billion between 1970 and 1978. From the Shah's perspective, the purchase of sophisticated arms from the United States would make Iran a major military force capable of projecting its power beyond the Persian Gulf and into the Arabian Sea and the Indian Ocean. From the U.S. policy-makers' perspective, massive arms sales to Iran would contribute to balancing the United States' trade deficit, would stabilize the employment picture in an otherwise unstable aerospace industry, and would serve America's strategy of converting Iran into a surrogate of Western interests and the "gendarme" of the Gulf.[13]

The surrogate strategy was put into practice in 1973 with the Iranian military intervention in Oman in order to bolster the pro-Western Sultan Qabus' regime against a guerrilla movement in Oman's Dhofar province. The Omani rebellion against Qabus was directed by the Popular Front for the Liberation of Oman (PFLO), a leftist insurgency movement that had staged a decade-long struggle to overthrow the Omani royal family. The Iranian expeditionary force of 2,000 men, the Iranian government claimed, was instrumental in the military defeat of the PFLO guerrillas.[14] Iran's military performance in Oman was to be the ultimate vindication of the surrogate strategy in Southwest Asia, despite the limited and questionable success of that performance.

Crumbling from Within

For all their apparent power, the Imperial Armed Forces were never able to obtain the needed legitimacy in the eyes of the Iranian people. They were generally perceived not as patriotic forces designed to defend the country against foreign aggression but, rather, as a military unit performing primarily the twin tasks of maintaining the Shah in power and serving U.S. interests in the region. The presence of 10,000 Americans working in military-related projects in Iran reinforced the perception of U.S. domination of the Shah's regime among many Iranians. Many Iranians, as well as some members of the Congress of the United States, began to question the implications of the major U.S. military presence in Iran and the close identification of the Shah's armed forces with the U.S. posture in the region. A U.S. Senate report concluded that, for the most part, the Shah's military forces would not be able to utilize effectively the sophisticated weapons purchased from the United States in the absence of a long-term U.S. presence in the country and "an excessive degree of U.S. technical assistance."[15] The U.S. military presence in Iran also contributed to the deterioration of morale among the Iranian armed forces personnel.[16] This outcome was partly due to the fact that several high-ranking Iranian officers had been placed under the nominal command of lower-ranking U.S. advisors who were receiving salaries and fringe benefits that were at least three times higher than those received by their Iranian counterparts.

Despite these shortcomings, the armed forces (or at least the command structure) were thought to be solidly behind the Shah, even during the heyday of the revolutionary uprising. For example, both General Manuchehr Khosrowdad, the Air Corps commander, and General Mehdi Rahimi, the military governor of Tehran, were among the young, ambitious, and highly skilled senior military officers who remained loyal to the Shah even after his departure from Iran in January 1979. As both later confessed shortly before they were executed by the new revolutionary regime, they would have staged a coup to save the Pahlavi monarchy had the Shah asked them to do so. In fact, the loyalty of many top military officers to the Shah did not allow them to "collaborate on any scheme without his express order as long as he was in Iran, and the time available for making plans and provisions after he left was not sufficient. As a result, the idea of a military coup d'etat never moved beyond the level of talk."[17]

The Shah's departure from the country brought to the fore the weakness of his military command structure and intensified rivalries among the heads of the branches of the armed forces. A strong rivalry developed between General 'Abbas Qarabaghi, the chairman of the Joint-Chiefs-of-Staff, and other top military officers, particularly General Oveissi, the Ground Forces commander. The Navy behaved as if it were independent of the other forces, as did the Imperial Guard. Consequently, the much-needed cooperation and coordination of activities of the various branches and sub-branches of the armed forces never materialized.[18]

The loyalty of the rank-and-file of the Imperial Armed Forces remained another thorny issue facing the faltering Pahlavi dynasty. This was particulary true in the case of the Shah's Ground Forces, whose entire rank-and-file consisted of conscripts. The conscripts, who came primarily from the lower and lower-middle classes, proved to be highly susceptible to Ayatollah Khomeini's religious-nationalistic edicts to desert and join ranks with the revolutionary forces. By November 1978, widespread desertions had become commonplace among the Army conscripts. These were followed by open defiance of the Army command and militant acts of disloyalty. The first serious act of open rebellion occurred on December 11, 1978, in the Lavisan barracks near the Shah's palace in north Tehran, where a group of Ground Forces conscripts entered the officers' mess hall and killed as many as fifteen senior officers and injured many more.[19] This incident set a precedent for other similar acts and prompted a general mutiny by army soldiers in major Iranian cities. In the northwestern provincial city of Tabriz, for example, several soldiers "laid down their arms and allowed opposition demonstrators to take over their vehicles, armored personnel carriers, or trucks."[20]

The mutinies of the Ground Forces spilled over to the other branches of the armed forces. For example, on January 24, 1979, a group of Air Force junior and warrant officers from Tehran's Farahabad garrison joined the anti-monarchy protesters on the capital's streets by proclaiming, "We have joined the people on the orders of Imam Khomeini."[21] This event prompted the arrest and execution of a dozen Air Force personnel and the declaration of a state of emergency within the armed forces—a definite sign of the impending collapse of the Shah's forces.[22]

Still another indication of the eventual demise of the Shah's armed forces was the elimination, for the first time, of the loyalty oath to the Pahlavi monarchy at the graduation ceremonies of Iran's military academies. For example, during the commencement exercises of the Officers College in Tehran on February 5, 1979, the cadets pledged loyalty only to God, the Quran, and the country's independence. Conspicuously absent from the pledge was any reference to the Shah and his dynasty, in spite of the fact that the Shah was still constitutionally the commander-in-chief of the armed forces. In the words of General Manuchehr Biglari, Commandant of the Officers College:

> After completing his initial training and grasping his responsibilities toward his country, every Iranian soldier, as a mature and true Muslim, takes an oath to sacrifice his life for his country's independence and to protect its fundamental rights which are actually an expression of our national and religious beliefs.[23]

In short, the disintegration of the Imperial Armed Forces from within was as much a factor in the defeat of the Pahlavi monarchy as were the mass revolutionary uprisings throughout the country. In fact, as Hassan Nejad has observed, the fall of the Shah's regime was largely due to "the gradual immobilization and demoralization of an army which, because of its recruitment system, organization, and the purpose for its establishment, had, at best, a precarious and illusive loyalty to the regime."[24] It was not a series of military confrontations with the revolutionary forces that brought about the demise of the Shah's armed forces; on the contrary, the armed forces were paralyzed by inter- and intra-service rivalries and by the weakness of the command structure, both of which were exacerbated by the leadership vacuum created after the Shah's departure from Iran. It is within this context that one can understand the issuance on February 11, 1979, of the so-called declaration of neutrality by the chairman of the joint-chiefs-of-staff. This declaration was certainly a last ditch attempt by the Shah's military to salvage the remnants of its crumbling edifice.

The New Revolutionary Armed Forces

After the Imperial military's "declaration of neutrality," which was tantamount to surrender, the government of Shahpur Bakhtiar, the Shah's last prime minister, collapsed and the new provisional revolutionary Islamic government came to power on February 11, 1979. Both Ayatollah Khomeini and Mehdi Bazargan, the new prime minister, were cognizant of the need to have strong armed forces to maintain internal order and to thwart foreign military threats. Therefore, the total dismantling of the Shah's armed forces was not on the priority list of the provisional Islamic government.

However, leftist military personnel staged a massive demonstration in front of Ayatollah Khomeini's Tehran headquarters a week after the downfall of the Imperial Armed Forces demanding the total disbandment of the Shah's military forces and their replacement by a "national revolutionary army." Calling the Shah's military command inherently counterrevolutionary, the young militant officers and their sympathizers issued a resolution demanding that revolutionary masses be given arms to nullify the threat of a counterrevolution: "Responsible people should be given arms," the resolution stated, "with which to protect the police stations and other installations, under the supervision of an elected committee [representing] lawyers, merchants, clergymen, and the Army officers of good reputation."[25] Furthermore, the militant officers vehemently opposed the appointment of General Muhammad Vali Qarani as the new chief of the Army's general staff. Ayatollah Khomeini, in order to maintain discipline within the military and prevent widespread insubordination, sided with General Qarani. In a statement issued to the young officers, Khomeini stated that for years General Qarani had been condemned by the former regime and had spent time in prison on charges of plotting to overthrow the Pahlavi monarchy. Ayatollah Khomeini's defense of Qarani was indicative of the new regime's intentions to reconstitute the armed forces as judiciously as possible and to "ensure that the armed forces were not subject to a wholesale reign of terror."[26]

The Purge Process

In the immediate aftermath of the Revolution, the armed forces, which had fallen into disarray because of massive rank-and-file desertions and the collapse of morale during the revolutionary upheaval, began to be reconstituted. Necessary to this reconstitution, was the purging of some senior officers from the Imperial Armed Forces. However, as Gregory Rose has shown, the first purge period (February–September 1979) was not "aimed at dismantling the pre-revolutionary armed forces."[27] Contrary to popular perception, the purge process in the first period was minimal, affecting only a handful of top military personnel who were closely associated with the last months of the Shah's regime in its last months.[28] These personnel were replaced by junior officers with family or functional ties to the clergy, or by senior officers who themselves had been purged by the Shah. The latter category included such people as General Qarani; General Sa'id Mahdiyun, the first post-revolutionary Air Force chief; and Rear Admiral Ahmad Madani, who was given the defense portfolio in Bazargan's government.[29]

The misperception about massive purges of the armed forces personnel resulted in, among other things, a breakdown of discipline in the armed forces, with some junior officers and conscripts seeking to veto the appointment of their commanders and openly disobeying the orders of their supervisors. Numerous revolutionary councils emerged in military installations and operated as a power center parallel to the existing command structures.[30] As a result, the military was further weakened at a critical time, when its loyalty was being questioned and its services were needed to quell uprisings among the Kurds and Turkoman tribes in northwestern and northern Iran, respectively. The military's paralysis and the danger facing the territorial integrity of the country compelled Ayatollah Khomeini to issue an eight-point edict. In it, Khomeini stated,

> As the Commander-in-Chief of the armed forces, I express my unequivocal support for all branches of our fighting forces. I will neither allow nor tolerate any criticism of our armed forces. Nor will I tolerate insubordination within the ranks of the armed forces. All those who disobey their commanders or endeavor to weaken the military in any fashion will be considered counter-revolutionary and will be dealt with in our revolutionary courts.[31]

In the first purge period, the execution of military personnel was not as massive as some critics have suggested. In fact, from mid-February to late September 1979, the execution of military personnel constituted approximately 21 percent of the total announced executions of 404 people in the country.[32] A more extensive purge within the armed forces, however, did occur when Mustafa Chamran, the deputy prime minister in charge of revolutionary affairs, was given the defense portfolio in September 1979. Chamran was the first civilian appointed to head the Defense Ministry. He was also a great orator and had established impeccable Islamic revolutionary credentials not only in Iran but also in Lebanon, where he was instrumental in setting up the military wing of the Amel Shi'ite militia movement.

Under Chamran's auspices, the (second) purge of the Iranian armed forces was aimed at ideological purification of military personnel at all levels. Chamran contended that the existing military order had been created by the "satanic" Pahlavi regime and, therefore, was not amenable to reform. These purges, however, were to be conducted in an "Islamic and revolutionary" manner based on the officers' belief in the tenets of the Revolution and the concept of *velayat-e faqih* (government of jurist) under the leadership of Ayatollah Khomeini.[33]

The purges in the armed forces were undertaken under the provisions of a bill passed by the Revolutionary Council (the de facto parliament) authorizing general purges in all governmental organizations. Under Chamran's leadership, the Defense Ministry set up numerous revolutionary committees to review credentials of its uniformed personnel and to recommend retention or dismissal. By September 1980, at the time of the Iraqi invasion, the second phase of the purge of the armed forces had come to a conclusion. During this phase, more than 10,000 personnel from the Ground Forces were purged, whereas those purged from the Navy and the Air Force totaled only 2,000.[34] This imbalance was largely due to the size of the Ground Forces and the fact that neither the Navy nor the Air Force had been involved to any significant degree in supporting anti-Shah mass demonstrations. Moreover, it is significant to note that, despite the intensification of the purge process under Chamran, the impact of the second purge period at the field-grade level was rather limited. As Gregory Rose has observed, "it is the field-grade which fills the crucial brigade and battalion command and staff positions necessary for performance of complex combat operations, and the purge's impact at this level appears to have been not so great."[35] All in all, about 29.4 percent (4,000) of the field-grade officers were affected by the second purge period.[36]

Another factor that contributed to the purges in the armed forces was the failed attempt to rescue the U.S. hostages in Iran and the suspicion that some Iranian military officers were in collusion with the Americans during the rescue endeavor. Perhaps the most prominent Iranian casualty of the U.S. rescue operation was General Bahman Amir-Baqeri, the Air Force chief-of-staff who was removed from his post and later arrested and condemned to life imprisonment. Baqeri's "crime" was carrying out an order from President Bani-Sadr to destroy the remaining U.S. helicopters left in the desert near Tabas and, in the process, destroying documents that had been left in the helicopters.[37]

The military purges reintensified following the discovery of two military coup plans in June and July 1980. The first was a minor plot code-named "Operation Overthrow," which was centered in the Piranshahr military base in Kurdistan. The second was an attempt by a larger group of Ground Force and Air Force officers to stage a coup against the regime. This attempt, code-named "Red Alert," originated in the Shahrukhi Air Base in the western city of Hamadan. According to Hujjatul Islam Muhammad Reyshahri, the chief of the military tribunal, some 600 officers were involved in the coup attempt. They had intended to bomb Khomeini's residence in north Tehran, Bani-Sadr's presidential headquarters, and the Fayzieh Theological Seminary in Qum.

Although the Revolutionary Guards managed to uncover and crush the coup attempts, they nevertheless heightened the regime's fear of military intervention in politics. Within a few weeks after the July coup attempt was blocked, 140 executions of military officers were announced. Moreover, the post-July 1980 purges were increasingly being couched in constitutional terms as an attempt to Islamicize the armed forces. To be sure, the preamble of the Constitution of the Islamic Republic calls for the establishment of a *maktabi* (doctrinaire) military:

> In creating our defensive forces, religious faith and adherence to religious doctrines should be the principal criteria for the recruitment of personnel in the military and the Revolutionary Guards Corps. Our defensive forces, therefore, should be entrusted not only with the duties of safeguarding our country's frontiers; they should also be capable of waging doctrinal *jihad* (holy war) in the name of God and for the extension of His domain.[38]

In other words, the doctrinal military would be blessed with the grace of God to carry on His battles of truth against "the army of falsehood."

A final factor that helped to accelerate the military purges in the Islamic Republic was the desire of the country's leadership to remove social and class barriers between the officers and the soldiers. Several commentators have argued that the failure of the Egyptian armed forces in the Arab-Israeli wars was caused in part by the wide class disparity between officers and recruits. Similarly, the poor performance of the superior Iraqi armed forces against their Iranian counterparts in the Gulf war has been explained partly in relation to the rigid Iraqi class structure and the wide social gap that exists between Iraqi officers and soldiers.[39] In the same vein, the defense planners in the Islamic Republic of Iran had correctly argued that the Shah's military, which mirrored the class rigidity of pre-revolutionary Iran, was not a citizen's military, and that it was incapable of engaging in protracted warfare without the loss of morale—which, in the final analysis, is the crucial element of the human factor in warfare.

As the Iran-Iraq war has clearly demonstrated, men more than machines dictate the course of events on the battlefield. In the words of David Evans and Richard Campany, two Pentagon staff officers:

> All the F-14s and M-60s purchased by the Shah have not had one-tenth the impact on the war that the tens of thousands of illiterate young Iranian peasants have. Spending money on the machinery of war—the focus of so much effort and debate in the West—remains secondary; the central issue is the willingness of the troops to fight, their belief in their cause, and their confidence in the officers.[40]

The importance of the human factor in modern warfare at the regional level accounts for the outperformance of the Iranian armed forces over those of Iraq in every major category, from tactical improvisations on the battlefield to combat skills and the general level of operational command. The Iranian armed forces, relying primarily on six divisions and lightly armed Revolutionary Guards, have been able to keep fourteen Iraqi divisions with superior military hardware at bay.[41]

The Revolutionary Guards

The Islamic Revolutionary Guards Corps (IRGC), or *Sepah-i Pasdarani-i Inqelab-i Islami*, a small irregular force that emerged as the guardian of the nascent Islamic revolution, has witnessed phenomenal growth since its inception in May 1979. Numbering some 250,000 uniformed personnel, the IRGC now has a cabinet-level ministry that reports directly to Ayatollah Khomeini. Aside from its broad mandate to safeguard the gains of the Islamic revolution, the IRGC's powers have been ill-defined. According to article 150 of the Islamic Republic's Constitution, the functions of the IRGC "will be determined by law in conjunction with the duties of other military forces of the nation and with regard to the principle of brotherly cooperation and coordination among all military forces."[42] Expressing his desire to have been a *Pasdar* (Guard) himself, Ayatollah Khomeini has called the IRGC the "eyes and ears of the revolution."[43]

However vague its functions in the past, the IRGC has become a cardinal factor in the regime's stability in post-revolutionary Iran. It has been instrumental in containing a myriad of domestic uprisings; it has also played a pivotal role in the Iran-Iraq war. As Morris Janowitz has noted in his study of the role of the military in developing countries, the coercive arm of the state in Third World nations "requires a perspective that encompasses more than the military, one that can include coercive institutions, such as police and paramilitary formations, and the various forms of repression."[44] In view of our preceding analysis of the Iranian armed forces, the importance of the establishment of the IRGC as a paramilitary coercive arm of the state becomes more pronounced. The IRGC, however, considers itself not a coercive apparatus of the Islamic Republic but an organization of warriors with functions similar to those of the combatants of the early Islamic era. According to an IRGC publication, this similarity is reflected in "self-sacrifice and bravery, and in volunteering to sacrifice one's life in order to let his fellow combatant live. On the whole, the similarities are in the mastery and skill of war, in attacking the heart of the enemy, in being brave, and in their [*Pasdaran*] humbleness toward Allah."[45]

The beginnings of the IRGC date back to the early days of the Iranian Revolution, when armed militias of local *Komitehs* (neighborhood defense committees) were organized into a paramilitary force to maintain order in major cities. The war with Iraq, however, catapulted the IRGC into a formidable defensive force. The *Pasdaran's* membership rose from 5,000 in 1979 to 50,000 in 1981 and to 150,000 in 1983. The IRGC's current strength is estimated to be 250,000 men organized into 53 brigades.[46] Although the IRGC has yet to gain its own air and naval units, it has its own infantry and tank units. Furthermore, a growing number of IRGC personnel have been undergoing training at military academies and air and naval facilities in Iran and abroad. Since 1983, an ever-increasing number of entering cadets in the Iranian air force and naval academies have come from the ranks of the IRGC. A special IRGC military academy—the Imam Hussein University—is now in its formative stage of development and will soon accept its first group of *Pasdaran* for military training. Its intention is to train Revolutionary Guards in all facets of warfare and to educate them in Islamic religious history. Ultimately, in fact, it will be integrated with the regular military's national academy. Even without the benefit of a military academy, Muhsen Reza'i, the IRGC commander, claims that the *Pasdaran* have already taken "quantum leaps" in producing "sophisticated" anti-tank weapons and light artillery hardware which are being used in the Iran-Iraq war.[47]

Structures and Functions of the IRGC

The structure of the IRGC revolves around two components—the Command and the Ministry. The Command has operational control over *Pasdaran* units;

the Ministry handles matters dealing with administration and logistics. This distinction is parallel to that the service commands (Ground Forces, Navy, Air Force) and the Ministry of Defense. Ideological matters in both the Command and the Ministry fall under the jurisdiction of Ayatollah Khomeini's representative, who reports directly to him on developments within the IRGC.

The *Pasdaran* perform domestic as well as external military functions. Those units that perform domestic duties are called *Pasdarani-i Komiteh-i Inqelb-i Islami* (Islamic Revolutionary Committee Guards). They range in function from being "guardians of social morality" to basic police. The neighborhood *Komitehs* are the basic structural units of the Islamic Revolutionary Committee Guards. The *Komiteh* members also function as police among other things. They monitor the movement of their neighborhoods' residents and identify suspected enemies of the Islamic Republic. Although the *Komiteh* members and the regular police units have overlapping functions in many areas, the former have developed a reputation for performing their task more efficiently than the latter.

As was mentioned earlier, the *Pasdaran* units were also engaged in the forefront of the Iranian defense lines against the Iraqi forces and continue to be involved in containing armed resistance by certain segments of the country's ethnic minorities, especially the Kurds. In carrying out its duties, the IRGC utilizes the services of its affiliate, *Basij-i Mustaz'afin* (Mobilization of the Oppressed) militias. The *Basij* has its origin in Ayatollah Khomeini's call, in the aftermath of the U.S. hostage crisis, to establish an "army of 20 million" to defend the country from invasion from abroad.

The *Basij* members are volunteers who are teenaged boys from families with deep religious sentiments and unmitigated support for the Islamic Republic. They have been the linchpin of the so-called human-wave attacks against the Iraqi positions along the border areas. The *Basij* trainees, who number some 3 million boys, are augmented by the Women's *Basij* Organization which has provided self-defense and military training to some 100,000 Iranian women. The *Basij* sisters, as the female trainees are called, are being organized into resistance cells centered in neighborhood mosques. Currently, the duties performed by the *Basij* sisters have been limited to providing back-up services to the soldiers and *Pasdaran* at the war front, including the provision of social services to war widows and the conveyance of positive developments at the war front to the general public. The female *Basij* trainees, however, are expected to join their male counterparts in armed resistance to defend the country's territorial integrity as the need arises.[48] The *Basij* organization has also been given a mandate by the Islamic leadership to provide military training for all Iranian students in the country's elementary and secondary schools. The director of the *Basij* organization, Muhammad 'Ali Rahmani, envisions that in the near future his organization could have as many as 4.5 million trained students who will be ready to join other *Basij* members at the war front.[49]

IRGC Versus the Regular Armed Forces

The establishment of the IRGC was initially viewed by the regular armed forces with some degree of apprehension because they perceived the *Pasdaran* as a possible rival to themselves. Indeed, in the earlier stages of the Revolution, the religious leadership had not overcome its distrust of the military. As a result, with the exception of utilizing the military to contain ethnic strife, particularly in Kurdistan, the regime eschewed the use of the armed forces personnel in managing domestic disturbances in such major metropolitan areas as Tehran, Isfahan, and Tabriz. Instead, it opted to rely on *Pasdaran* units whose loyalty to the new political system was not in doubt. As the war with Iraq intensified, tactical disagreements over the conduct of the war brought the tensions between the regular armed forces and the Revolutionary Guards to the fore. A principal cause of disagreement between the armed forces and the IRGC had been the latter's insistence, at least in the first four years of the Iran-Iraq war, on the viability and desirability of the human-wave assault tactics designed to repel the Iraqis. However, more often than not, the IRGC and armed forces personnel have coordinated their activities on the battlefield and have largely overcome the initial distrust of each other's motives.

The question that poses itself at this juncture is this: Can the armed forces play a major role in reshaping the political map of Iran? The answer, at least in the immediate future, should be no. Several factors continue to mitigate against the military's role in undermining the Islamic regime in Iran:

1. The successive purges of the officer corps of the armed forces since 1979 have resulted in the total overhaul and transformation of the military command positions. Today, officers who hold key positions in the armed forces are those who have been promoted since the establishment of the Islamic Republic and have occupied their posts because of their proven loyalty to the principles of the Islamic Republic. For example, Colonel Isma'il Sohrabi, the chairman of the Joint-Chiefs-of-Staff, displayed his loyalty to the regime by his exploits in suppressing the Kurdish uprising in 1979–1980. Similarly, Colonel Sayyad Shirazi, the commander of the Ground Forces, was an army captain who made his name as a particularly efficient deputy division commander of the 64th Infantry Division who put down the Kurdish uprising in northwest Iran.[50] Both Sohrabi and Shirazi are prototypes of young army officers whose battlefield exploits and ideological steadfastness have endeared them to the country's Islamic establishment. They have also developed a stake in maintaining the regime.

2. The Revolutionary Guard's countervailing influence serves as a constant check on the military's ambitions. The rivalry between the Revolutionary Guards and the regular armed forces has been fostered not only by battlefield experiences but also through the Revolutionary Guards' attempts to hinder military involvement in politics.

3. The intricate control of the Islamic establishment has been accomplished primarily through four groups in the armed forces: (a) the Political-Ideological

Department, which is headed by a senior cleric and is responsible for the indoctrination and political-religious education of armed forces personnel; (b) the Information and Guidance Department, whose major responsibility is to gather information on armed forces personnel through an extensive network of informers and infiltrators; (c) the Islamic Association, a large and more open clergy-dominated group within the military whose task is to identify military personnel whose allegiance to the principles of the Islamic Republic is in doubt; and (d) the Strike Group, a lightly armed but highly dedicated force composed of military police and Revolutionary Guards, who are entrusted with the task of breaking up groups or arresting individuals who have been targeted as suspects by the other three control organizations.[51] These factors have created obstacles to a credible challenge to the foundations of the Islamic Republic by the country's military.

Revolutionary Guards as "Exporters" of the Iranian Revolution

From the outset, the revolutionary leaders of Iran have expressed the view that the Iranian Revolution is not a nationalistic revolution and, therefore, that it transcends the country's geographic frontiers. At the same time, they have discounted military force and military intervention as the means to "export" the Revolution to other countries. In the words of Ayatollah Khomeini, exporting the Revolution implies that "Islam be spread everywhere. We have no intention of interfering militarily in any part of the world."[52] This assertion notwithstanding, the IRGC views itself as being on the cutting edge of liberation movements in general and Islamic movements in particular. As the IRGC has asserted, the "active and widespread connection with the liberation movements make up a large part of the IRGC's activities, and we hope, with the continuation of this policy, we can effectuate the Almighty's promise: the fulfillment of the rights of all the world's oppressed people."[53]

The ideals of the Iranian Revolution as reflected in the above statement have prompted many observers in the West to speculate about the "destabilizing" effects of the Iranian Revolution or to talk about the "export" of the Revolution to other countries in the Gulf region and beyond. The presence of several hundred Revolutionary Guards in the Bekka Valley in Lebanon has been erroneously associated with the "exporting" of the Iranian Revolution to Lebanon, where the Shi'ites constitute the largest single religious group in the country. The IRGC personnel entered Lebanon shortly after the 1982 Israeli invasion of the country; their principal mission there has been to help provide protection for the downtrodden Lebanese Shi'ite community and to bolster the Shi'ite militia's combat effectiveness vis-à-vis their adversaries. The impact of the Iranian Revolution on the Lebanese political scene is not exclusively the result of the presence of a handful of Revolutionary Guards. Rather, because of the traditionally close ties between the Shi'ite communities in Iran and Lebanon, the Iranian Revolution has merely provided "an exemplar for concerted Shi'ite political action against oppression."[54]

Moreover, as I have argued elsewhere, revolution is not a commodity that can be easily exported from one country to another through regular or paramilitary armed actions. In the absence of certain internal socioeconomic and political preconditions, no revolution can be "exported" successfully and by any means from one sovereign nation-state to another.[55] Furthermore, according to the Iranian government, some forty radio stations operating from abroad continue to aim propaganda and foreign culture at Iran. As Prime Minister Mir Hussein Musavi stated recently,

> No one objects when the United States tries to export its culture to our country, . . . but when we speak about Islam and say Muslims should return to Islam, they say that we intend to export our revolution. If the export of the Revolution means that we proclaim the message that the dignity of Muslims depends on their return to Islam, then we accept that we export the revolution.[56]

Conclusion

The transformation of the Iranian armed forces and their augmentation with the IRGC and other paramilitary units should be analyzed not merely in terms of military strategy and organizational efficiency but also in the broader context of the framework of domestic and foreign policies of the Islamic Republic. The "Islamization" of the Iranian military and the establishment of the IRGC alongside the regular armed forces have produced a fighting force that has "stunned Iraq—and military experts around the world"[57]—with its resiliency and war-fighting capability. Indeed, the reconstructed Iranian forces are especially suited for managing low-intensity and protracted conflicts that seem to have been emerging as a major form of warfare in the late-twentieth-century Middle East.

Notwithstanding the widespread perception in the West that Iran's armed forces have been decimated by the revolutionary regime, it can be argued that the country's capability to withstand foreign aggression has been enhanced. As James Bill and Carl Leiden have contended, Iran under the Shah was "a military client state of the United States. . . . Despite the incredible buildup of the Iranian forces, they remained under the Shah basically untested."[58] The post-revolutionary Iranian armed forces, on the other hand, have reduced their dependent status while gradually enhancing their professionalism and battlefield capabilities. The capture in February 1986 of the Iraqi port city of Faw was a vivid illustration of coordinated and professional military planning by both the regular armed forces and the Revolutionary Guards.

Another dimension (albeit an intangible one) of the transformation of the Iranian armed forces has been reflected in their willingness to engage in protracted struggle in defense of the country in spite of seemingly insurmountable odds. The dictum of the great nineteenth-century Prussian military strategist, Karl von Clausewitz, that the outcome of war is determined by two factors—the "sum of available means" and the "strength of will"—certainly rings true when one compares the performance of the Shah's armed forces with that of the post-revolutionary military. During the Shah's reign, the first factor was present whereas the second one was largely absent. On the other hand, the Islamic Republic's armed forces, despite the difficulties they encountered in obtaining advanced weaponry, have performed well because of their "strength of will." It is this "strength of will" that many Western observers have referred to in connection with manifestations of "the resurgence of Islam," "Islamic fundamentalism," and other similar clichés and platitudes. These phrases are

> so powerfully evocative that they make us lose sight of the real struggle that men and societies are engaged in. We think of great crusades, of a powerful desert wind devastating the achievements of progress, of societies being dragged back into the middle ages. But things may not be what they seem. People summon the spirits of the past to help them achieve very precise goals.[59]

A further impetus to a more assertive role for the Iranian military and the IRGC forces might come from outside attempts to destabilize the Islamic Republic. The Reagan administration's increasingly uneasy relations with the Third World, its commitment to the use of military force to deal with complex political issues,[60] and its gratuitous provocations and denunciations of the Islamic Republic as a "terrorist country"[61] should not be ignored by those who will ultimately have to shoulder the burden of Iran's defense. An additional impetus for covert military actions against revolutionary Third World regimes such as Iran has come from a number of conservative sources in the United States, the most important of which has been the recommendations of the Heritage Foundation, a conservative "think tank" with close connections to the Reagan administration.[62] If such recommendations are translated into U.S. policy, then the Iranian armed forces and paramilitary personnel will need to develop appropriate tactics to deal with the United States' armed intervention in Iran.

Notes

1. Hujjatul Islam 'Ali Khamene'i (then Deputy Defense Minister for Revolutionary Affairs and currently the president of Iran), *Ettela'at*, August 18, 1979, p. 11.
2. Manfred Halpern, *The Politics of Social Change in the Middle East and North Africa* (Princeton, N.J.: Princeton University Press, 1963), p. 251.
3. Ibid., pp. 253–261. See also J. C. Hurewitz, *Middle East Politics: The Military Dimension* (New York: Praeger, 1969), p. 102–120.
4. Gregory Rose, "The Post-Revolutionary Purge of Iran's Armed Forces: A Revisionist Assessment," *Iranian Studies*, vol. 17, nos. 2–3 (Spring/Summer 1984), pp. 153–194, and William F. Hickman, *Ravaged and Reborn: The Iranian Army, 1982* (Washington, D.C.: Brookings Institution, 1982).
5. *International Herald Tribune*, November 16, 1978, p. 2.
6. Ervand Abrahamian, *Iran Between Two Revolutions* (Princeton, N.J.: Princeton University Press, 1982), p. 435.
7. Ibid., p. 436.

8. See *The Economist* (London), November 11, 1978, p. 13. See also Haleh Afshar, "The Army," in Haleh Afshar, ed., *Iran: A Revolution in Turmoil* (Albany, N.Y.: State University of New York Press, 1985), pp. 186–189.

9. Robert Graham, *Iran: The Illusion of Power* (New York: St. Martin's Press, 1979), p. 143.

10. The Shah later blamed General Fardust for betraying his trust and siding with the opposition during the revolutionary upheavals of 1978–1979.

11. Farhad Kazemi, "The Military and Politics in Iran: The Uneasy Symbiosis," in Elie Kedouri and Sylvia G. Haim, eds., *Towards a Modern Iran* (London: Frank Cass and Company, 1980), p. 236.

12. Quoted in Michael T. Klare, *American Arms Supermarket* (Austin, Texas: University of Texas Press, 1984), p. 108.

13. Ibid. See also Thomas M. Ricks, "U.S. Military Missions to Iran, 1943–1978: The Political Economy of Military Assistance," in Leila Mao, ed., *U.S. Strategy in the Gulf: Intervention Against Liberation* (Belmont, Mass.: Arab- American University Graduates, 1981), pp. 56–60.

14. Alvin J. Cottrell, "Iran's Armed Forced Under the Pahlavi Dynasty," in George Lenczowski, ed., *Iran Under the Pahlavis* (Stanford, Calif.: Hoover Institution, 1978), pp. 407–413.

15. U.S. Senate, "The Middle East and Iran," *Congressional Record*, Proceedings of the 95th Congress, 1st Session, February 10, 1977 (Washington, D.C.: Government Printing Office, 1977), p. 13.

16. Echo of Iran, "The Fall of the Imperial Army," *FYI Political Digest*, February 26, 1979, p. 4.

17. Gholam R. Afkhami, *The Iranian Revolution: Thanatos on a National Scale* (Washington, D.C.: Middle East Institute, 1985), pp. 122–123.

18. Ibid., pp. 121–133. For an insider's account of the paralysis of the Imperial Armed Forces during the Iranian Revolution, consult General 'Abbas Qarabaghi, *Haqayiq Dar Barih-i Buhran-i Iran* [Facts About the Iranian Upheaval] (Paris: Suhayl Publications, 1984).

19. *Financial Times*, December 14, 1978, p. 4.

20. *Financial Times*, December 19, 1978, p. 40.

21. Quoted in *Kayhan International*, January 25, 1979, p. 1.

22. *Kayhan International*, January 29, 1979, p. 1.

23. Quoted in *Kayhan International*, February 6, 1979, p. 1.

24. Hassan M. Nejad, "The Social Revolution in Iran: A Theoretical Model," paper presented at the 1984 Annual Meeting of the International Studies Association, Atlanta, Georgia, March 27–31, 1984, p. 32.

25. Quoted in *Kayhan International*, February 17, 1979, p. 8.

26. Rose, op. cit., p. 158.

27. Ibid.

28. Ibid., pp. 160–183, and Shireen Hunter, "The Iran-Iraq War and Iran's Defense Policy," in Thomas Naff, ed., *Gulf Security and the Iran-Iraq War* (Washington, D.C.: National Defense University Press, 1985), p. 170.

29. Hickman, op. cit., p. 8.

30. Hunter, op. cit., p. 171.

31. *Ettela'at*, August 23, 1979, p. 12.

32. Hickman, op. cit., p. 9.

33. *Kayhan*, September 29, 1979, p. 1.

34. Hickman, op. cit., pp. 14–16.

35. Rose, op. cit., p. 187.

36. Ibid., p. 186.

37. See Hickman, op. cit., p. 15. See also Shaul Bakhash, *The Reign of the Ayatollahs: Iran and the Islamic Revolution* (New York: Basic Books, 1984), p. 118.

38. *Matin-i Kamil-i Qanun-i Asasi-i Jumhuri-i Islami-i Iran* [The Complete Text of the Constitution of the Islamic Republic of Iran] (Tehran: Hamid Publications, 1983), p. 14.

39. See, for example, Y. Harkabi, "Basic Factors in the Arab Collapse During the Six-Day War," *Orbis*, vol. 11, no. 1 (Fall 1967), pp. 677–691; W. Seth Carus, "Defense Planning in Iraq," in Stephanie Neuman, ed., *Defense Planning in Less-Industrialized States* (Lexington, Mass.: D.C. Heath and Company, 1984), pp. 29–51; and Robert E. Harkavy and Stephanie G. Neuman, eds., *The Lessons of Recent Wars in the Third World; Approaches and Case Studies*, vol. 1 (Lexington, Mass.: D.C. Heath and Company, 1985), pp. 18–20.

40. David Evans and Richard Campany, "The Lessons of Conflict," *The Atlantic*, vol. 254, no. 5 (November 1984), p. 32.

41. For a succinct analysis of the combat performance of the Iranian forces in the Iran-Iraq war, see Mark Heller, Dov Tamari, and Zeev Eytan, *The Middle East Military Balance 1983* (Tel Aviv: Jaffee Center for Strategic Studies, Tel Aviv University, 1983), pp. 310–315.

42. *Matin-i Kamil-i Qanun-i Asasi*, op. cit., p. 80.

43. *Pasdaran*, August 28, 1979, p. 1.

44. Morris Janowitz, *Military Institutions and Coercion in the Developing Nations* (Chicago, Ill.: University of Chicago Press, 1977), p. 20.

45. *Message of Revolution*, May 1983, p. 11.

46. *Christian Science Monitor*, August 7, 1985, p. 17.

47. *Iran Times*, October 4, 1985, p. 4.

48. *Iran Times*, October 18, 1985, p. 5.

49. *Iran Times*, October 25, 1986, p 5.

50. Fred Halliday, "Year IV of the Islamic Republic," *MERIP Reports*, vol. 13, no. 1 (March–April 1983), p. 5.

51. Ibid. See also Eric Hooglund, "The Gulf War and the Islamic Republic," *MERIP Reports*, vol. 14, nos. 6–7 (July–September 1984), p. 36.

52. Quoted in James A. Bill, "Resurgent Islam in the Persian Gulf," *Foreign Affairs*, vol. 63, no. 1 (Fall 1984), p. 118.

53. See *Message of Revolution*, May 1983, p. 9. See also Dilip Hiro, "Riding the Wave of Islam's Past," *The Nation*, January 9, 1985, p. 145.

54. Augustus Richard Norton, "Changing Actors and Leadership Among the Shi'ites of Lebanon," *Annals of the American Academy of Political and Social Sciences*, vol. 482 (November 1985), p. 116.

55. Nader Entessar, "Changing Patterns of Iranian-Arab Relations," *Journal of Social, Political, and Economic Studies*, vol. 9, no. 3 (Fall 1984), p. 356.

56. Quoted in *Iran Times*, May 9, 1986, p. 15.

57. Elaine Sciolino, "Iran's Durable Revolution," *Foreign Affairs*, vol. 61, no. 4 (Spring 1983), p. 905.

58. James A. Bill and Carl Leiden, *Politics in the Middle East*, 2nd ed. (Boston: Little, Brown and Company, 1984), pp. 253–254.

59. Fouad Ajami, *The Arab Predicament: Arab Political Thought and Practice Since 1967* (New York: Cambridge University Press, 1982), pp. 177–178.

60. See, for example, Sanford J. Unger, *Estrangement: America and the World* (New York: Oxford University Press, 1985); Richard E. Feinberg, *The Intemperate Zone: The Third World Challenge to U.S. Foreign Policy* (New York: W.W. Norton

and Company, 1983); George W. Ball, "Reagan's Ramboism—The Fantasy of Star Wars and the Danger of Real Wars," *Christian Science Monitor*, April 28, 1986, p. 18; Robert R. Bowie, "Reagan's Foreign Policy—It's Now Based on Interventionism," *Christian Science Monitor*, April 29, 1986, p. 14; and Jeff McMahan, *Reagan and the World: Imperial Policy in a New Cold War* (New York: Monthly Review Press, 1985), pp. 87–122.

61. See, for example, R. K. Ramazani, "Iran: Burying the Hatchet," *Foreign Policy*, no. 60 (Fall 1985), pp. 73–74.

62. Center for Defense Information, "America's Secret Soldiers: The Buildup of U.S. Special Operations Forces," *Defense Monitor*, vol. 14, no. 2 (1985), p. 15.

6

The Islamic Republic and the World: Images, Propaganda, Intentions, and Results

Annabelle Sreberny-Mohammadi and Ali Mohammadi

Introduction

This chapter focuses on the use of visual images, particularly political cartoons, as a propaganda vehicle for creating sympathy and support abroad for the ideological perspectives of the Islamic Republic of Iran.[1] Analysis of the form and content of these images reveals the ideological ambiguities and confusions of the Islamic Republic (specifically in the area of foreign relations), evaluates how well such visualizations "travel" across cultural/political boundaries, and by that means assesses the possible level of efficacy that such messages may have on foreign audiences.

Political cartoons and caricatures are increasingly recognized as an important form of visual communication. A burgeoning research literature now explores the rhetorical and semiotic dimensions of such forms.[2] An older approach analyzes their content and functions in the context of particular historical epochs,[3] especially times of revolutionary upheaval[4] and, of course, political campaigns.[5]

The sociological, historical, and communicative analyses of cartooning and caricature are useful in revealing the culture that produces such images, the symbolic resources available within a culture, and the potential meaning of such symbols within specific sociopolitical environments.[6] Such studies reveal ethnocentric or ideological biases in the depiction of events, issues, and personalities by indigenous cartoonists as in depictions of Ayatollah Khomeini by U.S. cartoonists or in the presentation of U.S. involvement in the Middle East by Soviet caricaturists.[7]

Many studies implicitly see political cartoons as a form of persuasive communication. Yet most deal with the nature and effects of political cartoons within a single, essentially Western, intellectual and cultural traditions and primarily with the effects of such representations within a single national political system. An examination of the political cartoons of the Islamic

Republic raises two fundamental questions. One is whether the visual representations emanating from within a very different cultural milieu are structured in ways similar to political cartoons in the West. The second is whether and in what manner these cartoons would be received by their intended Western audiences. Thus we have to deal with the question of the universality of visual rhetoric and the cross-cultural decoding of visual representations.

Unlike rhetoric and verbal propaganda, an agreed-upon taxonomy for identifying and classifying the available means of graphic persuasion is as yet unclear.[8] Among the most useful schemata are Gombrich's analysis of the techniques of cartooning, and Medhurst and DeSousa's analysis of the *topoi* of visual cartooning (i.e., what constitutes the content of such visualizations).

In a seminal article on the nature of the "cartoonist's armoury," Ernest Gombrich has described a number of visual forms that have recurred time and again in the history of Western political cartooning.[9] The question posed by this chapter is whether these forms were indeed the same weapons that artists working within a very different religio-cultural and political environment would use.

The first "weapon" in the cartoonists' armory that Gombrich describes is the visualization of figures of speech. Here, verbal metaphors, such as politicians possessing "feet of clay" or "rocking the boat," provide inspiration for cartooning. The second process is that of condensation and comparison, whereby complex ideas or a whole chain of ideas are transformed into a single "pregnant" image, playing with comparisons or similes to present the cartoonist's special point of view. The third weapon is portrait caricature, which typically involves plays on physiognomic features to depict politicians and even countries in a usually derogatory manner that overemphasizes certain characteristic traits. A fourth technique is to utilize the "political bestiary," whereby attitudes toward certain animals become attached to individuals through their visualization as various beasts of nature. The symbols for U.S. political parties is an example of this technique. A fifth weapon is the use of natural metaphors, such as light and dark, to portray good and evil. A sixth technique is the power of contrast, whereby situations are made vivid through representations of differences in size, and through comparative visualizations of political rhetoric and reality.

Medhurst and DeSousa attempt to categorize the inventional *topoi*, the sources of inspiration from which cartoonists draw, in their attempt to reveal the essential themes that appear with regularity. They discovered four major inventional *topoi*: The first is the political commonplace of everyday themes and events available to any cartoonist in a modern nation-state; the second source encompasses literary or cultural allusions, fictional or mythic characters, and themes from any literary or media form; the third encompasses the personal and character traits of politicians, such as honesty or dishonesty, morality, charisma, age, regional origin, and so on; and the fourth concerns situational themes—idiosyncratic and transient situations of immediate importance, but with little long-term salience.

Gombrich argues that the cartoonist possesses powerful visual tools. His analyses are drawn from the history of European and North American cartooning, but their implications appear to be universal; these techniques are indeed everywhere the substance of the cartoon form. The taxonomy offered by Medhurst and DeSousa derives from a North American context, in particular, yet there is nothing in their discussion to suggest an awareness of or concern with cultural bias in their schema. There is no discussion of the possible limitations of their schema; they construct these four *topoi* as the essential substance of the political editorial cartoon.

Our task here is to examine whether indeed the Islamic cartoonists utilize the same "weapons" and sources of inspiration and to analyze how universally comprehensible their images are.

Communications During and After the Iranian Revolution

During the Revolution, various innovative forms of "small media," such as audio-cassette tapes and photocopied leaflets, played a critical role in mobilizing the popular movement.[10] These aural and print forms were used to orchestrate the demonstrations, to agitate and politicize, to express solidarity, and to facilitate mass participation in the movement.

But beyond these forms, as yet undocumented and unresearched, there developed a plethora of spontaneous visual communicative forms such as elaborate calligraphic graffiti, multicolored posters, and spray-painted stencil images. These transformed city walls into a dynamic canvas of the unfolding popular movement. A series of bloody photographs of young "martyrs" killed for the Revolution had an agitating effect in Tehran, arousing anger against the violent regime. Other forms, such as political cartoons and comic strips, provided humorous relief from the tensions of the period, as well as a satiric commentary on events.

Political graphics and visual materials continue to play an important role in post-revolutionary Iran. Huge paintings of Ayatollah Khomeini and other religious figures adorn entire facades of large buildings. Posters, calligraphy, even postage stamps are used to carry the message of the Islamic Republic at home and abroad. Political cartoons also appear in newspapers and magazines more regularly now than during the Pahlavi period.

Although there is a growing literature on the political ideologies and rhetoric of the Islamic Republic, little attention has been paid to the visual representations of Islamic ideology by the Islamic Republic.[11] Yet visual images can be extremely powerful and may be particularly effective among nonliterate populations. Visual images can provide condensed, simplified, and vivid symbols.[12] The old adage that one picture is worth a thousand words (which the Islamic Republic itself uses in its magazines) is often very correct, but not always. For visual images, like language, derive meaning from their contexts, from their cultural milieu, and from pre-existing understandings.

Islamic rhetoric has already added some new metaphors to the vocabulary of international politics, such as the depiction of the United States as the

"Great Satan." Our study aims to discover whether a specifically Islamic visual rhetoric can be discerned, how universal the taxonomies discussed earlier indeed are, and how a non-Islamic, non-Iranian audience could be expected to interpret and react to these images and the substantive perspective on international affairs presented through them.

Our focus is on the visual images presented in *Imam* magazine, a monthly publication written in English and published by the embassy of the Islamic Republic in London. It is a major vehicle of international propaganda for the Islamic Republic and is specifically intended to

> introduce fundamental Islamic doctrines, the Prophetical traditions, to present Muslim viewpoints on current affairs, and to give a concrete shape to the ideological views of Muslim personality and ideals of true Islamic polity and egalitarian society.[13]

Imam is sent, free of charge, to anyone who expresses interest, although in 1984 a bank account was established that allowed for voluntary financial contributions. The magazine, designed to appeal to a foreign audience, is a high-quality publication with glossy, full-color covers and a lavish amount of visual content that includes photographs, cartoons, and graphics; it also features a strong focus on issues pertaining to international relations and international communications.

We examined twenty-four issues of *Imam* from January 1980 (when it started publication) through December 1984, including all visual content. In particular, we analyzed a total of 1,253 visual images made up of photographs, collages, stencil profiles, line drawings, cartoons, and abstract graphics. In this chapter, we shall concentrate on visual representations of foreign countries and international issues, which were depicted in 573 images or 46 percent of the total number of images. These selected images were mainly political cartoons.[14]

Political Cartoon Representations of Foreign Countries: An Analysis

Inasmuch as the central stance of the foreign policy of the Islamic Republic is aggressive nonalignment, expressed through the slogan "Neither East nor West," it is instructive to examine how the two superpowers are portrayed.

The Soviet Union

Thirty-nine images, 6 percent of the total, dealt with the Soviet Union. How was it portrayed? One dominant theme was the depiction of the Soviet Union as an imperialistic power vis-à-vis Afghanistan. A number of cartoon images use the map of Afghanistan to highlight the problem. For example, in Image 1, Brezhnev is a smiling tailor, very simply sewing Afghanistan

Image 1

like a patch onto the Soviet bloc, the annexation of territory being depicted as a very clean and easy process.

In another more violent depiction, Brezhnev is a soldier placing the hammer and sickle over the bloody map of Afghanistan. The barbed wire surrounding the map is the "iron curtain" encircling the country. In yet another image, the map of Afghanistan forms the background to Andropov, who is driving a tractor that is plowing up the land with the sickle of communism. The outcome is not economic development but the preparation of another grave for the "Muslim martyrs" of Afghanistan, turning the entire country into a cemetery.

After the metaphors of Brezhnev the tailor and soldier come symbolic depictions of the Soviet Union. The internationally accepted symbol of the hammer and sickle is often used to represent the Soviet Union, vivid in Image 2, where it is shown dominating both Poland and Afghanistan through military power. Yet the concentration of the editors has clearly slipped in this instance, for the signs are marked in Persian, not English, and the implications of the image are thus unclear for a Western audience. The problem with all depictions of this kind is that, typically, the superpower is shown simply as an invading force, and there is no room for any analysis of the internal political dynamics in each country that leads to such relations with the Soviet Union. Complex political and international issues are reduced to simple stereotypes with agitational power but little accuracy.

The Islamic Republic clearly sees the two superpowers as equally guilty imperialists. In Image 3, the two superpowers are depicted as greedy predators

Image 2

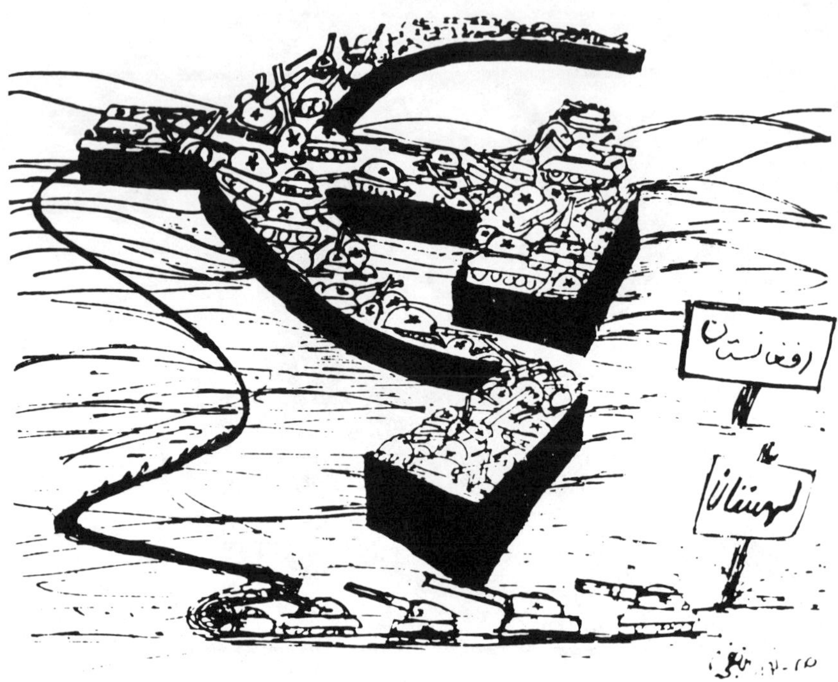

Image 3

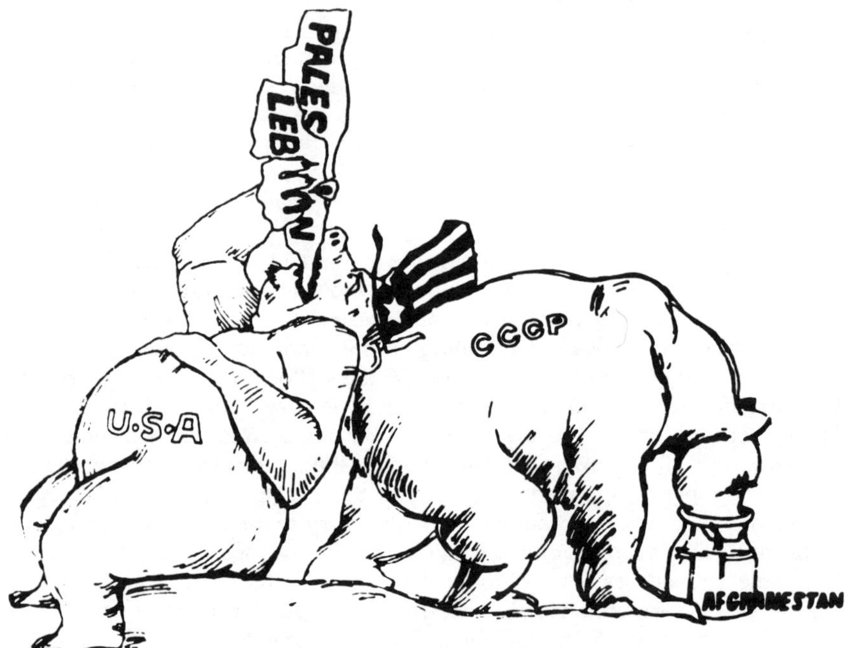

Image 4

in the context of the "political bestiary." The Russian bear licks up Afghanistan while the U.S. pig swallows Palestine and Lebanon. There are additional connotations, derived from Islamic conceptions, that the pig is not only greedy but also ritually unclean (*najes*), contaminating these Islamic nations, whereas the bear is deceitful (*makkar*); these connotations add to the power of the metaphor for those aware of them.

Some cartoons imply that the superpowers are in cahoots. In Image 4, for instance, Brezhnev is shown in his coffin, surrounded by Uncle Sam, Israel's Begin, and Iraq's Saddam Hussein, who weep while the rest of the globe smiles. This image implies the existence of a kind of coalition between the superpowers—but in the current atmosphere of Reaganite anti-communism, it is a most peculiar vision. Similarly, the treatment of Jews in the Soviet Union makes Israel no great friend of the Soviets. Thus, in this case, the Islamic Republic is painting a most eccentric picture of international relations, depicting a global conspiracy few would recognize.

In some graphics, such as Image 5, the straight path of Islam, represented by arrows and Arabic calligraphy that says "*La Ella'ha el Allah*" (there is nothing but God), cuts through and demolishes the power of the hammer and sickle. These highly condensed symbolizations of entire national cultures attempt to signify the omnipotence of Islam and its willingness to take on all foes, which makes for an expansionist and aggressive foreign policy outlook and a readiness to tackle any situation without any real calculation of cost or consequence.

Image 5

The essential issues raised in the depiction of the Soviet Union thus pertain to the nature of "social imperialism" and the problem of Afghanistan.

The United States

The United States is depicted in 150 images—more than four times the number of those relating to the Soviet Union. Uncle Sam—again, like the hammer and sickle, an internationally recognized symbolic condensation—is the most common image of the United States. In Image 6, Uncle Sam

Image 6

is pouring a bottle of something down someone's throat. The image is hard to interpret by itself: What is being poured and who is receiving it? A white Uncle Sam overpowering a person of color? The image relies for its meaning on the textual message about nationalism. Yet it is a confusing image, for there is the strong connotation that medicine is being administered—medicine, which, though nasty in taste, ultimately has a healing effect. There is also the possibility that oil is being poured, given the funnel stuck down the person's throat: Does this mean the Third World gorges on its own natural resources? The confusion of the visual image is countered by the starkness of the language underneath. Nationalism is clearly seen as an affliction imposed on the Third World by the United States, which divides nations from each other. The debate about the relationship of Islam and nationalism is a long one; here, nationalism is clearly presented very negatively.

Ubiquitous Uncle Sam! In Image 7, he is seated on a milking stool, milking the earth of its oil. The implication is that the United States is responsible for the economic ravage of natural resources.

The United States is also metaphorically depicted as an eagle, both the national bird of the United States and its national symbol. In Image 8,

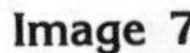

Image 7

Reagan is transmogrified into the national bird, extending a withered olive branch in one hand while clutching weapons in the other.

The other visual representations used to depict the United States are the Stars and Stripes and the Statue of Liberty, both of which are internationally familiar symbols. In Image 9, the hands of Liberty are tied up by a U.S. hand, revealed as such by the stars on the sleeve. Yet, this time, the text seems to be at odds with the image; it speaks primarily about economic deterioration, although the West is also said to have paid the price of "abandonment of all moral, ethical, and humanitarian values." The essential objective is the devaluation and belittlement of the "West" in general, and the United States in particular, as possessing neither freedom nor economic stability. Presumably, both freedom and stability are flourishing under the Islamic Republic. For an unsophisticated public, what comprehension of the

Image 8

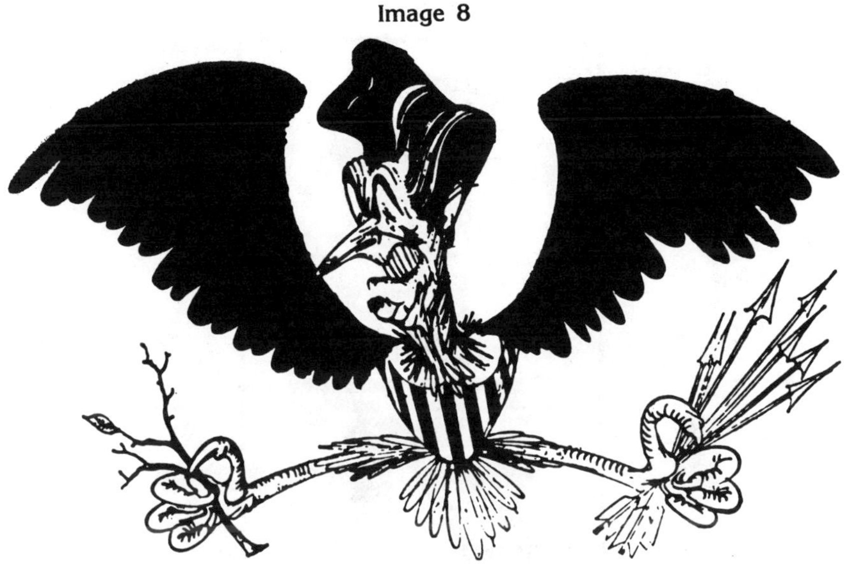

dynamics of the West can be gained by such a representation? And who in the West would accept such a crass stereotype? This is not to say that there are no problems pertaining to freedom and human rights in the West—but such a crude and one-sided depiction can do nothing to help readers understand the roots of those problems.

The depiction that grew out of the seizure of the U.S. Embassy was the United States as universal snoop, with a global CIA force spying on and intervening in Third World affairs. Indeed, a number of images represent the United States as involved in clandestine activities. In Image 10, a visual representation of a figure of speech, the Persian term *posht-e pardeh* ("behind the curtain"), is used to describe foreign conspiracies that exist everywhere. Here, the curtain carries an image of the eagle to represent the United States, and behind the curtain lurk CIA agents with smoking guns, a pile of skeletons, and, more sinister still, an immense radar disk.

The United States is frequently portrayed in a bloody manner, as the perpetrator of violence, often directed against Islam. In Image 11 the U.S. flag represents U.S. policy; the strips of the flag have been turned into hangmen's nooses, whereas the stars have become the Star of David, the symbol for Israel. Thus, the cooperation between the United States and Israel is presented as having a deadly impact.

The depictions of the United States are always negative: imperialist, clandestine, criminal, cruel, superpowerful, and ubiquitous. By implication, there is nothing to be learned, used, or gained from relations with the United States.

Image 9

Israel and the Arab States

The images of Israel are almost always related in some way to the United States. The Islamic Republic, despite its protestations that it is neither racist nor anti-Semitic, continually uses symbols of Judaism to represent Zionism and reproduces tracts from the forged "Protocols of the Elders of Zion" to "prove" the expansionist nature of Zionism. Accordingly, the visual representations often portray Israel either as a globe-girdling snake with a Jewish skull cap or as a scorpion. In one of the latter depictions, Image 12, a key stands erect on the horizon. The key opens the way to truth and is frequently used to represent Islamic power, which here is standing firm against Zionism. The key is an evocative symbol in Shi'ite Islam; the faithful attach padlocks on a door at the shrine of Mashhad and, through true prayer, anticipate them to be opened by God.

The Star of David is used to represent the state of Israel. In Image 13, the United Nations closes its eyes as a huge Israeli bomb is dropped on a

Image 10

Muslim city. The transformation of language used by the Islamic Republic to describe certain international struggles is vividly portrayed here; the struggles in the Middle East are depicted in a single condensation of Muslim against Jew.

The Arab states come off no better in the foreign policy outlook of the Islamic Republic. In Image 14, Begin, with whip in hand, tries to flog the almost-dead horses labeled Saudi Arabia, Egypt, Iraq, and Jordan, as they lurch in opposite directions and threaten to dismember the dove of peace. The Arab states are shown as powerless, following the whippings of the Israeli commander. Not even the Palestinians receive a positive treatment. Although the image of an Arab is often used to depict the victims of U.S.-Zionist aggression, Arafat himself is presented as a compromiser, one who sells out the Palestinian cause. Thus, for example, in Image 15, Arafat and King Hussein of Jordan balance precariously on the edge of a scimitar, the symbol of the power of Islam, thus suggesting that if they are not extremely careful, the sword will cut them down.

Image 11

Iraq

One hundred and sixty-eight images, or 14 percent of the total, depict the Iran-Iraq war. The dominant metaphor, portrayed through repeated imagery, is that of Iraq's Saddam Hussein as a puppet of the United States.

In Image 16, the figure of Saddam Hussein stands for the Iraqi state, shown as a clockwork toy operated by the United States key. Here, the key has a meaning very different from the one mentioned before: It represents the political dominance of one country over another. In Image 17, Uncle Sam removes the mask of Saddam Hussein to reveal his true identity—as

Image 12

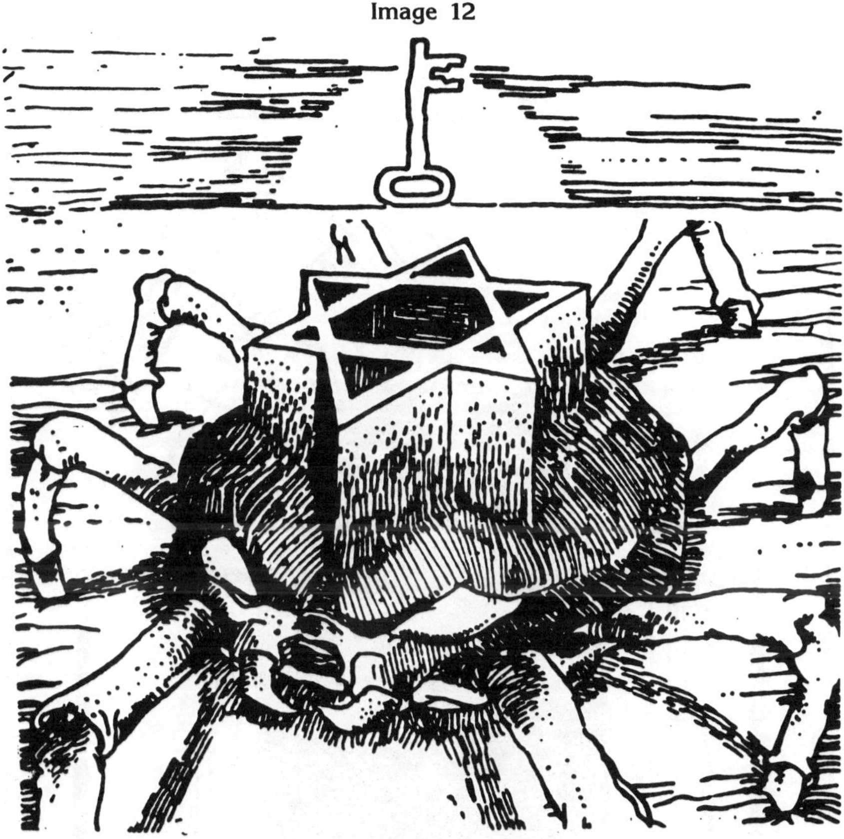

an American. This and many other images imply that it is United States interests that are predominant in the continuation of the war. Image 18 portrays Saddam as crawling out from under the United States' hat (which has protected him) and suing for peace. The implication is that, despite the United States' support, he cannot win and wants to surrender.

The United States is not alone; both the Soviet Union and the Arab world are cooperating to save Saddam from falling over the brink, as depicted in Image 19. The image of superpower support is powerful but inadequate, given that there is never any discussion about either their different interests in the area or their mutual desire for neither side to win (or to lose) this war.

Western Europe

Only twelve images pertain to Western Europe, and these focus on Great Britain and France. Image 20 depicts the Western alliance as blindly walking to the edge of a precipice. Reagan leads, followed by Thatcher and other

Image 13

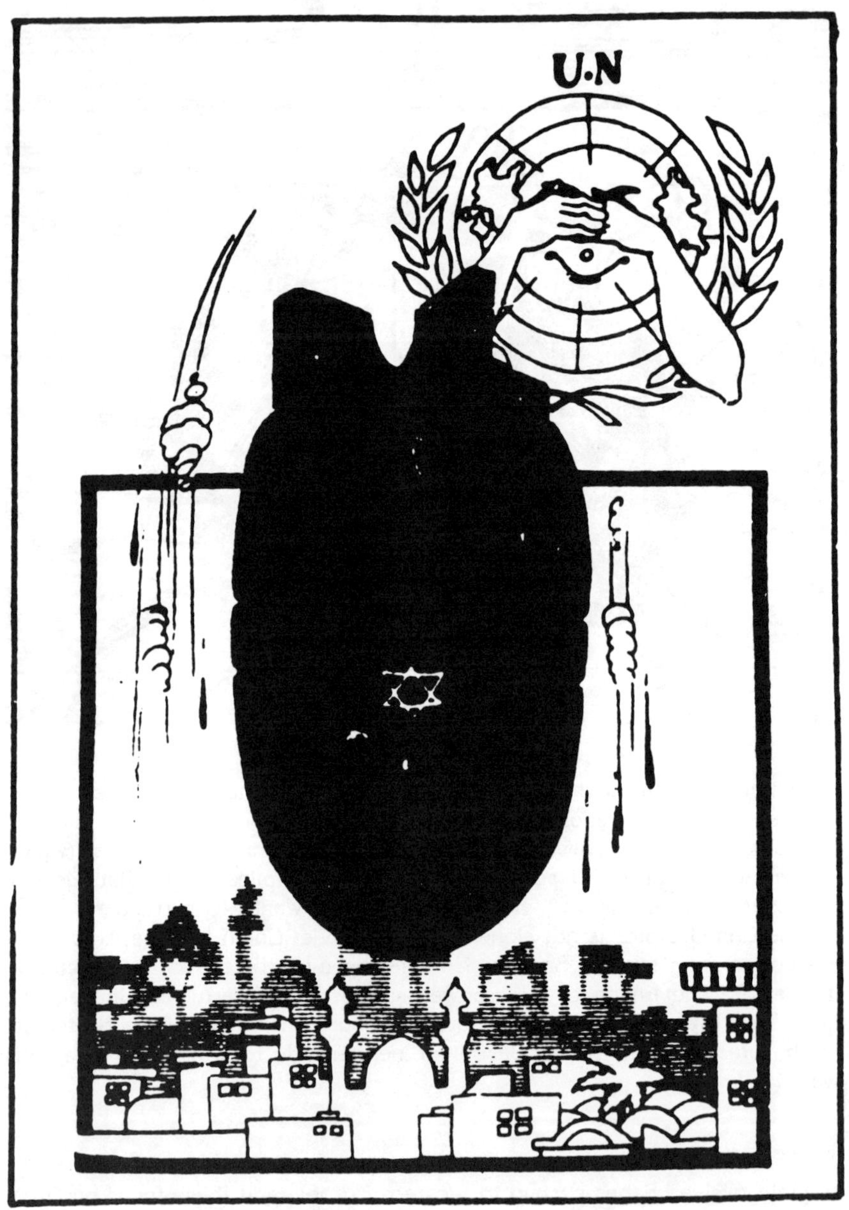

Image 14

European leaders, all wearing dark glasses. A theme found in *Imam* is clearly being sounded here: The West is "irredeemably doomed" with false morality, borrowed technology, and sham democracy. The intention of the cartoon is to diminish the tantalizing power held by the West and to produce a negative myth of the West. It is interesting to note the depiction here of the West as weak and crippled, in stark contrast to the images of power and dominance that predominate in other cartoons.

Image 21 represents one kind of power: The figure in the black coat is British, as evidenced by the top hat combined with the pounds sterling he dreams of; with his financial power, he can manipulate the military that is a clockwork held in his hands. As a depiction of the military-industrial connection, this image is quite neat, although it offers no explanation of

Image 15

why and how the money is to be realized. The accompanying text refers to nationalism as the means by which the powers have set nations against each other, describing nationalism as "the basis of all the misfortunes of the Moslems because it sets our nation against others and others against us" (as if the variety of problems facing the Middle East could be reduced to a matter of competing nationalisms).[15]

Western Media

It is worth noting the manner in which the Western media are portrayed, for, in conjunction with the military and economic power of the West, the Islamic Republic clearly considers the Western media to be an essential element of the system and an international actor that is hostile to Islam and the Islamic Republic.

The Western media are portrayed as a monolithic voice espousing the "Western worldview." Various images express the messages of the different news agencies as being hammered into the skull—literally hammered home in an apparently inescapable way, as in Image 22. But they also collectively represent the voice of corruption and anti-religion. In Image 23, for instance, *Time*, *Stern*, *Newsweek*, and Western radio and television combine to form the voice of the devil, who trumpets out his tune throughout the world.

Image 16

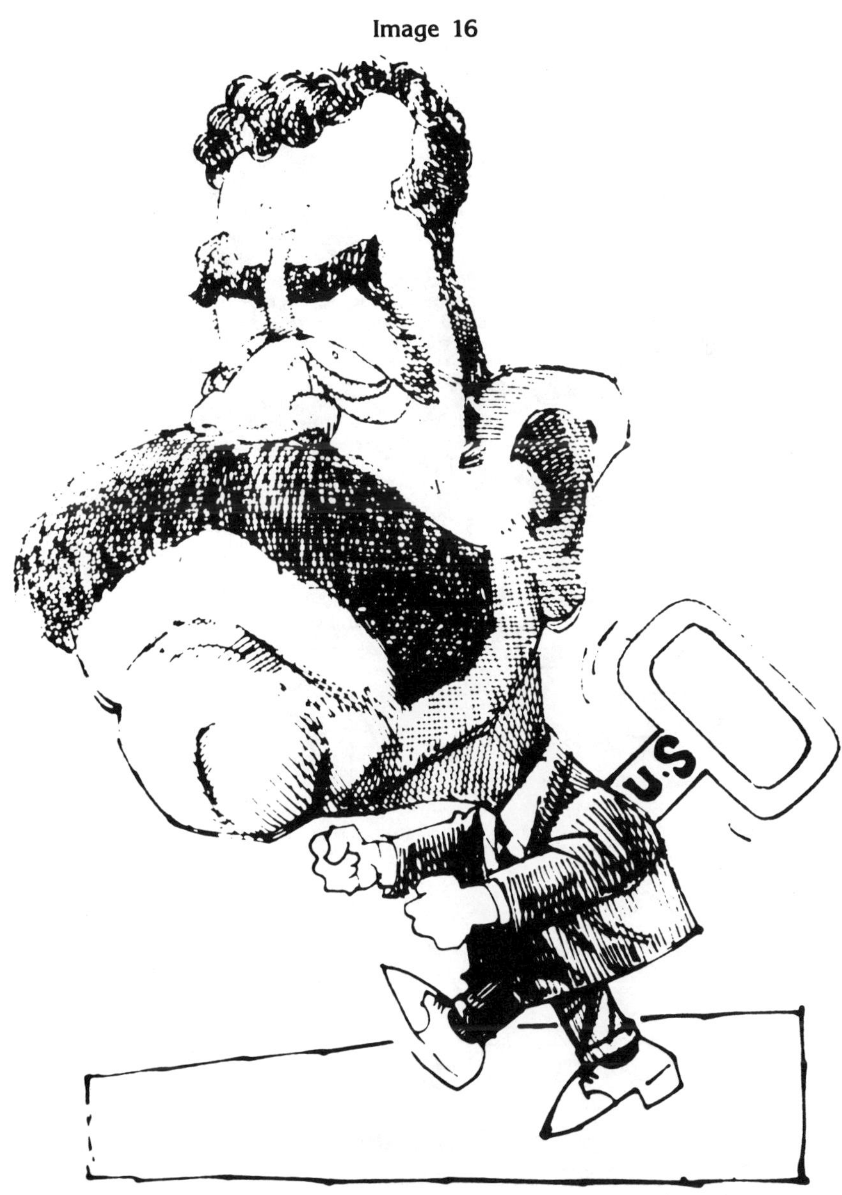

Image 17

Image 18

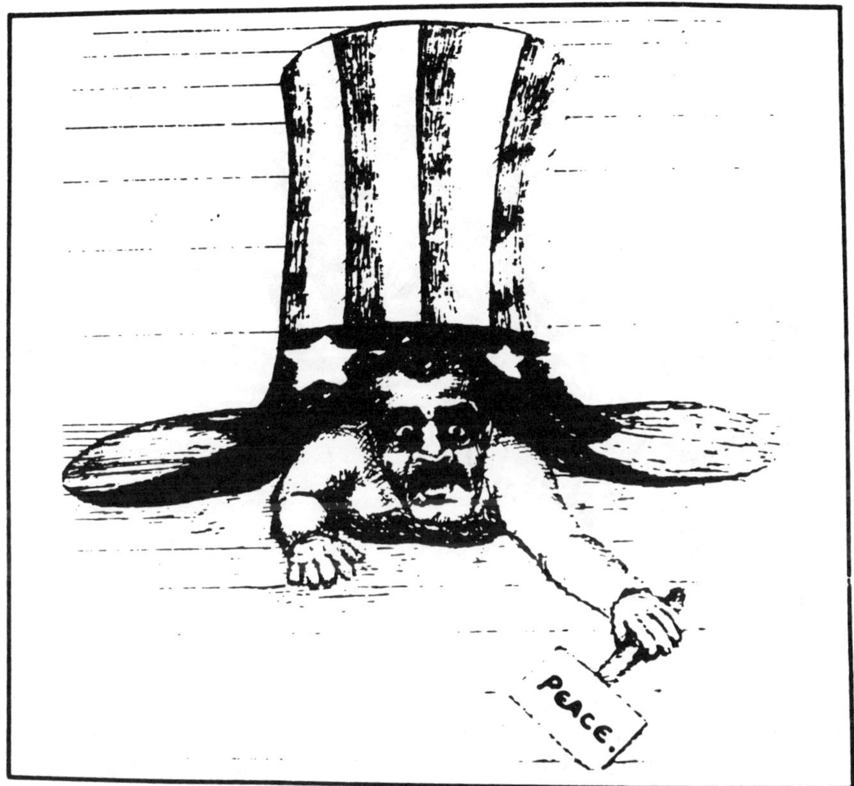

Although international debate continues over the global impact of the Western media (particularly about the big news agencies) on international news flows, the totally one-sided, negative, and conspiracy-based images from the Islamic Republic do little to contribute to an understanding or analysis of the origin of the power of the media.

Islam and Iran

For a contrast to the previously mentioned negative and comic images, we now turn to the depictions of Islam and Iran; 258 images, or 20 percent of the total, relate to Iran. First, there are few images that deal with Iran *per se* or which are related to nonreligious architecture or culture, to secular politicians, or to nationalist images. Thus "Iran" has almost disappeared in the efflorescence of the Islamic Republic.

Second, this is the only category in which photographs predominate. Thus, while every other nation, problem, or issue is constructed in cartoon form and with strong ideological and frequently satirical overtones, the real

Image 19

horror of the Iran-Iraq war is shown through a camera lens that appears to represent the "authentic" eye. Thus a photograph showing children killed in an Iraqi bombing in Khuzestan carries the caption, "Pictures speak the truth where words lie." This suggests a certain invidious naiveté about the unmediated truth of photography through which Iranians are presented as innocent victims of aggression. But Iranians are also brave soldiers, ready for martyrdom and prepared to defend themselves. Thus the war is shown through many photographs of young soldiers armed both with weapons and the Quran. For example, in Image 24, an innocent-looking girl child in Islamic dress brandishes an automatic weapon.

Militancy is depicted through various Islamic symbols. We counted 69 images that relate only to Islamic militancy. Image 25 is a neat example of a graphic in which a number of condensed symbols of power are presented. The skyline of a mosque, the power and heart of Islam, is drawn so that it resembles the Arabic letters of Allah (God) and the curvature of the building remind one of the power of the sword and the Islamic crescent. Power is also represented by the fist, which by now is an international symbol of resistance possessing no special Islamic connotations. Flags are important as symbols of solidarity and identity as in Image 26, where the white-robed Mahdi appears on horseback.

Without a doubt, the single most prevalent individual among these pictures was Ayatollah Khomeini; he was represented in 48 photographs or silhouettes,

Image 20

Image 21

Image 22

at least one of which appeared in every single issue, usually on the inside front cover or on the second and third pages, after the editorial. He is generally portrayed as a figure of power and militancy, particularly against the United States, the Soviet Union, Britain, and Israel.

Conclusion

A number of image categories have not been considered in this chapter, such as the presentation of economic issues and reconstruction in Iran (for which there were very few images) or the images of peace (there is only a sprinkling of doves and tulips). Not all visual content in the magazine is represented by political cartoons. We counted a number of neutral graphics and abstract designs; yet the majority of the images are political cartoons,

Image 23

and repetition of such images and symbols, month after month, has a powerful cumulative impact.

What seems to be portrayed is a world of total manipulation, one power always dominating another (although the roles shift and even reverse in different images). The world is visually depicted in the two colors of black and green, representing satanic corruption and falling power (despite the ubiquity of the superpowers) against the triumphant emergence of Islam. Even though both superpowers are presented as imperialistic, a strong feeling comes across that the United States, with its great power, is involved in every corner of the world and can be blamed for famine in Africa, the oil crisis, the rise of nationalist movements, the Iran-Iraq war, and more.

Only Islam has value. All other nations and systems are useless, corrupt, and ultimately weak against the power of Islam. Thus the visual depictions of foreign policy issues clearly reflect the rhetoric of fundamentalist Islam as articulated by the Islamic Republic.

Image 24

Image 25

The question is whether these images help people understand the dynamics of the real world. Or do they merely foster limited and inaccurate stereotypes that are simply the other side of the limited and inaccurate stereotypes to be found in the Western media about Third World countries and the Middle East affairs?

Gombrich's taxonomy does appear to have cross-cultural validity. Figures of speech, such as "behind the curtain" and "flogging dead horses" (in their Persian constructions, of course) are transformed into political, visual images, although specific cultural connotations do not always travel well (e.g., the concept of the impurity of the pig is not shared in the Christian West). Internationally well-known symbols, such as the hammer and sickle and the Stars and Stripes, are used as condensed representations of nations. Medhurst and DeSousa's categories are also reflected in the presentation of major political themes, current specific events, and the characters of internationally known political figures. The cultural allusions and mythical figures are most evident in the imagery of Islam—particularly in representations of the faceless Mahdi, the key to salvation. Again, these are images

Image 26

that travel poorly across cultural boundaries, although they are clearly recognizable as political cartoons.

Most of the images are international ones, made more comprehensible with occasional English-language labels. One must remember that international copyright laws have never been acknowledged in Iran, and it is possible that some of these images have indeed been cribbed from international sources. But it is also possible that the similarity between the cartoons in this study and those that are internationally known is due to the internationalization of communications, especially mass media images.[16] Overall, in analyzing these images from *Imam*, it appears that they are largely political cartoons and carry certain cultural connotations that may or may not be shared or understood internationally.

It is only when Islam is under consideration that new images from a distinctive cultural tradition are utilized (not surprisingly). Here might lie the seeds for a different visual code and symbolization. Yet, for the most part, their meanings are comprehensible, even if deeper levels of nuanced interpretation are lost. We have seen that the messages of the images can be contradictory, and that a reading of the text is sometimes required for better comprehension. Many of the cartoons are indeed funny and provocative, but stereotypical in the extreme; when the text and the analysis offer no more explanation or elaboration than these images do, the ideological position becomes essentially one-dimensional.

It may well be that "political propaganda thrives on polemics conveying a negative image of the opponent. . . . Political issues are defined and presented . . . as choices between alternatives courses proposed by 'well-intentioned' and 'evil' actors. . . . Thus a real dialogue is effectively cut off."[17] Such crude and self-evident "propaganda" is unlikely to be very effective outside the Islamic Republic, and the constant and monolithic quality of the internal propaganda may also have quite unanticipated effects. It is the one-sided, negative manner of depicting anything non-Islamic, hammered home again and again, that is likely to render this propaganda ineffective in gathering new recruits for the Islamic cause. Although such images may please those already in sympathy (preaching to the already converted), they are more likely to antagonize and alienate Western audiences.

Imam is only a tiny fragment in the modern and traditional communication systems created by the Islamic Republic at home and abroad to foster a hegemonic ideological position for Islam. In both scope and domain, the extent of its reach into various spheres of social life is yet to be seen. Islamic propaganda, however, appears to be one of the most universal ideological forces the world has known. Everything falls within the religious orbit in Iran, from teachings on personal hygiene to international relations, and everyone must be included. Islam is highly vertical in nature, stemming from a few initiates who possess the powers of interpretation; and it is societal, if not global, in compass. But potential eclipse lies in its simplicity, one-dimensionality, and intolerance for any other outlook.

Notes

1. An earlier version of this chapter (with slide illustrations) was presented at the Conference on Post-Revolutionary Iran, Center for Iranian Research and Analysis, Rutgers University, April 1985.

2. See, for example, Alette Hill, "The Carter Campaign in Retrospect: Decoding the Cartoons," *Semiotica*, vol. 23, nos. 3–4 (1978); Kathleen Turner, "Comic Strips: A Rhetorical Perspective," *Central States Speech Journal*, vol. 28 (1977); Ernest Gombrich and Ernst Kris, *Caricature* (Harmonsworth: Penguin, 1940).

3. M. Dorothy George, *English Political Caricature 1793–1832: A Study of Opinion and Propaganda*, 2 vols. (Oxford: Clarendon Press, 1959).

4. See W. A. Coupe, "The German Cartoon and the Revolution of 1848," *Comparative Studies in Society and History*, vol. 9 (1966–1967); Victor Alba, "The Mexican Revolution and the Cartoon," *Comparative Studies in Society and History*, vol. 9 (1966–1967); and the many references in the broad collection of visual representations by Robert Philippe, *Political Graphics: Art as a Weapon* (New York: Abbeville Press, 1980).

5. See Hill, op. cit.; Michael DeSousa and Martin J. Medhurst, "Political Cartoons and American Culture: Significant Symbols of Campaign 1980," *Studies in Visual Communication*, vol. 8 (1982).

6. See Martin J. Medhurst and Michael DeSousa, "Political Cartoons as Rhetorical Form: A Taxonomy of Graphic Discourse," *Communication Monographs*, vol. 48 (1981).

7. Michael DeSousa, "The Satisfaction of Pretended Insight: The Iranian Crisis in Selected United States Editorial Cartoons," SCA Convention, Kentucky, 1982; Yeshayahu Nir, "United States Involvement in the Middle East Conflict in Soviet Caricatures," *Journalism Quarterly*, vol. 54 (1977).

8. For an elaboration of this argument, see Medhurst and DeSousa, "Political Cartoons," op. cit.

9. Ernest Gombrich, "The Cartoonist's Armoury," in his *Meditations on a Hobby Horse* (London: Phaidon Press, 1963).

10. See Annabelle Sreberny-Mohammadi, "The Power of Tradition: Communications and the Iranian Revolution," Ph.D. dissertation, Columbia University, 1985; Hamid Mowlana, "Technology Versus Tradition: Communication and the Iranian Revolution," *Journal of Communication*, vol. 29, no. 3 (Summer 1979).

11. See D. Ray Heisey and J. David Trebing, "A Comparison of the Rhetorical Visions of the Shah's White Revolution and the Ayatollah's Islamic Revolution," *Communication Monographs*, vol. 50 (June 1983); David Menashri, "Shi'ite Leadership: In the Shadow of Conflicting Ideologies," *Iranian Studies*, vol. 13, nos. 1–4 (1980).

12. E. Gombrich, "The Cartoonist's Armoury," op. cit.

13. This description of editorial policy was found on the inside front page of *Imam*.

14. The single largest category of images dealt with the theme of "Islam" (258 images), including images of Khomeini, the clergy, and militant Islam. These domestic themes were powerfully explored through visual techniques other than cartooning, such as photography, stencil drawings, and so on.

15. *Imam* (August 1980).

16. See the excellent collection of internationally known cartoons in Robert Philippe, *Political Graphics*, op. cit.

17. Paul Kecskemeti, "Propaganda," in Ithiel de Sola Pool, ed., *Handbook of Communication* (Chicago: Rand McNally, 1973), p. 863.

PART TWO

From Ideology to Pragmatic Policy

7

The Political Economy of Islamic Planning in Iran

Sohrab Behdad

Introduction

In the aftermath of the 1979 Revolution, the Islamic Republic of Iran (IRI) has not yet been able to put into operation its first economic development plan; in the absence of such a plan, the state has managed the economy partly through annual budgeting and partly on the basis of ad hoc policies. To appreciate the gravity of the problem, one must consider both the extent of the state's involvement in the economy and the IRI's proclaimed commitment to restructuring it.

In the two decades preceding the Revolution, the state expanded its involvement in the economy[1] in step with the increase in oil revenues and used economic planning as a means of intervention.[2] The involvement, which was further expanded immediately after the Revolution by government nationalization of all banks and insurance companies and of most large-scale manufacturing and mining enterprises, has continued under the IRI.

The expanded public sector has made economic development planning indispensable—a fact clearly recognized by the new regime: The Islamic Constitution explicitly states that "the economic system . . . is to be based on orderly and correct planning."[3] Nevertheless, the economy remains unplanned and its policies are largely ad hoc. Technical problems do not appear to constitute a serious problem.[4] Iran has had extensive experience in economic planning. The long delay in the formulation of its first economic plan reflects, I propose, the conflicting approaches within the IRI toward the organization of the economy and regarding the objectives and strategy of the plan.

The author is grateful to Paul King, Hooshang Amirahmadi, and Manoucher Parvin for their comments and corrections.

Mainstream Islamic Economics

The literature on "Islamic economics" is vast, diverse, and methodologically scholastic. It attempts to shape economic systems according to the law of God. More precisely, Islamic economics is a study in Islamic jurisprudence (*fiqh*). The most modern version of this position, as formulated predominantly by Pakistani, Indian, and Arab scholars,[5] attempts to apply modern mainstream economic (i.e., neoclassical-Keynesian) synthesis to the economic categories of Islam within the constraints imposed on economic behavior by Islamic law.[6] I refer to this relatively cohesive body of knowledge as mainstream Islamic economics. Thus, M. A. Choudhury defines Islamic economics as "a new economic order" in which the central issue is *efficient allocation* of resources in the light of a more transcendental consideration—that of a righteous community promoting the law of God on earth" (emphasis added).[7] The principle of Divine Unity and Brotherhood "is the central principle" taught by this type of economics. "Islamic economics," states Choudhury, "teaches man how to relate and deal with other men in light of his relationship with God."[8] The issue, then, concerns the consequences of this cardinal principle for the social relations of production.

According to Choudhury, "the second principle of Islamic economics is that of work and compensation for work performed."[9] Wage is related to the amount of work and to the category of labor and is "constrained by the minimum of the rent [in this case, the Islamic term for wage] determined for the category of labour in demand."[10] The wage rate, as well as the wage differentials, are determined by the market. Thus, mainstream Islamic economic wage theory is nearly identical to that of neoclassical economics.[11] Wage labor is accepted as the legitimate form of participation of workers in the production process, and the market determined wages are said to constitute the fair share of labor in the social product.[12] (Working conditions may be specified by an Islamic state.)[13]

Agricultural rent is prohibited *only* on uncultivated land, but once "labour and capital" have been applied by its owner, "it would be an act of injustice toward the land owner to have him forego, for nothing in return, the exchange value created in land by his labour and capital."[14] A *hadith* (saying of the Prophet) suggests that rent in cash should be preferred to rent in crops.[15]

Interest is prohibited in all forms. The main reasons for this are oppression (*zolm*) of the poor through transfer of wealth from them to the rich, and the fact that interest guarantees a return to capital whereas entrepreneurial profit is subject to risk. Interest also creates an idle class.[16] The interest-free banks recently established by a number of "Islamic states" represent practical steps in eliminating interest.[17] The main notion in Islamic banking is that money capital may garner a share in profit by taking the risk of investment and may not be guaranteed a fixed return (interest rate). The Islamic bank becomes a partner in the investment ventures of the borrowers in forms acceptable to Islam. Savers are to be paid from the profits of the bank.

Prices are determined by the market mechanism. A "just price" for factors of production or products can result from the "free working of the market forces" only if the market is "freed of monopoly, hoarding, speculation, and other non-Islamic practices."[18] If the equilibrium price indicates to the neoclassical economists only the optimum allocation of resources, such an equilibrium is also "just" to the mainstream Islamic economists.

Certain modifications are necessary, however, to make the market mechanism "conform to the *ideals of Islam as much as possible*" (emphasis added).[19] But these modifications should not affect the character of the market in any substantial way. In some cases, the proposed Islamic modifications will require more strict regulations than are now available in the market economies (e.g., regulations controlling monopolies). In other cases (especially in the case of labor law on matters of minimum wage, child labor, and collective bargaining), the Islamic modifications may even imply deregulation.

Islamic economists are unanimous in their belief that ownership of property belongs to God.[20] "Man holds property in trust for which he is accountable to Him," asserts M. N. Siddiqi, a prominent Islamic scholar in the mainstream tradition.[21] The right of the individual to hold property, wealth, or means of production is accepted and respected. A source of conflict in Islamic economics, however, is the notion of God's ultimate ownership. If the implication is that divine ownership supersedes the right of the individual to property, then a state representing the will of God (i.e., the Islamic state) may impose limits on individual property rights. How restrictive these limits will be depends on the extent to which the property rights of the individual interfere with the realization of God's will as judged by the Islamic state.

Mainstream Islamic economics recognizes the authority of the Islamic state to control and limit private property rights. Siddiqi quotes Abd al-Qadir Audah ("the martyr") as saying that "though Islam allows ownership without limit . . . the society . . . can, when the public interest demands, abrogate the individual *ownership of benefits of a property, subject to the condition that a suitable compensation is paid to the owner of the benefits involved*" (emphasis added).[22] Note that the benefits of ownership, and not the property right itself, can be abrogated—and then only after payment of "suitable compensation." This view is not much different from the concept of the "eminent domain" right of the state in developed capitalist economies. Under "eminent domain," the state may intervene in the economy when the need arises.

As there exist numerous conflicting *sunnahs* (traditions) and *hadiths* concerning the limitation on private property rights, the question becomes an open one and is largely ideological in nature.[23] The debate revolves largely around land ownership. There is little limitation on manufacturing, merchant activities, or ownership except when such factors "interfere" with the working of the market. A few Islamic economists have suggested that Islam prohibits ownership of land beyond what can be cultivated directly by the owner.[24] But this view is rejected by mainstream Islamic economics as an "extreme socialist position."[25]

The state in an Islamic society should always be ready, according to mainstream Islamic economists, to intervene in the economy to prevent excessive gains (*riba*) and the abuse of property. Such intervention is said to have significance for the issue of equity in society. The most important means of achieving such equity are *zakat* (taxes on wealth), *sadaqah* (voluntary charity), *ganimah* (war booty), *kharaj* (tax on lands conquered during war), and *ushr* (*zakat* on crops).[26] In modern states, where little property can be gained through wars, equity is to be achieved principally through taxation and charity.

In sum, mainstream Islamic economics presents a design for the economy consistent with the market mechanism and capitalist production relations. Production is for profit. Labor is for hire in return for wages. Market mechanisms determine prices and wages, and they reflect an "optimum" and "just" allocation of resources. The state may regulate the market to ensure the working of this model of pure competition. But disagreements arise regarding the extent of the state's control over the economy and the legitimacy of the state's right to abrogate private property rights.

Islamization of the Iranian Economy

Only limited systematic attention was paid to Islamic economics in pre-revolutionary Iran.[27] The Persian translation of *Iqtisaduna* (Our Economics), written in Arabic by Sayyed Muhammad Baqir Sadr (first published in 1961), received scant attention from the Muslim intelligentsia and then not until the early 1970s. Similarly, Abol Hasan Bani Sadr's *Eqtesad-e Tawhidi* (Economics of Divine Unity), first published abroad in 1978, received attention only in the last few months before the fall of the Shah. Other prominent ideologues of the Islamic Revolution, namely Ali Shari'ati,[28] Ayatollah Mahmud Taleqani,[29] and Murtaza Mutahhari,[30] although they have dealt with economic matters, did not attempt to present a model for an Islamic economy. Their economic analysis (especially that of Shari'ati and Taleqani) is limited to condemnation of oppression, inequality, and poverty.

Islamic economics as a model for the organization of economic relations entered the Iranian arena of social and political thought in the very last phase of the Revolution. However, its actual development occurred only during the early construction phases of the Islamic state. The Islamic leadership of the Revolution did not publish an economic program prior to the fall of the Shah. It was only in response to the journalists in Paris that Ayatollah Khomeini made reference to an Islamic economy for Iran.[31] The construction of an Islamic economy was thus characterized by spontaneous and improvisational efforts to a much greater degree than was the construction of the political structure of the Islamic government.[32]

Islamic or not, economic reconstruction was a top priority on the post-revolutionary agenda. All the opposition forces, Islamic and non-Islamic alike, focused on the economic consequences of fifty years of Pahlavi rule. Economic demands were also a major force in bringing millions of underprivileged masses to the streets in opposition to the Shah. Such demands were particularly pronounced in the resolution of the Ashura March (December 11, 1978). Specifically, the resolution demanded social justice, the right of workers and peasants to the full benefit of the product of their work, an end to exploitation of man by man, and "elimination of oppressive profiteering, foreign exploitation, and dependency on imperialism of East and West."[33] These demands reflected the already widespread slogans in the movement.

By February 1979, before the Provisional Revolutionary Government had come to power, most of the large enterprises had already been taken over by the newly formed workers' councils.[34] Banks had been attacked by demonstrators since November 1978, and many of the owners and managers of the banks and other large enterprises had fled the country, leaving huge debts behind. Thus, the nationalization of banks and large manufacturing establishments became inevitable. In June and July of 1979, all of the private banks and many of the largest manufacturing enterprises were nationalized.

The expropriation wave continued throughout 1979 and beyond. The Revolutionary Islamic Courts ordered the expropriation of the wealth of those who were considered "corrupt on earth" (i.e., those who had gathered "excessive" property through "illegitimate" means). Takeovers by workers' councils continued, spreading to urban housing and agricultural lands. Many of these takeovers were directed by rival political organizations, including the newly formed local Revolutionary Committees. As excessive wealth is a relative concept, the local car dealers in certain small towns and villages or farmers with 20-hectare plots were considered large capitalists or landlords, and their properties were expropriated.

In the days immediately following the Revolution, two general tendencies became apparent in the IRI regarding the economic question. One tendency, which for the sake of convenience I shall designate as "moderate," concerned the approval of only limited changes in the economic system. That is, private property rights were to be respected and protected, nationalization was to be limited to those cases in which "national interest" was involved or in which the original owners had fled the country, and state control over the economy was to be limited to the provision of a proper atmosphere for the activity of the private sector. This "voice of moderation" was supported by the propertied class, including bazaar merchants, industrialists, and landlords. Mahdi Bazargan (the first prime minister following the Revolution), his cabinet, and members of his Freedom Movement of Iran were among the propagators of this tendency. A significant faction of the urban middle class also supported it. As of the summer 1981, when the Muslim fundamentalists took complete control of the political regime, this position became represented (albeit with a stronger religious flavor) by a powerful minority within the regime. All the *maraji'-e taqlid* (sources of imitation), with the exception of Ayatollah Khomeini and Ayatollah Montazeri, supported the "moderate" view. Given that laws and policies of the state in the IRI must be in accordance with Islamic principles, and given that high-ranking ayatollahs are the indisputable authorities on Islamic jurisprudence, their political position can to be considered a serious challenge to the religious authority of the state.

The opposing tendency, which I have designated as the "populist-state control" orientation, has included such prominent individuals as the late Ayatollah Beheshti, the master designer of the IRI; Hashemi Rafsanjani, the speaker of the Parliament; and Ayatollah Montazeri, recently selected as the future leader, or Imam (the position that Ayatollah Khomeini now holds). Advocates of this tendency supported the populist path and the limitation of private property rights. They were also behind many of the agitations against and takeovers during Bazargan's government, which was branded as "non-Islamic."

In addition, this faction of the IRI supported the establishment of various Revolutionary Foundations in an attempt to create grass-roots support for a fundamentalist Islamic regime. These organizations include the Construction Crusade (active mainly in the rural sector), the Housing Foundation (established to provide housing for the homeless), the Martyr Foundation (established to support the families of the martyrs of the Revolution and the war), Mobilization of the Oppressed (created for purposes of war mobilization), the Revolutionary Committees, and the Revolutionary Guards.[35] With the exception of the Housing Foundation, which had been made part of the Ministry of Housing and Urban Development, the foundations have remained independent and the most effective instruments of the IRI's power.[36] After establishing their grip over the state, the proponents of this tendency gradually abandoned their populist orientation but retained their support for extensive state control of the economy. The faction also cut back on its grass-roots agitations against the state, adhered closely to the Constitution, and concentrated its efforts on the passage of laws in the Parliament.

The Constitution and the Economic Question

The Constitution of the IRI, written by the Assembly of Experts between August and November 1979, was approved in a referendum on December 2–3, 1979.[37] The Constitution "sets forth the cultural, social, political, and *economic foundations* of Iranian society" (emphasis added).[38] The most important and controversial aspects of the Constitution are the principle of *welayat-e faqih* (the government of the jurist) and the prescribed economic model. Whereas the former generated heated debates in the Assembly of Experts, the latter was passed without much discussion or disagreement[39] but became controversial in the years that followed. The radical revolutionary organizations considered the Constitution too conservative to be acceptable. Moderates were also opposed to the Constitution with regard to the notion of the *welayat-e faqih* and articles concerning economic matters.

In evaluating the Constitution, we must consider the spirit of the post-revolutionary conditions, and the dominating influence of Marxism on the Iranian Islamic opposition movement during the rule of the Shah. The influence of Marxism, in particular, is clearly observed in the works of the popular Islamic writers of the pre-revolutionary period. Although they all attempted to distinguish in their analyses between radical Shi'ism (or, to use Shari'ati's term, Alavi Shi'ism) and the ideology of capitalism, on the one hand, and that of socialism on the other, the borderline between the two has not been clearly established. Their terminologies, categories, and, at times, their analyses closely resemble those of Marxism.[40] The Constitution of the IRI reflects this general characteristic of radical Islamic thought (albeit in its mildest form).

The Constitution asserts that "the Iranian Revolution . . . has been a movement aimed at the triumph of all oppressed and deprived persons over the oppressor."[41] It then goes on to reject both capitalism and socialism: "Government does not derive from the interests of a certain class,"[42] and "the economy is a means, not an end. This principle contrasts with other economic systems where the aim is concentration and accumulation of wealth and maximization of profit. In materialist schools of thought, the economy represents an end in itself."[43] The Constitution also declares "economic independence" from foreign domination and elimination of "poverty and deprivation" to be among the basic goals of the IRI.[44]

The most controversial aspects of the Constitution regarding economic issues have been Articles 44 and 49. The first defines the limits of activity of the private sector. The economy is to consist of three sectors: state, cooperative, and private.[45] The state sector is to include "all the large-scale and major industries, foreign trade, major mineral resources, banking, insurance, energy, dams and large irrigation networks, radio and television, post, telegraphic and telephone services, aviation, shipping, roads, railroads, and the like." The nature and extent of the activity of the cooperative sector is not clarified in the Constitution. It states only that cooperatives will be established in cities and the countryside for "production and distribution . . . in accordance with Islamic criteria." The activity of the private sector is thus limited to those factors "that supplement the economic activities of the state and cooperative sectors."

Further limitations are imposed on private property. Article 47 states that "private ownership, *legitimately acquired*, is to be respected. *The relevant criteria are determined by law*" (emphasis added).[46] Article 49 sets the general criteria for legitimate ownership by defining what is illegitimate.[47] The government has the responsibility of confiscating what is considered illegitimate wealth. Articles 47 and 49 are concerned with all present wealth accumulated in the past, even though most of the stated criteria cannot be objectively defined, especially for past practices. Under these conditions, all wealth of substantial size may be considered illegitimate.

Ayatollah Khomeini—foreseeing the conflict between the two tendencies (i.e., between the "populist-state control" tendency, which is powerful within the regime, and the "moderate" tendency, which is backed by the authority of the Grand Ayatollahs), and attempting to avoid a confrontation on the terrain of Islamic jurisprudence outside the political structure—selected the majority of jurists in the Council of Guardians from among those who represented the view of the Grand Ayatollahs. According to Article 96 of the Constitution, legislation passed by the Parliament must be approved by this council for compatibility with both the "ordinance of Islam" and the Constitution before becoming law.

Nevertheless, conflicts arose between the two tendencies regarding the passage of laws dealing with urban land ownership, mineral rights, confiscation of property of those who have fled the country, and, most important, nationalization of foreign trade and redistribution of rural land. The confrontation in its most visible and substantial form took place between the majority of deputies in the Parliament, who passed bills, and the majority of jurists in the Council of Guardians, who kept rejecting them as non-Islamic.

The problem first surfaced over the Bill for Procedure of Transferring Ownership and Development (*ehya'*) of Land, which was passed by the Revolutionary Council on September 16, 1979, and amended by the same council on December 2 (the Parliament had not yet convened). The bill originally provided for redistribution of "uncultivated" land (*mawat*, meaning dead land) and government-owned lands among the peasants.[48] The amended version of the bill called for redistribution of the previously mentioned types of property but also of "the large pieces of land under control of large landlords whose ownership with the criteria of the previous regime is seemingly legitimate." The amended bill defined "large pieces of land" as those "bigger than three times of what is required to sustain a farming family."[49] This so-called Section C was opposed by the "moderate" tendency within the regime, as well as by a number of Grand Ayatollahs. To give religious legitimacy to the bill, Ayatollahs Beheshti, Montazeri, and Meshkini reviewed the bill upon the request of Ayatollah Khomeini and signed it. None of the three approving ayatollahs were, however, a "source of imitation," and their approval did not resolve the matter. Confronted with the opposition of the fundamentalist "moderates," Ayatollah Khomeini asked the Groups of Seven (formed in the villages according to the requirements of the bill) to stop redistribution of cultivated lands. The issue was delayed so that it could be dealt with by the Parliament.

When the Parliament convened in June 1980, it first embarked upon the issue of nationalization of urban land. It was the simplest of all controversial economic bills. The unused urban land is generally considered *mawat* or *bayer* (the latter was previously developed but has become *mawat* through time). Although confiscation of this type of land is permitted by some "sources of imitation," the Council of Guardians rejected the bill passed by the Parliament as non-Islamic. Ayatollah Hashemi Rafsanjani and some influential members of the government appealed to Ayatollah Khomeini for help. In a letter to the Parliament (October 11, 1981), Ayatollah Khomeini, pointing to the "secondary rulings" (*ahkam sanaviyeh*) in the condition of "urgencies" (*zorurat*),[50] gave the Parliament the authority to decide the "urgency" of matters, including the bill in question. This move was one of strong support for the "populist-state control" tendency, which had the majority in the Parliament. The Parliament then decided that the bill was urgent. Subsequently, the bill gained the approval of the Council of Guardians after its duration was limited to five years (the period of "urgency"). Moreover, instead of confiscating lands, they may be purchased from the owners at the officially determined price.

The Council of Guardians has refused to approve several versions of bills passed by the Parliament concerning redistribution of agricultural land (even under the "secondary rulings" provision) and nationalization of foreign trade (even though it was explicitly mentioned in the Constitution as involving the state sector).[51] The Council of Guardians has thus far been consistent in taking an uncompromising position in support of private property rights. Within the structure of the government, an increasingly vocal minority in the Parliament and a number of powerful individuals have supported the position of the Council of Guardians. The opposing tendency, however, has relied on its control over the executive branch of government for implementing either policies based on the bills passed by the Revolutionary Council during its period of tenure (these bills must be ratified in the legislative process) or policies with no legal foundations. It is in the light of this general atmosphere that attempts for the formulation of the First Economic Plan of the IRI will be considered.

The Early Planning Attempts: The ORP Program

Immediately after the Provisional Revolutionary Government (PRG) was formed, it set up the Office of Revolutionary Projects (ORP). It invited planning experts and interested individuals to participate in the formulation of the general policy frameworks of the government. By August 1979, it had prepared a draft of the ORP Program.[52] Although the formulation of this program appears to have been an important issue, the list of participants who prepared this draft does not include individuals of significant political influence (then or later) from the Freedom Movement of Iran or the fundamentalist coalition of the regime.[53] The participants were individuals who apparently had different political orientations, were dominated by the moderates, and participated in various committees according to their expertise or interest. The ORP Program set out to define the goal of the Revolution, the structure of property relations, and the outline of the plan to be formulated.

The Goal

The goal of "the Islamic Revolution of Iran" is defined by the ORP Program to be the "establishment of a social, political, and economic system based on the teachings of Islam and toward a classless Society of Divine Unity (*jame'-ye bi tabaqe-ye tawhidi*)."[54] The Society of Divine Unity is explained as one in which the actions and thoughts of individuals are directed toward God, who owns everything. The "classless" element of the society is not, however, explained or referred to in the rest of the program. But there are indications as to what it might imply. On explaining the ultimate objectives of the program on the General Environment for Ownership and Management, the ORP program states that in the

> Society of Divine Unity the basis of ownership is the product of work of individuals and *surplus value* or *profit* gained in any economic activity, after appropriation of a proportion for development and innovation in that activity and payment of society's share—*beyt al-mal*—is distributed among the work force. *The Islamic government determines the share of the society and the workers from the profit in each case.* (emphasis added)[55]

This explanation of the notion of distribution resembles that put forth by socialism. The terminology is also remarkably close to that of Marxism (except for the reference to *beyt al-mal*, which is strictly an Islamic term). This is not to say, however, that the general direction of the program is either socialist or Marxist. Where the structure of property ownership in the economy is concerned, the conditions of the program projects are much closer to those of a market economy in crisis than to a socialist economy.

The Structure of Property Ownership

According to the ORP Program, the economy was to be composed of three sectors:

1. Free or People's Sector: This sector was to include "small" establishments and the participation of the "people." The government was to be responsible for providing "the environment for development and progress" of this sector through formulation and implementation of "explicit policies on ownership of means of production, extent and limits of wealth, and the preventive mechanisms against accumulation (*takathor*)."[56]

2. Mixed or People-State Sector: This sector was to be made up of the "medium" and "large" establishments "with participation of the people and supervision or investment of the government." What the program implied was the joint participation of the state and "people" in the same establishments. The program maintained that "in the next two years the establishments which are now owned by the government or are private," must become mixed, be reorganized, and "come under [government's] supervision." The activities in this sector would be subject to the laws of the market; yet, inasmuch as "these establishments are monopolies or quasi-monopolies, their profits should be *just* and according to the economic criteria and not based on their monopoly power." The program also suggested that the participation of the state in this sector should gradually be decreased through the provision of a condition of confidence and the transfer of investments of the "free sector" to the "mixed sector."[57]

3. State Sector: According to the program, all the heavy industries and strategic activities, and those in which the "people's sector" is not willing or able to participate, must be organized in the state sector. At the same time, this sector would be reduced in size and in the scope of its activities

by the gradual transfer of activities from the state sector to the other two sectors.[58]

From the standpoint of ownership and the role of the state in economic activities, the ORP Program reflected the view of Bazargan's Provisional Revolutionary Government. State takeover and control of many large establishments were viewed as inevitable in the immediate post-revolutionary period, when many capitalists had fled the country. These establishments were to constitute the "state-people's" sector. "People's" participation in this sector meant the participation of those owners (often the smaller shareholders) who remained in the country. State ownership and control over these establishments, as well as over the "nonbasic" industries in the state sector, would eventually be reduced. The program did, however, propose the redistribution of "large" landholdings among peasants.[59] It also included a proposal for nationalization of ownership of mines although mining activities were left for the "free" or "mixed" sectors.[60] On the other hand, it neither proposed nationalization of foreign trade nor specified the type of ownership under which the banking system should eventually fall.

The Proposed Outline of the Plan

The program proposed three phases for the development plan of the IRI: an initial two-year phase (from March 1980), an intermediate eight-year phase (two four-year plans), and a final twelve-year phase (three four-year plans). The program emphasized the development of the agricultural sector with an eye toward providing the "basic necessities" of society and assistance to be given to "well-to-do small landholding farmers." The main agricultural policy proposals, in addition to the redistribution of "large" landholdings, pertain to stabilization of agricultural prices, establishment of cooperatives, and infrastructural development.[61] The core of the proposed industrial policy of the program was development of intermediate, capital goods–producing, and "basic and strategic" industries. In the second phase of the program, "industrial dependency" was to be examined and "relative self-reliance" was to be achieved. By the end of the final phase, no more crude petroleum and natural gas would be exported.[62] The program also proposed both an increase in inter- and intrasector integration of the economy and the development of a "proper" infrastructure.

In sum, although the ORP Program proposed or implied certain radical reforms, in its totality it outlined the views of the "moderates" for revitalizing the economy through the direct, but decreasing, participation of the state. The scope of the activity of the private sector was much wider, in comparison to what the Constitution later defined, and the legitimacy of private property was in no way questioned. The state sector was only a supplement to the private sector, and the "mixed" sector was an intermediate solution to the existing post-revolutionary crisis in ownership. On the land question, the program took an unequivocally radical position, which was inconsistent with the policy of the Bazargan government. In short, the program was of various orientations. It was later lost amidst the factional politics and struggles of the religious fundamentalists against the Bazargan government (fall 1979) and, subsequently, against the government of Bani Sadr (June 1981).

Formulation of the First Economic Plan

Once attention was directed toward the economic question after the fall of Bani Sadr, the sharp differences in the approaches of various tendencies in the fundamentalist coalition became apparent. The deadlock that developed on the question of private property rights prevented the passage of laws that had significant implications for the development strategy of the national economy. In a tactical move designed to expedite the resolution of the economic question, Prime Minster Bahonar and his cabinet asked the Plan and Budget Organization (PBO) to initiate the process of formulation of the first economic plan of the IRI. By August 1981 the PBO had prepared the draft of "The National System of Planning," which was approved by the Economic Council (composed of the prime minister and a number of other ministers) in December.[63] According to this document, planning was to encompass a twenty-year period divided into four five-year plans. The system was designed to gather the planning information and to solicit objectives and demands from different segments of the economy at various stages from the village councils to the ministries. The plan drafted by the PBO, upon approval of the Economic Council, was to be reviewed by the Cabinet and then submitted for the Parliament's approval.[64]

Moreover, upon the directive of the Economic Council in November 1981, ten ad hoc committees were formed in the PBO to consider the objectives of the plan in an attempt to reach a consensus among various interest groups on the critical economic issues. Three of these committees were designated to deal with the scope and the limits of activities in each of the three "fundamental" economic sectors as defined by the Constitution (i.e., in the state, cooperative, and private sectors). Among the ten committees, only the "Committee on the Quantitative Goals of the Economic-Social Development," composed mainly of the PBO planners, prepared a report independent of the deliberation of the other committees. Those other committees faced the same deadlock that already existed on these critical issues within the regime.

The report served as the outline of the plan.[65] It was merely an exercise in calculating numbers. Nothing was specified about the existing economic structure. A number of target rates of growth for various sectors were set, and the necessary rates of capital formation for achievement of these growth rates were calculated from similar estimates in the previous (i.e., pre-revolutionary) plans.[66] Oil exports were to remain the main source of capital formation, and the minimum projected level for the year 2002 was estimated to be 2.5 million barrels per day (mb/d). In effect, the PBO planners took the position of the "moderates" by avoiding the issue of conflict that had been pushed forth by the "populist-state control" tendency within the regime.

The outline of the plan was criticized severely by the Economic Council.[67] The Economic Council made the following observations: (1) the proposed outline did not specify "the relationship between the quantitative goals and the Islamic values" and that "it is not clear what type of a society these goals are designed to achieve." (2) Self-sufficiency in agriculture must be one of the goals of the plan, and the projected oil export in the final phase of the planning period was "too much." According to the Economic Council, heavy reliance on oil exports (85 percent of total exports) by the end of the long-term plan was "a reflection of dependence on the oil revenues." (3) The goals of the plan should have been to achieve economic independence, to abolish poverty, and to provide education, health, social security, housing and employment. "Economic independence" was defined by the Economic Council as the economic condition such that, "if the channels of entry of commodities to the country are ever closed, the national economy would not collapse"; that is, economic independence is viewed as a vulnerability in times of war or severe international confrontation. Although the expression of this view reflects the concern of the Economic Council about the U.S. trade embargo in Iran, there is a surprising lack of concern regarding the consequences of the war mobilization against Iraq.

The PBO drafted a new five-year plan (1983–1987)[68] based on the directives of the Economic Council. It was approved by the Economic Council and the Cabinet and then submitted to the Parliament in August 1983.[69] The proposed plan, which included at the outset a critique of the "dependent development of the Iranian economy" during the Shah's rule,[70] considered economic-social development a means for achieving the goals of an Islamic society ("liberation of Man from non-God") based on Islamic laws and principles. The general orientation of the plan was "improvements in education and propagation of the Islamic culture, . . . achievement of economic independence," and "social welfare."[71] In more concrete terms, the plan emphasized the importance of agriculture as the central core of development, the creation of intersectoral linkages, and the growth of industries making intermediate and capital goods. The rapid growth of consumption was to be prevented.[72] The estimates and projections of the plan, which were similar to those of the initial draft, were devoid of any consideration of existing economic conditions in Iran and the dilemmas in the organization of the national economy.

The plan set an average annual growth rate of 9 percent for the economy in the first five years of the planning period. This rate was to be achieved by 7 percent average annual growth in agriculture, 14.1 percent in industry, and 9.8 percent in construction.[73] The plan projected that the economy would attain self-sufficiency in agricultural products by 1991 (i.e., by the end of the second plan), and that there would be a housing unit for each household by the year 2001 (at present, 2 million households are without a house, and the population is growing at 3.1 percent per year).[74] Only a total mobilization of the economy, or another oil bonanza, could bring about such results. With the continuation of the war with Iraq, deep internal social conflicts, and the fall in the international price of oil, the plan was no more than a fantasy.

The plan also projected that, under the worst circumstances, the price of oil would remain at $29. Thus, according to the plan, Iran had to export 2.2 mb/d in 1983 and had to increase this total to 2.5 mb/d by 1987.[75] Moreover, the plan expected nonoil exports to supplement oil revenues by growing at 48.7 percent annually.[76] Not only the projection about the world oil market but also the projected increase in the nonoil export earnings proved utterly unrealistic.

It is worth noting that the Economic Council was divided on the planning decision. A number of ministers taking the hard line "populist-state" control position insisted that formulation of a plan without passage of laws dealing with property relations was not meaningful. The "moderate" position was that planning was not necessary anyway. The ministers in the former position pressed for high goal attainments in the plan projections, and those in the latter position chose not to extend the cooperation of their ministries with the PBO. The proposed plan was a compromise that the Economic Council could finally reach. It also received the approval of the Cabinet, the majority of whose member ministers held a position between the two ends of the conflicting spectrum mentioned above.

The resolution of the conflict in Parliament was more difficult because the "populist-state control" tendency was stronger there than in the Cabinet. The proposed plan remained in the hands of a special committee for two and a half years. In January 1986, the Outline of the General Perspectives of the First Plan[77] was brought to the floor for the first round of discussions. It was passed with little debate. This new version is a remarkably modest plan that, more than anything else, reflects the war mobilization effort of the IRI. Military strength, internal security, and law and order are included among the most important objectives of the plan. It does not set any growth targets or make any substantial commitments. "Improvements" are to be "attempted gradually" through increases in the "utilization of capacities and capabilities" and "reorganization" efforts. Target growth rates are not set, and definite goals are not specified. Undefined "attempts" are supposed to be made toward "self-sufficiency" or "self-reliance." "Determination of the legal and operational extent of ownership in different sectors" is another aim. Meanwhile, the private sector is to be encouraged as a means for increasing investment. The activities of the agricultural sector are defined as completely outside the limits of government's direct involvement, and construction of housing is specified as the responsibility of the private sector.

The new minister of planning and budget explained the new orientation of the plan.

> In the new point of view, the determining element is not growth . . . [but] existing capabilities. . . . We have estimated the financial, physical, and exchange equilibriums and thus we have changed both our viewpoints on planning . . . and our planning procedure. . . . In this period we will not start any major investments; the emphasis is on finishing the existing (projects).[78]

Conclusion

The new version of the plan, as passed in the first round of discussions in the Parliament, reflects a compromise between two conflicting tendencies within the regime on the economic question; but it also reflects a retreat on the part of the "populist-state control" tendency. First, the decision on the extent of state control over the economy will be postponed. The direct involvement of the state in the economy is, however, explicitly restricted in certain areas, and the expansion of the activity of the private sector is encouraged in certain other areas. Second, the overly ambitious targets of the proposed plan are to be toned down. Both are compromises on the part of the "populist-state control" tendency, which has had its stronghold in the Parliament. These compromises are made in the face of realities that the regime has confronted in mobilizing an economy in crisis[79] for carrying on a war of attrition with Iraq. The "populist-state control" tendency, which also subscribes to an Islamic version of "permanent revolution," has retreated, specifically by giving in to the pragmatism of the "moderate" tendency.

In the past, the strategy of the "moderates" has been one of passive, yet uncompromising, resistance to setting any legal limitations on private property rights; the opposing orientation has mobilized its political forces against this resistance. The Council of Guardians has thus far been the most effective stronghold of the "moderates" and has done little more than simply obstruct the passage of legislation, which it has found to be an infringement on private property rights.

The "populist-state control" tendency has relied on the instruments of power at its disposal—mainly on its control over the executive branch and the Revolutionary Foundations—to carry out its policies. It has also relied on mobilization of its grass-roots forces by extending privileges to, and promising changes for, the benefits of the Mostaz'afin.[80] However, as delivery of these privileges has become exceedingly difficult for the state in a stagnating economy and in the face of the economic and noneconomic costs of the war, the grass-roots mobilization of the "populist-state control" tendency has become increasingly less effective. The proponents of that tendency have thus been forced to retreat from their past position and are gradually toning down their promises and initial commitments to the Rule of Mostaz'afin.

The conflict, however, is far from being resolved. The "populist-state control" tendency has not accepted complete retreat. It is still holding strong within its position of power in the regime. Yet, times are changing in favor of the "moderates." Security for the activities of capital is an indispensable requirement for bringing about an undisturbed reproduction process. The regime has come to realize this fact, especially now that some of its strongest supporters have much more to lose in the face of conditions unfavorable to the private sector (relative to conditions at the time of the Revolution).

The turnabout is a complicated one in this time of post-revolutionary conditions, especially following a revolution of the depth and momentum of that in Iran in 1979. The war, whose continuation is based on mobilization of the very same Mostaz'afin, who have been promised everything from jobs, housing, land, and better health care to dowries and subsidized pilgrimages to the holy shrines, makes this turnabout difficult. In the meantime, the war itself is considered something of a blessing for containing the existing social conflicts and mass discontent.

In short, the resolution of internal conflicts in the face of political realities and economic constraints appears to be far from complete. The direction of this process is nevertheless clearly identifiable. Total resolution of the problem will take some time, or perhaps some abrupt shifts and shufflings in the regime. In the meantime, ambiguity, ad hoc decision-making, and scant planning will remain the features of the economic policies of the IRI.

Notes

1. In 1977, government expenditures accounted for 40 percent of the gross national expenditures, and government investments made up 56.4 percent of the gross fixed domestic capital formation. See Bank Markazi, *National Accounts of Iran, 1959–1977*, 1981, pp. 100–101, 380, 410.

2. See G. B. Baldwin, *Planning and Development in Iran* (Baltimore, Md.: Johns Hopkins University Press, 1967); J. Bharier, *Economic Development in Iran 1900–1970* (London: Oxford University Press, 1971), ch. 5; R. G. Looney, *Economic Origins of the Iranian Revolution* (New York: Pergamon Press, 1982), chs. 2 and 3; and H. Razavi and F. Vakil, *The Political Environment of Economic Planning in Iran, 1971–1983* (Boulder, Colo.: Westview Press, 1984), ch. 2.

3. This and all other references to the IRI's Constitution are taken from *Constitution from the Islamic Republic of Iran* (CIRI), trans. H. Algar (Berkeley, Calif.: Mizan Press, 1980).

4. Although a number of senior planners have left the PBO in the post-revolutionary years, the planning machinery has remained technically functional.

5. See Muhammad Nejatullah Siddiqi, *Muslim Economic Thinking: A Survey of Contemporary Literature* (Leicester, U.K.: Islamic Foundation, 1981); and Kurshid Ahmed, ed., *Studies in Islamic Economics: Papers Presented to the First International Conference on Islamic Economics, February 1976* (Leicester, U.K.: Islamic Foundation, 1980).

6. This analytical approach is applied throughout M. N. Siddiqi's *Muslim Economic Thinking*. See also M. A. Mannan, *Islamic Economics: Theory and Practice* (Delhi, India: Idarah-i Adabiyat-i Delli, 1970).

7. Masudul Alam Choudhury, "Principles of Islamic Economics," *Middle Eastern Studies*, vol. 19, no. 1 (1983), p. 93.

8. Ibid.

9. Ibid., p. 94.

10. Ibid.

11. M. A. Mannan doubts the validity of the marginal productivity theory because it "has been subjected to various criticisms" (from what point of view?); he also argues that the theory "remains valid only under conditions of perfect competition." Under actual conditions, however, "competition is never perfect." Therefore, the workers "under capitalism, are likely to get wages much lower than their marginal product." According to Mannan, "this exploitation . . . is foreign to the Islamic faith." See Mannan, op. cit., p. 155.

12. Maxime Rodinson, *Islam and Capitalism* (Austin, Texas: University of Texas Press, 1978), p. 16.

13. M. A. Mannan suggests that the "fixation of wage and productivity formulae will be a matter of correct adjudication" in an Islamic state. See Mannan, op. cit., p. 156.

14. Choudhury, op. cit., p. 94.

15. Ibid.

16. Siddiqi, op. cit., p. 63.

17. On Islamic banking, see M. N. Siddiqi, *Issues in Islamic Banking* (Leicester, U.K.: Islamic Foundation, 1983).

18. Ibid., p. 17.

19. Ibid., p. 59.

20. See Siddiqi, *Muslim Economic Thinking*, op. cit., p. 7; and Choudhury, op. cit., p. 94.

21. Siddiqi, *Muslim Economic Thinking*, op. cit., p. 7.

22. Ibid.

23. Rodinson, op. cit., pp. 19–20.

24. Ibid.

25. Siddiqi, *Muslim Economic Thinking*, op. cit., p. 7.

26. Choudhury, op. cit., p. 95.

27. See Homa Katouzian, "Shi'ism and Islamic Economics: Sadr and Bani Sadr," in Nikki Keddie, ed., *Religion and Politics in Iran: Shi'ism from Quietism to Revolution* (New Haven, Conn.: Yale University Press, 1983), pp. 145–165.

28. See Ali Shari'ati, *On the Sociology of Islam: Lectures*, trans. H. Algar (Berkeley, Calif.: Mizan Press, 1982); and Shari'ati, *Marxism and Other Western Fallacies: An Islamic Critique*, trans. R. Campbell (Berkeley, Calif.: Mizan Press, 1982).

29. See Mahmud Taleqani, *Society and Economics in Islam* (including the chapter entitled "Islam va Malikiyat—Islam and Ownership"), trans. R. Campbell (Berkeley, Calif.: Mizan Press, 1982).

30. See Murtaza Mutahhari, *Fundamentals of Islamic Thought: God, Man, and Universe*, trans. R. Campbell (Berkeley, Calif.: Mizan Press, 1982). His "Islam and Capitalism," which *Ettela'at* published in a series of articles in the summer of 1981, created a controversy among the *ulama*. In these articles, it is argued that modern capitalism poses new problems that are not clearly dealt with in the *fiqh*—an argument that was considered a revisionist departure from orthodoxy. The book has not yet been published.

31. See, for example, Ayatollah Khomeini's interview with *Tempo* (Indonesia), January 13, 1979, reprinted in *Payam-e Enqelab*, vol. 3 (Tehran: Payam-e Azadi, 1361 [1982]), p. 244. This collection includes the declarations, speeches, and interviews of Ayatollah Khomeini from 1961 to the present, in eight volumes so far.

32. On the formation of the political structure of the Islamic government, see Shaul Bakhash, *The Reign of the Ayatollas* (New York: Basic Books, 1984), ch. 4.

33. Reprinted in Akbar Khalili, *Gam be Gam ba Enqelab* [Publication of the Radio and Television Organization of the IRI] (Tehran: Soroush, 1360 [1981]), pp. 114–116. The resolution is often referred to by Ayatollah Khomeini as a referendum against the Shah.

34. Shahrzad Azad, "Workers' and Peasants' Councils in Iran," *Monthly Review*, October 1980.

35. The Mostaz'afin Foundation is also officially included among the Revolutionary Foundations, but it makes few efforts in the direction of mobilization and serves

largely as a trust for most of the expropriated properties. The Revolutionary Islamic Courts have been controlled primarily by the "populist-state control" faction.

36. The Revolutionary Guard Corps has recently become a ministry.

37. Bakhash, op. cit., ch. 4.

38. CIRI, op. cit., p. 13.

39. Bakhash, op. cit., pp. 83, 87–88. For details of the debates in the Assembly of Experts, see Islamic Consultative Assembly (the Parliament), *The Complete Report of the Debates in the Assembly for the Final Review of the Constitution of the Islamic Republic of Iran, Vol. I, 1st–31st Sessions* (Tehran: Islamic Consultative Assembly Printing Office, November–December 1985). Two additional volumes are forthcoming.

40. Some authors have attributed this parallel to the attempt of Islamic scholars and political activists to attract to Islam the young activists under the influence of Marxism. See, for example, Katouzian, op. cit., p. 147, and Bakhash, op. cit., p. 167.

41. CIRI, op. cit., p. 19.

42. Ibid., p. 19.

43. Ibid., p. 21.

44. Ibid., p. 43.

45. Ibid., pp. 44–45.

46. Ibid., p. 46.

47. Ibid.

48. *Ruznameh-ye Rasmi Keshvar* [Official Bulletin of Government], No. 10092, 24/7/1358 (October 16, 1979).

49. Ibid., No. 10238, 1/2/1359 (April 22, 1980).

50. For example, the eating of the meat of a dead animal goes against the primary rulings; however, in a condition of urgency, one may eat that meat to remain alive—a secondary ruling.

51. For a detailed account of the confrontation between the Parliament and the Council of Guardians on these issues, see Bakhash, op. cit., pp. 191–194 and ch. 8.

52. Office of Revolutionary Projects, "Summary of the Preliminary Report on Determination of the Economic-Social Policies in the Islamic Republic of Iran," *Murdad* (1358) [August 1979], mimeo.

53. Ibid., pp. 71–75.

54. Ibid., p. 5.

55. Ibid., p. 46.

56. Ibid., pp. 6, 13.

57. Ibid.

58. Ibid., pp. 6, 34.

59. Ibid., p. 29.

60. Ibid., p. 62.

61. Ibid., pp. 29–31.

62. Ibid., pp. 31–36.

63. PBO, "The National System of Planning, Approved by the Economic Council 10/10/1360 (December 31, 1981)," mimeo.

64. See Alinaqi Mashayehki, "Review of the National System of Planning in Action and Some Constructive Suggestions," *Barnameh va Towse'e*, vol. 1, no. 1 (Winter 1985); and Razavi and Vakil, op. cit., pp. 116–119.

65. PBO, "The Quantitative Goals of Economic-Social Development in the Islamic Republic of Iran for 1361–1381 [1982–2002]," *Esfand* (1360) [February-March 1982], mimeo.

66. This estimation method was explained to me by a number of the planners involved.

67. PBO, "The Summary of Views and Directives of the Economic Council on the Quantitative Goals of Economic-Social Development in the Islamic Republic of Iran for 1361–1381, Approved 30/1/1361 (April 19, 1982)," mimeo.

68. PBO, "The First Five-Year Macro Economic-Social-Cultural Plan of the Islamic Republic of Iran, 1362–1366 (1983–1987), Approved by the Economic Council, 9th *Shahrivar* (1361) [August 31, 1982]," mimeo.

69. PBO, "The Bill for the First Economic-Social-Cultural Development Plan of the Islamic Republic of Iran, 1362–1366, Approved by the Cabinet of the Islamic Republic of Iran 20/4/1362 (June 11, 1983)," in four volumes, mimeo.

70. Ibid., vol. 1, pp. 1.1–1.4.

71. Ibid., pp. 1.5–1.10.

72. Ibid., pp. 1.11–1.8.

73. Ibid., p. 2.15.

74. Ibid., pp. 2.2, 2.5.

75. Ibid., p. 2.3. In May 1986, Iran's exports of petroleum had declined to less than one mb/d, at a price at least 50 percent less than anticipated in the "worst" situation.

76. Ibid., p. 2.12.

77. Islamic Consultative Assembly, "The Bill for the First Economic-Social-Cultural Development Plan of the Islamic Republic of Iran."

78. Mas'od Zanjani (in the Parliament), quoted in *Kayhan* (Daily), January 7, 1986.

79. Sohrab Behdad, "Crisis in the Iranian Economy," paper presented at the Middle East Economic Association meeting, December 27–30, 1985.

80. The conventional mass media (radio, television, major newspapers), as well as much of the Friday Prayer network of propaganda, is under the control of this tendency. Ali Akbar Hashemi-Rafsanjani, speaker of the Parliament, used the Tehran Friday Prayer for explaining the position of this tendency on the economic question. These sermons are printed in the five volumes of *Social Justice: Economic Problems*, published by the Organization of National Industries of Iran, in 1982–1983.

8

War Damage and Reconstruction in the Islamic Republic of Iran

Hooshang Amirahmadi

Introduction

The Iranian Revolution of 1979 had a number of interrelated goals, one of which was national prosperity on the basis of economic development. The realization of this goal required peace and political stability. Although political instability in post-revolutionary Iran had been anticipated, hardly any Iranian had predicted the war with Iraq. That war has effectively put an end to economic development.

But history only rarely fits expectations. In less than two years after the victory of the Revolution, and to the surprise and horror of the Iranians, the Iraqi regime began its war against Iran. The war is now in its eighth year (having endurerd for a longer period than World War II) and has caused massive destruction (to a much greater degree than the Vietnam War). Dwelling on the roots of the war will serve no purpose in this chapter, which is focused on destructions and reconstructions in Iran.

Extent and Types of Damage

On September 22, 1980, the Iraqi army invaded Iran along a front 1352 kilometers (850 miles) in length, penetrating at certain points as deeply as 80 kilometers (50 miles) into Iranian territory. In less than a few weeks, more than 14,000 square kilometers (5400 square miles) of Iran had come under Iraqi occupation. The map in this chapter indicates the five Iranian provinces under Iraqi attack. They include W. Azarbaijan, Kurdestan, Bakhtaran, Ilam, and Khuzestan. This last region, which was among the few well-developed provinces and is the oil capital of the country, has suffered the most. The provinces are densely populated, and most of the population consists of national minorities. Four other neighboring provinces have also suffered in varying degrees, along with the many cities in various central, southern, and western parts of the country that have been hit by missiles or bombs on several occasions.

In general, the war has cost Iran heavily in human and material terms for the simple reason that it has been fought mainly inside the borders of Iran. Although Iraqis have been forced out of almost all occupied territories, the war still goes on and damages continue to accumulate. Such damages have been particularly devastating for Iranian production. Specifically, production has been negatively impacted as a result of human damage, damage to settlement systems, material damage, and financial/budgetary damage.

The human damage includes the many thousands who have been killed, disabled, or maimed. Others have disappeared at the war front, or have been captured. More than 5 million people have also lost their homes and jobs, and about 2.5 million of these have been forced to migrate to war-free zones where they live in refugee camps or self-prepared shacks. To this list of human damage must be added the millions who had to serve in the war including military personnel, paramilitary forces, and irregular or professional volunteers from various segments of society. It is important to note that much of this human damage has occurred among the young and the most productive working people of Iran.[1]

Damage to human settlements has been equally devastating. Although only 5 (of 24) provinces have been involved in the war, a number of neighboring provinces, the adjoining 4 in particular, have suffered from missile attacks and bombs (see the map). Specifically, 51 cities and towns and 3,891 villages have been damaged to varying degrees. The cities of Haveizeh, Qasr-e Shirin, Musian, Sumar, Ozgoleh, and Khosrawi have been "totally levelled" and the cities of Khoramshahr, Nosud, Dehloran, Gilan-e Qarb, Abadan, Bostan, Mehran, Susangard, Shush, Dezful, Andimeshk, Naft-Shahr, Baneh, and Sar Pol-e Zohab, among others, have received "wide-ranging damage."[2] According to a government source, total monetary damage to the "urban sector" until September 1985 amounted to 234,782.6 million rials (U.S. $2.9 billion) (1 U.S. dollar equals about 80 rials). This total includes the damage to buildings and equipment belonging to municipalities and residents, but it excludes the damage to buildings constructed by the Ministry of Housing and Urban Development. The figure for this latter alone is reported at 247,439.4 million rials (U.S. $3.09 billion). Note that these figures do not include damage to commercial buildings (such as shops and other trading centers), to cultural, historical, religious, educational, and health care–related buildings, to industrial establishments, or to the infrastructures of various types in the cities, including the postal facilities.[3] According to official figures, more than 60 percent of the country's port facilities are not functioning as a result of war damage.[4]

The magnitude of the damage to villages in the five war provinces is indicated in Table 1. Thirty percent of the villages in the five provinces have been damaged, many of them beyond repair. In Khuzestan alone, for example, 356 "Arab-inhabited villages" are reported to "have been reduced to ashes and literally wiped out of the map."[5] The provinces of Bakhtaran

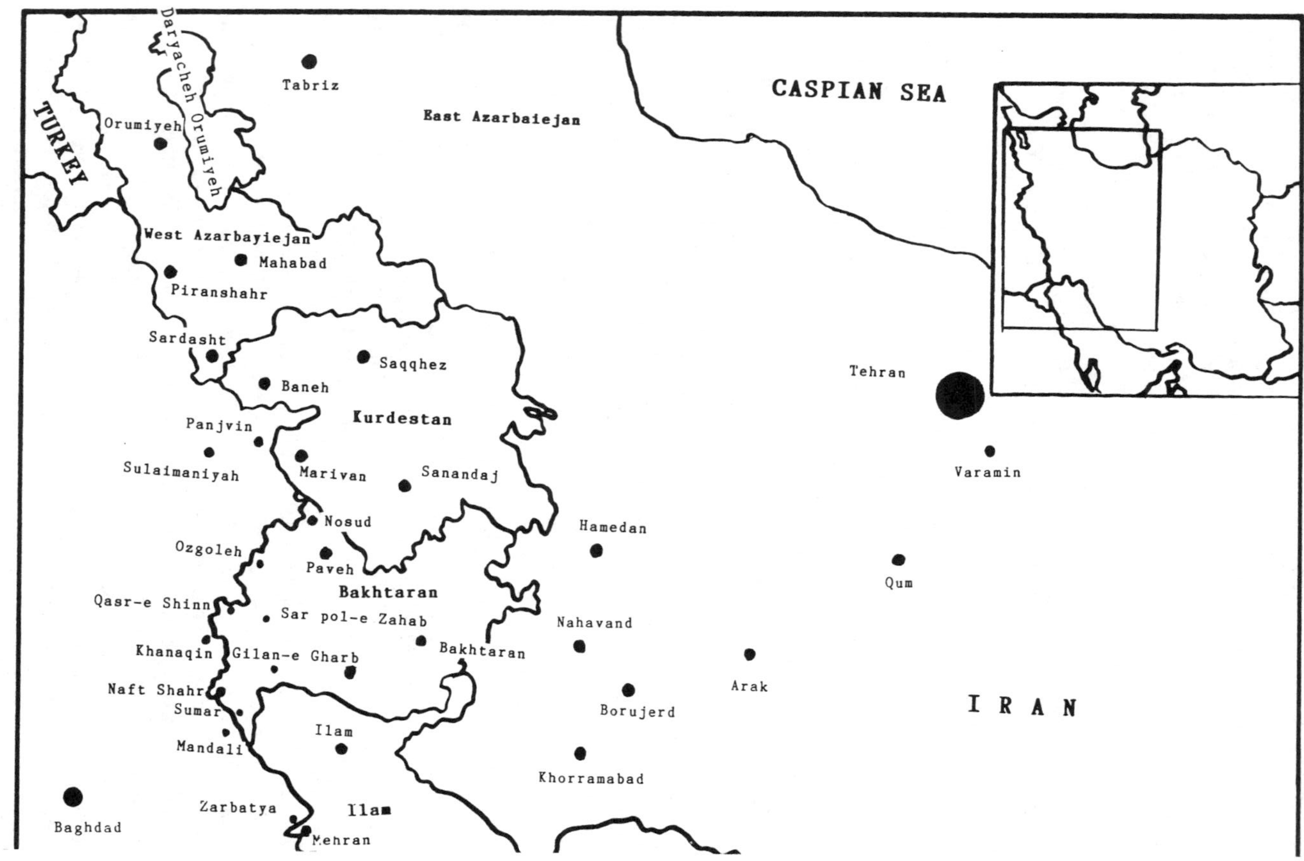
Daryacheh Orumiyeh
Tabriz
East Azarbaiejan
CASPIAN SEA
TURKEY
Orumiyeh
West Azarbayiejan
Mahabad
Piranshahr
Sardasht
Saqqhez
Baneh
Kurdestan
Tehran
Panjvin
Sulaimaniyah
Marivan
Sanandaj
Varamin
Nosud
Hamedan
Ozgoleh
Paveh
Qum
Bakhtaran
Qasr-e Shinn
Sar pol-e Zahab
Nahavand
Khanaqin
Gilan-e Gharb
Bakhtaran
Arak
Naft Shahr
Sumar
Borujerd
I R A N
Ilam
Mandali
Khorramabad
Zarbatya
Ilam
Baghdad
Mehran

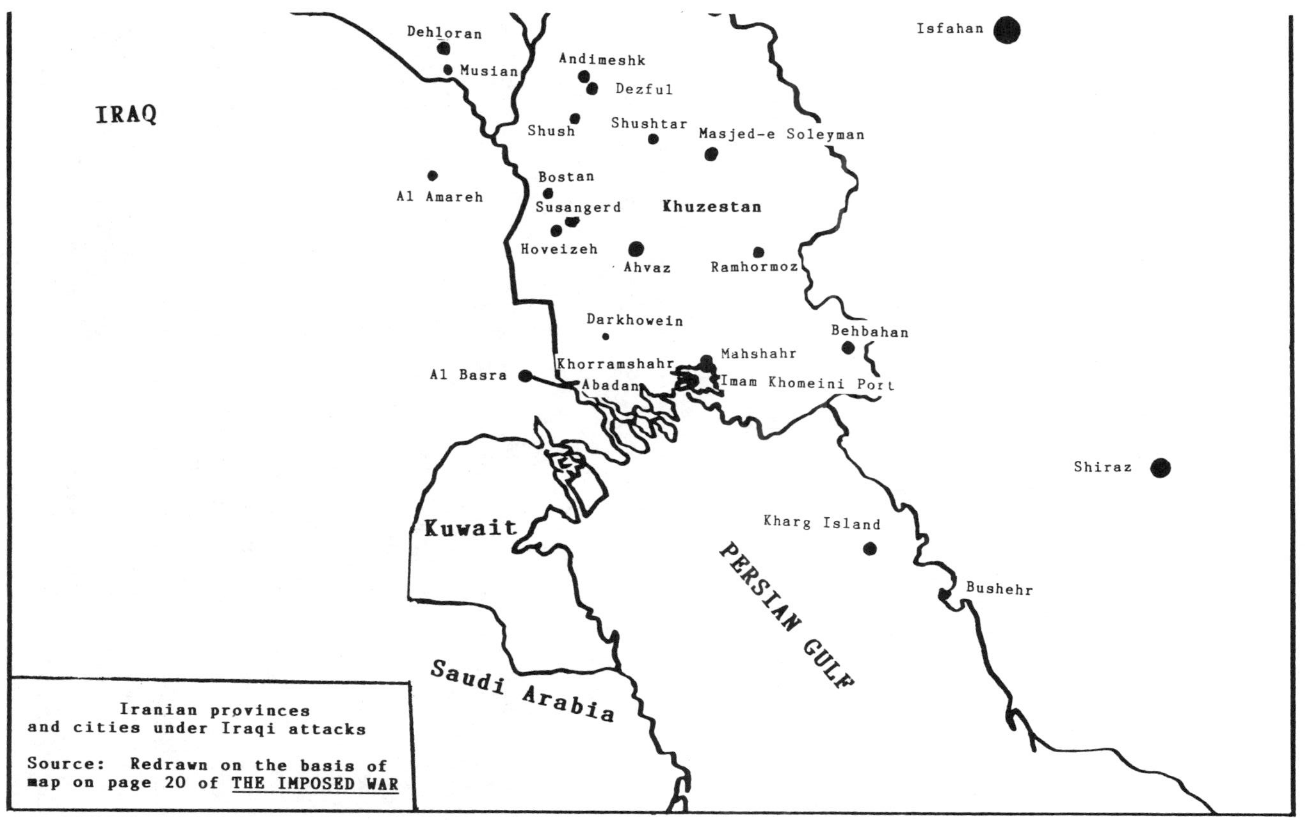

Iranian provinces
and cities under Iraqi attacks

Source: Redrawn on the basis of map on page 20 of THE IMPOSED WAR

Table 1 EXTENT OF DAMAGE TO THE VILLAGES IN THE FIVE PROVINCES IN THE WAR ZONE

PROVINCE	No. of TOTAL VILLAGES EXISTING(a)	DAMAGED	% DAMAGED	DAMAGE (million rials)
Ilam(b)	819	104	12.7	35,868.5
Bakhtaran	2764	341	12.3	44,805.3
Khuzestan	4316	497	11.5	64,726.9
W. Azarbaijan	3179	1705	53.6	194,446.8
Kurdestan	1929	1244	64.5	220,367.7
TOTAL	13007	3891	29.9	560215.2

NOTES & SOURCE:

Khoulaseh-e Gouzaresh: Baraourd-e Khasarat-e Eqtesadi-ye Jang, 1364, p. 317.

(a) On the basis of the National Census of 1355 (1976).

(b) Figures for Ilam and Khuzestan are taken from the 1362 (1983) report of damage. Data for damage inflicted on Qasr-e Shirin are included in figures for Bakhtaran.

and Kurdestan seem to have suffered the most, probably due to a combination of the war with Iraq and the activity of the Kurds, who have been fighting the central government since 1979 in their demands for regional autonomy. The total damage to the villages in the five provinces is reported at 560,215.1 million rials (U.S. $7.003 billion), a figure larger than the corresponding number for the cities.

More detailed accounts are available for the material damages accrued during the war (see Table 2). These damages are reported for seventeen sectors of the society, and for each sector from one to nine types of damage are included. As indicated in Table 2, the most recent official estimates (up to September 1985) put the total damage to various sectors of the society at 24,730,424 million rials (U.S. $309.13 billion) at current prices. This figure includes damage to human settlements, but it excludes damage to the armed forces and the population.[6] Considering that the foreign exchange earnings of the government from oil in the 1979–1984 period was U.S. $16.75 billion (average per annum), the amount of loss is equivalent to 18.5 years of Iranian oil export earnings.

The seventeen sectors (which numerically correspond to the categories in Table 2) are as follows:

1. Agriculture (all subsectors)
2. Manufacturing industries
3. Oil
4. Energy
5. Telecommunications
6. Housing and urban development (structures constructed by the Ministry of Housing and Urban Development)
7. Education and Islamic Guidance
8. Health and welfare
9. Roads, transportation, and customs
10. Banks (including assets, buildings, unpaid debts by customers, and opportunity costs)
11. Municipalities (including buildings and equipment belonging to municipalities and other buildings in cities; the damages also affected the properties, furniture, and so on, belonging to city dwellers)
12. Revolutionary foundations (the damages in this case affected the villages in five war-damaged provinces, and included the expenses incurrred by the Guard Corps [e.g., expenditures for provision of the basic needs of its fighters and payments to families of those killed, disabled, and injured in the war], the expenditures relating to war immigrants, the expenses incurred by war captives and asylums, and the cash and/or in-kind assistance contributed to the war fronts by the Imam's Assistance Committee, the Fifteen of Khourdad Foundation, and the Foundation for the Oppressed
13. Commerce and finance
14. Labor and justice
15. Red Crescent–Tehran Municipalities
16. Prime Ministry and Ministry of Plan and Budget
17. Gendarmery and police

The nine types of damage reported (in this case the letters correspond to those in Table 2) include the following:

A. Various buildings and public establishments
B. Machinery and equipment
C. Materials, goods, and other national wealth
D. Reduction in capacities and delay in operations
E. Obstacles and difficulties resulting from the war
F. Opportunity costs
G. Cash and in-kind assistance and payment of wages and salaries to those sent to the war front
H. Damage to machineries and vehicles sent to the war front
I. Assistance to expenses of war-inflicted population

Material damage may be grouped into the two categories of direct and indirect damage. The latter includes losses emanating from damage types

Table 2 ECONOMIC DAMAGE OF THE WAR UP TO SEPTEMBER 1985, current prices (million rials)

	TYPES OF DAMAGE									
SECTOR	A	B	C	D	E	F	G	H	I	TOTAL
1	267,338	16,991	2,625,488	57,994	86,705	434,741	4,833	242	121	3,494,453
2	86,206	18,906	16,200	103,533	1,445,148	623,504	7,929	191	42	2,301,659
3	334,954	469,323	271,401	1,130,820	2,035,482	8,577,080	25,721	5,516	1,419	12,851,716
4	77,091	46,174	4,833	92,478	112,393	39,832	769	672	315	374,557
5	1,550	2,925	9,718	96	7,134	2,548	419		40	24,430
6	234,397	846	733	3,275	8,178		11			247,440
7	30,889	2,223	1,608	493	676		14,278	257	1,105	51,529
8	23,957	4,279	10,055	6,786	35	2,148	35,959	2,221	666	86,106
9	49,980	27,322	41,042	35,428	20,414	271,379	11,074	24,796	2,899	484,334
10	296,681									296,681
11	209,104	3,966	11,645	340	1,550	192	2,951	260	4,774	234,782
12	3,160,378									3,160,378
13	12,733	4,214	17,114	14,622	19,293	10,627	166	9	96	78,874
14	529	72	314				16		46	977
15	958	4,494	155	250,032	50,946	281,163	70,564	264	104	658,680
16	58	251	23	193,690	314	4,000	81	11	10,485	208,913
17	151,523									151,523
TOTAL	4,938,326	601,986	3,010,329	1,889,587	3,788,268	10,247,214	174,771	34,439	22,112	24,730,424

NOTES & SOURCE:

Khoulaseh-e Gouzaresh: Baraourd-e Khasarat-e Eqtesadi-ye Jang, 1364.

For the list of sectors and types of damage see the text.

Figure 1

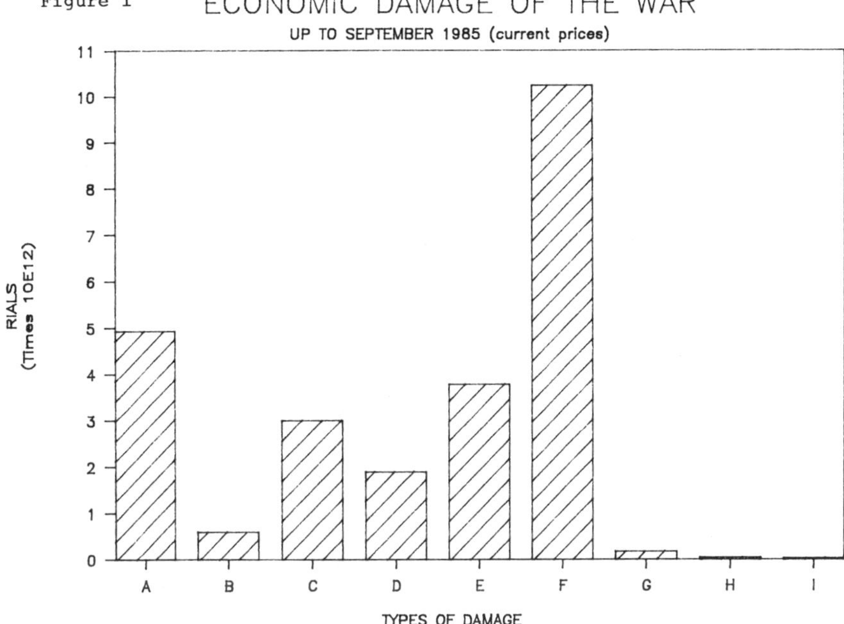

D, E, and F (see Table 2) and is estimated at 15,925,069 million rials (U.S. $199.1 billion) for the September 1980–September 1985 period, or about 64.4 percent of the total material damage of the war. Opportunity costs make up a sizable portion of the indirect costs. Direct damage, on the other hand, includes damage types A, B, C, G, H, and I and is estimated at 8,805,355 million rials (U.S. $110.1 billion) or 35.6 percent of the total damage. Machineries, buildings, materials, goods, and similar national wealth account for most of the direct costs. Figure 1 indicates the degrees to which various economic sectors suffered damage.

A more informative picture of the material damage is obtained when sectoral damage is considered. Table 2 gives the rial amounts of such damage for each sector, and Figure 2 depicts them graphically so that the relative size of damage to each sector can be visualized. It is clear that the oil sector (12,851,716 rials or U.S. $160.6 billion) has suffered the most, followed by agriculture (3,494,451 million rials or U.S. $43.7 billion), revolutionary foundations (3,160,378 million rials or U.S. $39.5 billion), industries (2,947,050 million rials or U.S. $36.8 billion), and the rest (2,276,828 million rials or U.S. $28.5 billion) grouped under "others." All of the figures represent current prices.

For some interesting comparisons, the reader may refer to Table 3 and Figure 3. It is clear that the war damages have been extraordinarily high when compared to the production level of the three main productive economic sectors for the 1985 and 1979–1985 period. Specifically, the total

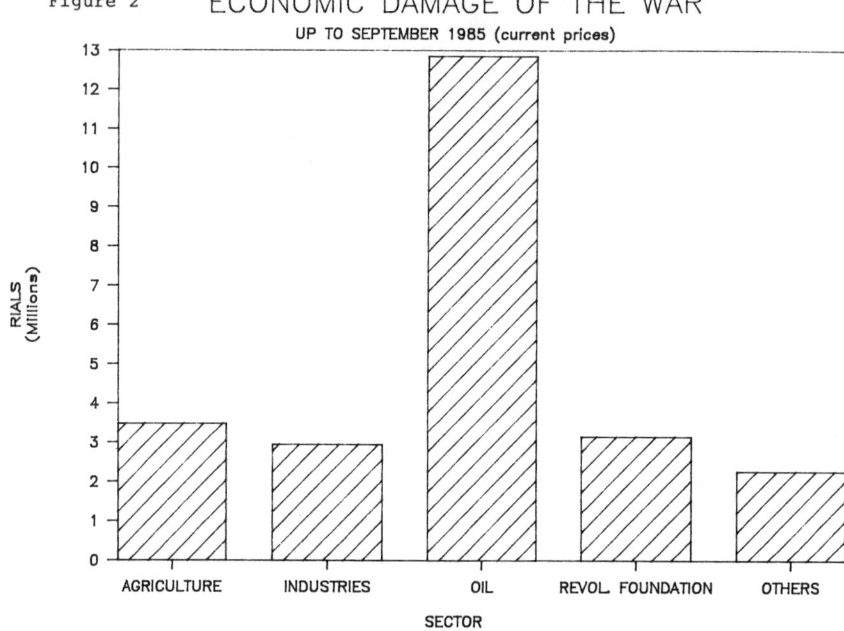

war damages to the three sectors' production levels exceeded their combined 1985 production level by 14.8 percent and was 48.8 percent of the sectors' 1979–1985 production. The oil sector's production has suffered the most, followed by that of agriculture and industries. Thus, the war damage to oil production totaled 597.5 percent of the sector's production in 1985 and 80.8 percent of its production over the entire 1979–1985 period. Comparable figures for agriculture were 143.8 and 24.8 percent, and for the industries, 86.8 and 14.6 percent. In addition, the destruction of 60 percent of Iran's refinery capacity has been reported.[7] Another relevant statistic may be obtained by comparing total GDP in 1985 (3,508,600 million rials, or U.S. $44 billion, at 1974 constant prices) with the total war damage. The latter exceeded the former by 15.8 percent; that is, the total war damage amounted to 115.8 percent of total 1985 gross domestic production.

Although these figures clearly reflect the tremendous impact of the war on levels of production, a more important insight may be obtained by considering the financial/budgetary damage of the war. Financial damage is measured in terms of war expenditures, including those paid out of the public budgets and those contributed by the population. The relevant figures are given in Table 2, under damage types G and I (174,771 million and 22,112 million rials, or U.S. $2.2 and $0.27 billion, respectively) and in Table 4, where payments made out of the public budget for war expenses are indicated. Current expenditures of the war for the 1981–1985 period amounted to 2,129,200 million rials (U.S. $26.6 billion) at current prices. If expenditures

Table 3 SECTORAL WAR DAMAGE AND PRODUCTION, 1985 AND 1979-85 (fixed 1974 prices)

		PRODUCTION			
SECTOR	TOTAL WAR DAMAGE TO SEPTEMBER 1985 (billion rials)	CONTRIBUTION TO GDP IN 1985 (billion rials)	CONTRIBUTION TO GDP IN 1979-85 (billion rials)	TOTAL WAR DAMAGE AS PERCENT OF 1985 PRODUCTION	TOTAL WAR DAMAGE AS PERCENT OF 1979-85 PRODUCTION
1. Agriculture	735.7	512.5	2969.6	143.6	24.8
2. Industries	620.4	714.7	4241.6	86.8	14.6
3. Oil	2705.6	452.8	3349.3	597.5	80.8
TOTAL	4061.7	1680.0	10560.5	241.8	38.5

SOURCE: Calculated by the author on the basis of Table 2 and Hooshang Amirahmadi, 1986, Table 1.

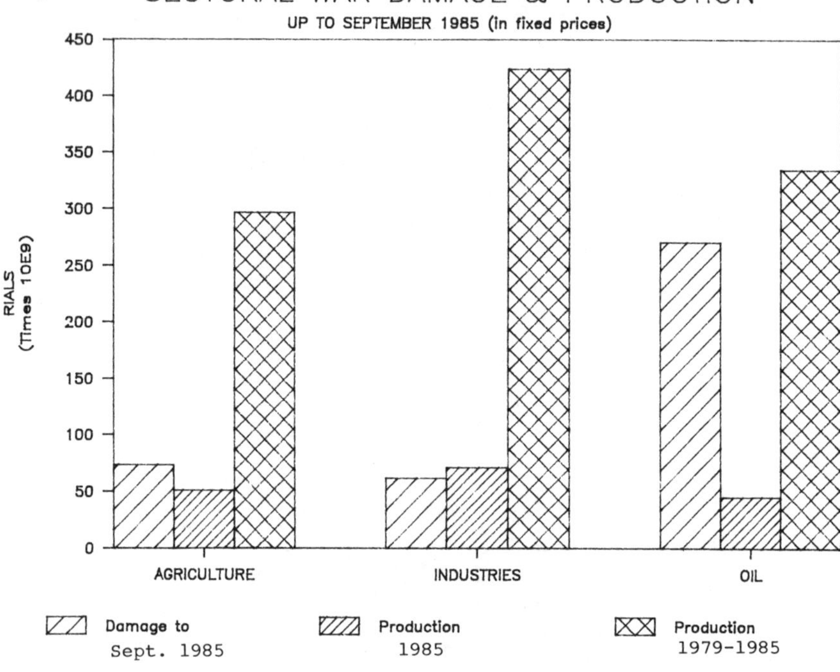

for reconstruction of war damage are also added, we arrive at the staggering figure of 2,400,400 million rials (U.S. $30.0 billion) for the period. Table 5 indicates the relative share of the war-related expenditures made by the public budget. In 1981, more than 14 percent of this budget was paid out in war expenditures; the comparable figure for 1985 was 10.3 percent. These figures largely underestimate the real war expenditures, not only because they are underreported but also because other "nonwar-related" expenditures were spent on activities that aimed to facilitate the war effort.

For a comparable picture of the war-related expenditures, we must look at military expenditures as well. Table 6 provides some interesting statistics in this connection. Although military expenditures have declined in the post-revolutionary years (compared with the pre-revolutionary period), they remain very high, as evidenced by the ratio figures given in the Table 6. For example, of the total oil revenues in 1980, about 50 percent went to the military budget. The figure was as high as 79.6 percent in 1981 and 53.5 percent in 1982. As percentages of GNP and nonoil GNP, the figures are also quite high; they account for slightly less than 10 percent in the case of GNP and for more than 10 percent in the case of nonoil GNP throughout the post-revolutionary years.

It is also important to consider the impact of the war on the public budget and, hence, the level of production. Specifically, the war has affected the budget in two ways: by reducing public revenues and by shifting the

Table 4 STRUCTURE OF PUBLIC EXPENDITURES (main items), 1976-85 (billion rials, current prices)

	1976	1977	1978	1979	1980	1981	1982	1983	1984	1985
CURRENT EXPENDITURES	1792.0	1874.0	1387.1	1552.0 [a]	1727.8 [b]	2032.4	2293.9 [c]	2548.7	2684.2	2739.1
War	0.0	0.0	0.0	0.0	0.0	381.0	445.2	503.0	400.0	400.0
Operating	1059.8	1047.3	1366.4	1520.2	1690.7	1606.3	1802.2	2010.4	2254.2	2305.3
FIXED INVESTMENTS	629.1	591.6	657.1	633.1 [d]	568.1	674.7	943.5	1163.5	1186.4	1135.8
Reconstruction of War Damage	0.0	0.0	0.0	0.0	0.0	0.0	70.1	91.1	60.0	50.0
National & Provincial Projects	629.1	591.6	657.1	633.1	568.1	674.7	844.7	1057.5	1126.4	1085.8
TOTAL EXPENDITURES & INVESTMENTS	2421.1	2465.6	2044.2	2185.1	2295.9	2707.1	3237.4	3712.2	3870.6	3874.9

NOTES & SOURCES:

1979-83 statistics are compiled from Gouzaresh-e Eqtesadi Va Taraznameh, Central Bank of Iran, Tehran, 1362, pp. 79 and 200-201; 1978. Statistics are from ibid., 1361, pp. 184-85; 1977 figures are from ibid., 1359, p. 73; 1976 figures are from ibid., 1355(2535), p. 27; 1984-85 figures are from Tazeha-ye Amari, Ministry of Plan and Budget, Statistical Center, Tehran, No. 3, 1363, p. 170 and No. 5, 1364, p. 135.

a. Includes 57.1 billion rials expenditures of the year 1978.
b. Includes 46.6 billion rials expenditures of the year 1979.
c. Includes 55.7 billion rials expenditures of various counties.
d. Includes 109.8 billion rials expenditures of the year 1978.

Table 5 STRUCTURE OF PUBLIC EXPENDITURES(main items),1976-85 (percentages)

	1976	1977	1978	1979	1980	1981	1982	1983	1984	1985
CURRENT EXPENDITURES	74.0	76.0	67.9	71.0[a]	75.3[b]	75.1	70.9[c]	68.7	69.3	70.7
War	0.0	0.0	0.0	0.0	0.0	14.1	13.8	13.5	10.3	10.3
Operating	43.8	42.5	66.8	69.6	73.6	59.3	55.7	54.2	58.2	59.5
FIXED INVESTMENTS	26.0	24.0	32.1	29.0[d]	24.7	24.9	29.1	31.3	30.7	29.3
Reconstruction of War Damage	0.0	0.0	0.0	0.0	0.0	0.0	2.2	2.5	1.6	1.3
National & Provincial Projects	26.0	24.0	32.1	29.0	24.7	24.9	26.1	28.5	29.1	28.0
TOTAL EXPENDITURES & INVESTMENTS	100.0	100.0	100.0	100.0	100.0	100.0	100.0	100.0	100.0	100.0

NOTES & SOURCES:

1979-83 statistics are compiled from Gouzaresh-e Eqtesadi Va Taraznameh, op.cit., 1362, pp. 79 and 200-201; 1978 Statistics are from Ibid., 1361, pp. 184-85; 1977 figures are from Ibid., 1359, p. 73; 1976 figures are from Ibid., 1355(2535), p. 27; 1984-85 figures are from Tazeha-ye Amari, op.cit, No.3, 1363, p. 170 and No.5, 1364, p.135.

a. Includes 57.1 billion rials expenditures of the year 1978.
b. Includes 46.6 billion rials expenditures of the year 1979.
c. Includes 55.7 billion rials expenditures of various counties.
d. Includes 109.8 billion rials expenditures of the year 1978.

Table 6 IRAN: RELATIONSHIP BETWEEN MILITARY EXPENDITURES, GNP, NON-OIL GNP, AND OIL REVENUE, 1972-83 (billion dollars)

					RATIO OF MILITARY EXPENDITURES TO:		
YEAR	MILITARY EXPENDITURES	GNP	NON-OIL GNP	OIL REVENUE	GNP	NON-OIL GNP	OIL REVENUE
1977	9.9	79.4	58.2	21.2	12.5	17.0	46.7
1978	12.1	76.1	56.8	19.3	15.9	21.3	62.7
1979	6.0	70.8	50.3	20.5	8.5	11.9	29.3
1980	6.7	74.5	61.0	13.5	9.0	11.0	49.6
1981	7.4	77.5	68.2	9.3	9.5	10.9	79.6
1982	8.5	85.4	69.5	15.9	10.0	12.2	53.5
1983	5.5	99.8	81.1	18.7	5.5	6.8	29.4

SOURCE: Adapted from Abbas Alnasrawi. "Economic Consequences of the Iran-Iraq War." Third World Quarterly, Vol. 8, No. 3 (July 1986), pp. 880-883. Combines Table 4 and part of Table 6.

budget structure toward more nonproductive spending. The reduction in revenues has occurred largely through the war's impact on oil production. Declining oil revenues, in turn, have led to reductions in oil-related taxes (such as taxes on imported goods and services). Thus, total oil-related incomes in the public budget declined from 83.2 percent in 1976 to 61.9 percent in 1984, contributing to a reduction in public income from 1,743,900 million rials (U.S. $21.8 billion) in 1976 to 2,645,200 million rials (U.S. $33.1 billion) in 1984.[8]

This reduction in public income, in the face of an expensive war and growing operating expenditures, led to a gradual decline in both the share of the development budget and the level of fixed capital formation, resulting in a reduction in sectoral productions. Thus, development expenditures, which accounted for 37.2 percent of the public budget in 1977, declined to 26.1 percent in 1984, reflecting a decline of about 30 percent. A growth rate of −4.7 percent was registered over the same period. As a consequence of this trend, gross domestic fixed capital formation dropped significantly, by 3.3 percent average per annum over the 1977–1983 period.[9]

Reconstruction Strategy for War Damage

Given the extent of the war destruction, the Iranians face a gigantic task of reconstruction of their homeland, particularly in the southern and the southwestern regions. Yet, the Islamic Republic does not have a workable comprehensive strategy to carry out the task. Various economic sectors, however, do have their own strategies and policies for reconstruction.[10] Nevertheless, the present reconstruction activities, while extensive in the areas of housing and infrastructure, remain partial and without clear direction.

In what follows, I will first explain the government's search for a suitable reconstruction strategy and then outline the pros and cons of the ongoing reconstruction activities and policies.

The Search for a Suitable Reconstruction Strategy

The most significant effort undertaken to date in the search for a suitable reconstruction strategy was the organization of the International Conference on Reconstruction of the War-Damaged Areas of Iran, which was held at Tehran University from March 6 to March 16, 1986. The conference was organized by Tehran University's Faculty of Fine Arts, in cooperation with the Ministries of Housing and Urban Development, Reconstruction Crusade, and Plan and Budget, and the Headquarters for Renovation and Reconstruction of the War-Damaged Regions. Sixty papers by participants (the author was among them) from thirty countries were presented. Among the participants from the Islamic Republic were the president, the prime minister, and several ministers, deputy ministers, and other high-level policy-makers. The participants were taken on a four-day tour of the war-damaged areas and were shown both the war damage and the ongoing reconstruction activities.

The idea of the conference emerged in 1983 when the government began to concern itself with the growing war destruction. The themes of the conference were three: (1) review of experiences worldwide; (2) exploration of the latest techniques for reconstruction; and (3) evaluation of the Islamic Republic's experience.

The views presented (including those of the speakers from the Islamic Republic) were diverse, indicating a lack of unity on the subject of reconstruction. The president emphasized that reconstruction in the Islamic Republic must be based on two principles: the use of modern technology, and the participation of the people. The prime minister, on the other hand, was more emphatic about the situation of the oppressed and the problem of the nonbureaucratic organization of the reconstruction process. Participants from the Ministry of Reconstruction Crusade were equally concerned with the oppressed people as were those participating from the Ministry of Housing and Urban Development. The most technocratic views came from the Ministry of Plan and Budget and from the participating university professors.

One tendency favored a decentralized reconstruction process in which the people make decisions, carry out the tasks, manage the affairs, and provide most of the resources. The proponents of this tendency gave an insignificant role to the government and were somewhat hostile to its bureaucracies. The opposite tendency is best described as "Islamic modernist": It favored large-scale government involvement, a more centralized and planned process, and the use of modern technologies. While the first tendency was quite emphatic and ideological about Islamic values, the opposite tendency was largely pragmatic. It was evident that the differences were philosophically, as well as methodologically, rooted. For example, proponents of the "Islamic traditionalist" tendency argued that "development cannot be taken to the people" and that government should provide the conditions for the "self-development" of private individuals.

While these two tendencies were quite distinct from each other, a large number of government officials could not be placed into either of the two categories. They stood somewhere in between, even though they occasionally sided with one or the other tendency on certain issues. It was not clear whether either of the two tendencies or the so-called "moderates" in between them would win the ideological competition any time soon. Whatever its practical impact, the ideological diversity has created a dynamic situation from which new ideas for reconstruction may emerge.

The conference produced a "Final Statement" in which the main themes agreeable to the majority of participants were incorporated. The statement took an apparently technocratic view of the reconstruction. Specifically, the use of "modern technologies" and "planning," including "regional planning," was highly recommended.

The statement also indicated that a suitable reconstruction strategy should set its objectives in line with those of the national economy. It further recommended the establishment of a national data bank and formation of a controlling/supervisory unit within the prime minister's office to oversee the reconstruction process. Although it emphasized the role of the government in reconstruction of the infrastructure, it specified that the state should not promote the idea of free housing for the poor or the war-inflicted population. Instead, the government was instructed to use its power and resources to increase the people's purchasing power.

Other important recommendations in the statement included the preservation and promotion of the national traditions and customs in the reconstruction process, correspondence of the regional reconstruction strategy with the region's needs and conditions (including historical and cultural ones), and participation of the people in designing their settlement environment, particularly in urban planning. Whether these recommendations will be incorporated in a yet-to-emerge reconstruction strategy remains to be seen.

One thing, however, is certain: the government remains interested in the intellectual aspects of developing a more suitable reconstruction strategy, as evidenced by the increased attention of the few large public universities to do research on reconstruction. In the fall of 1986, for example, the University of Shiraz established a "Center for Research on the War-Damaged Areas of Iran" to promote the following objectives: evaluation of the results of the International Conference, coordination of various research projects throughout the country, establishment of links between academic research and reconstruction activities, and promotion of the role of research as an infrastructure for reconstruction. The initial steps in realizing such objectives included two major national conferences in 1986 and 1987. These conferences brought a wide range of expertise and interest groups from universities, policy-making institutions, and implementing agencies to discuss a variety of issues related to the theory and practice of reconstruction in Iran. They dealt primarily with the role of various socioeconomic factors, social groups, and organizations and defined a more focused agenda for research.

Ongoing Reconstruction Activities in the Islamic Republic

Although partial and with no strategic direction, reconstruction activities in the Islamic Republic have been significant, particularly in the areas of housing and infrastructure. Industrial reconstruction, on the other hand, remains largely undeveloped. Although it is impossible to give a comprehensive view of such activities in so short a space, an outline of the major activities is useful.

The Nature of Reconstruction Activities. The reconstruction process can be thought of as divided into four stages: emergency, restoration, replacement, and developmental reconstruction. The emergency stage begins immediately following the occurrence of a disaster (e.g., after a missile attack or bombardment). Normally, search, rescue, mass feeding, housing, and clearance of debris are among the major coping measures undertaken at this stage. The objective of the restoration stage, which begins before the emergency stage is over, is to help the community return to its normal life. Those damaged structures that can be replaced are patched up and made usable again. Destroyed structures and capital stocks are reconstructed during the replacement stage, at a time when government involvement and planning become indispensable. Finally, any additions or improvements to the pre-disaster level of activities, structures, or investments are made at the developmental stage. Self-help actions, so powerful during the first two stages, tend to lose their relevance at this stage. Instead, large-scale government involvement should be directed toward a furthering of national goals. Comprehensive planning is thus required.

For the most part, reconstruction activities in the Islamic Republic remain limited to the first three stages and largely take the form of housing construction. For example, development reconstruction is not one of the responsibilities of the Central Headquarters for Renovation and Reconstruction of the War-Damaged Areas, the country's main organization for the reconstruction of war damage. According to its general administrator, the main responsibilities of the Headquarters include (1) preparing for probable bombardment and missile attacks; (2) maintaining order and discipline and preventing looting and stealing; (3) promptly removing the dead and injured; 4) attending to and curing the injured; (5) vacating damaged areas; and (6) starting repairs on structures with less than 50 percent of damage.[11] Recently, however, the Central Headquarters has determined that cities suffering damages of more than 50 percent must be rebuilt according to modern urban-planning standards. Moreover, the Supporting Headquarters (*Setad-ha-ye Mo'in*) located in certain provinces have been directed to undertake activities largely related to replacement and developmental reconstruction. The main responsibilities of these headquarters include: (1) mobilizing the needed establishments; (2) preparing the ground for extended reconstruction work; and (3) undertaking the necessary research and planning.[12]

The Islamic Republic has, in theory, favored a mixed approach. According to the terms of the Constitution, the economic system is composed of three sectors: government, cooperatives, and private. It also emphasizes sound planning. In practice, however, the economy remains largely unplanned despite the growing state and cooperative sectors. The same is true of the reconstruction efforts being made in the war-damaged areas. In the absence of planning, most of these reconstruction activities are focused on emergency relief measures, temporary restoration of damage, and replacement of such structures as houses, schools, hospitals, and religious places. Activities concerned with developmental reconstruction and renovation of damaged industries are rare. Indeed, both the Supreme Council and the Central Headquarters for Renovation and Reconstruction are largely concerned with budgeting rather than planning.

Organization for Reconstruction. The experience to date indicates that reconstruction is a civilian job and that popular organizations are the most important tools in its process. Following this principle, the Islamic Republic has created a multitude of such organizations. These include various *Setadha* (Headquarters), *Nehadha* (institutions), *Bonyadha* (foundations), *Shuraha* (Councils), *Gruhha-ye kar* (Work Groups), and *Comiteha* (Committees).

Though indispensable, popular organizations are not by themselves sufficient for the organizational and administrative tasks of reconstruction. Appropriate government agencies must be created to assist and complement them. Having come to this realization, the Islamic Republic has created many new agencies concerned with war and reconstruction. Included among these are *Vazarat-e Jihad-e Sazandegi* (Ministry of Reconstruction Crusade), *Bonyad-e Maskan* (Housing Foundation), *Bonyad-e Mostazafan* (Foundation for the Oppressed), *Bonyad-e Omur-e Mohajeran-e Jangi* (Foundation for the Affairs of the War Immigrants), and *Sepah-e Pasdaran* (Guard Corps). Previously existing organizations and ministries are also involved, including the *Helal-e Ahmar* (Red Crescent), *Owqaf* (the religious endowment institution), the *Astan-e Qods* (the organization in charge of the properties of the Eighth Imam), and the Ministries of Housing and Urban Development, Industries, and Commerce. Each of these organizations has its respective subdivisions at various levels.

The main organization in the country concerned with reconstruction is the Central Headquarters for Renovation and Reconstruction of the War-Damaged Regions. The organization oversees the work of many organizations but is in turn supervised by the Supreme Council for Renovation and Reconstruction, whose president is the prime minister. The other three members include Ayatollah Khomeini's representative and the ministers of interior and plan and budget. This last minister also acts as secretary of the Supreme Council. The Central Headquarters, on the other hand, is made up of fifteen ministers, with the minister of the interior as president. Other major organizations include the Ministry of *Jihad-e Sazandegi*, the Ministry of Agriculture, and the Central Bank.

The Central Headquarters is divided into *Setadha-ye Ostani* (Provincial Headquarters), *Setadha-ye Mo'in* (Supporting Headquarters), and *Setadha-ye Shahrestan* (County Headquarters). *Setad-e Mo'in* is composed of the provincial governor, *Jihad-e Sazandegi's* representative, a representative from the Ministry of Commerce, and the *Imam Jomah* (the Friday Imam), who acts as president. Among the other offices at the Headquarters are the Committees for the Return of the War Migrants, Ordinance, Determination of Damages, and Supervision of Reconstruction Projects.

Determination of Damage and Identification of Resources. War damage in the Islamic Republic is classified, as it should be, in terms of extent (partial or complete) and type (houses, furniture and appliances, vehicles, shops, factories, farms, etc.); it is also compensated (in full or in part) by means of cash payments, loans, drafts, or a mix of these.[13] Several organizations have been made responsible for the repair of different kinds of damage. They include the Imam's Relief Committee (*Comiteh-e Emdad-e Imam*), the Foundation for War Immigrants, the Headquarters for the Affairs of the War Victims (*Setad-e Omur-e Jang-zadegan*), and the Central Headquarters for Renovation and Reconstruction and its regional and local offices.

The Islamic Republic needs to expand its classification of damage and to establish a central independent organization with various specialized agencies, work groups, and research teams to centralize the damage-estimation activities and create a central data file system. The damage-estimation activities must be undertaken not simply for the purpose of determining compensations as they are currently required but also as part of an organized effort to collect information about loss and availability of resources, to set priorities, and to determine the proper timing for reconstruction of damage. The identification of resources for reconstruction is particularly important. Existing and potential resources must be distinguished, and the latter must be further identified in terms of their immediate and long-term exploitability. Resources must also be identified in terms of type, quality, amount, distribution, costs, ease of use, and national origin. Although work has continued in these areas, the results remain far from satisfactory.

Mobilization of Resources. Resources must be mobilized before they can be utilized, and mobilization is a largely government-led and organized act. The Islamic Republic has experimented with many ways of mobilizing for both the war and reconstruction. For example, the government organized "War Week" and the "Day of Struggle for Economic Development" as methods of mobilizing people. Popular organizations, self-help projects, and the patronage system are also being used extensively. For example, *Astan-e Qods* rebuilt Haveizeh, Tehran is paying for most of the expenses incurred for reconstruction of Khorramshahr, and Mazandaranis have paid for the reconstruction of Susangard.

The mobilizing efforts have been equally successful from a financial standpoint. According to the general administrator of the Central Headquarters for Renovation and Reconstruction of the War-Damaged Areas, of a total of 300 billion rials (U.S. $3.8 billion) spent for rehabilitation and reconstruction of the war-damaged areas over the 1361–1363 (1982–1984) period, 90 billion rials (U.S. $1.1 billion), or about 30 percent, came from popular assistance.[14] In another interview, the administrator adjusted the figure upward to 40 percent.[15] Other methods have included raising more taxes and channeling a large chunk of the public budget toward war-related expenses. This latter measure totaled 2,400.4 billion rials (U.S. $30 billion) over the 1981–1985 period.

Specific Projects. Almost immediately after the start of the war, the government began to be concerned with reconstructing the economic sectors. Special committees began drawing up plans and programs for the reconstruction of their respective sectors. For instance, the Ministry of Industries established the "Committee of Industry" which took responsibility for designing strategies and workable plans for the reconstruction of industries. The results of the activities of this important committee were published in April–May 1982 in a book listing hundreds of damaged and destroyed industries along with plans and projects for their reconstruction.[16] A similar committee took charge of housing and urban development. The Housing Committee Report was published in September 1984.[17] Although many such projects or plans were never implemented, enthusiasm for reconstruction was very high.

With the passage of time, however, such enthusiasm seems to have diminished. Indeed, increasingly fewer projects and programs have been designed or implemented since 1983, the peak year for reconstruction. Thus, the government budget for reconstruction of war damage increased from 70.1 billion rials (U.S. $876 million) in 1982 to 91.1 billion rials (U.S. $1.14 billion) in 1983 and thereafter declined to 60 and 50 billion rials (U.S. $750 million and $625 million respectively) for 1984 and 1985, respectively.[18] In the face of significant cuts in development expenditures, the 1986 and 1987 figures are probably much lower.

A second shift in the government activities concerning reconstruction has to do with priorities. Earlier, the economic sectors had been the focus of the officials, and the attempts being made in behalf of their reconstruction were quite significant, at least on paper (e.g., studies of damages, plans for reconstruction, and implementation strategies). More recently, however, such concerns have lapsed significantly in favor of more attention to reconstruction of social sectors, settlement systems, and housing. Attempts to reconstruct the infrastructure also persist.

The most significant ongoing reconstruction projects relate to settlement systems and housing. Many of the ruined or damaged cities and villages are under reconstruction, as are hundreds of houses. As previously noted, the participants of the International Conference on Reconstruction of War-Damaged Areas were taken on a four-day tour of such cities and villages in Khuzestan province. The city of Haveizeh, which had been totally leveled by Iraqi occupiers, has been completely reconstructed under the patronage of the *Astan-e Qods*. The project includes 1,800 housing units (each of which has two or three bedrooms and modern facilities), a public bath, a mosque, religious and secular schools, a large bazaar, and other social facilities. The plan of the new city includes right-angle crossings, wide streets, and modern sewage facilities. The project has cost over 1 billion rials (U.S. $12.5 million). It was undertaken to serve a political purpose as well; as a showcase, it provides the Iraqis the opportunity to see for themselves that, as the prime minister put it in his speech at the conference, "our power of reconstruction is much greater than the enemy's power of destruction." It would probably be impossible for the Islamic Republic to replicate the project elsewhere—a fact that became the main focus of criticisms from the international observers participating in the Tehran conference. Others have concluded that the project has not taken into account the existing way of life, traditions, and customs of the residents—a problem that was also observed in relation to projects in rural areas. In one instance, a farmer had erected a shack adjoining his newly built modern house in which to keep his cattle.

Other projects involving reconstruction of human settlements on a large scale have taken place in Dezful, Hamidieh, Susangard, and Dehlavieh, as well as in the smaller towns and villages of Khuzestan province. The most significant of these is the reconstruction plan for the city of Khorramshahr. Although conference participants were unable to visit the city (for security reasons), they were shown films and provided with extensive published materials on some of the activities there.[19] Because of the enormity of the project and its political-economic importance, a special *Setad-e Mo'in* (Supporting Headquarters) has been established for the city under the supervision of the deputy minister of housing and urban development. Since the liberation of the city in 1983, the *Setad* (in cooperation with the Mandan, Yekan, and Andishkar consulting firms, the Iran Housing Company, and the Industrial Management Organization) has undertaken comprehensive studies concerning the type and extent of damages the city has suffered under Iraqi invaders. It has also undertaken planning and design activities, and implemented a number of major reconstruction projects. The details of such activities are provided in the "Summary of Works and Studies Performed for Reconstruction and Planning of War Inflicted Port City of Khorramshahr," published by the *Setad-e Mo'in* of the city in 1986.

As noted, many of the reconstruction activities in the Islamic Republic, including those witnessed by the international observers, have concentrated on housing. The social infrastructures also continue to receive priority, but reconstruction of basic economic institutions has appreciably diminished in recent years. With the new constraints on the public development budget (e.g., the decline in oil revenue and the increase in defense expenditures), reconstruction activities in economic sectors will suffer further. Because much of the war damage is concentrated in these sectors, the Iranian economy may not return to normalcy, much less to any level of prosperity, in the absence of reconstruction and development.

Conclusions and Policy Implications

This chapter has shown that, while the war damage is extensive, the Islamic Republic lacks a workable reconstruction strategy; moreover, its activities for rebuilding the society remain largely limited to certain sectors such as housing and infrastructure. In the face of a continuing war and increasing accumulation of war destruction, these limitations could result in a further decline in sectoral production and in an intensification of such existing problems as homelessness, joblessness, inflation, and budgetary deficit. The consequences for the Iranian nation could be disastrous, to say the least.

Urgent actions are thus needed, but first the war must be stopped; although reconstruction during the war is warranted, a lasting reconstruction, particularly if it is to be developmental, requires a lasting and just peace. Reconstruction of the Iranian society must also follow the goals of the 1979 Revolution. In particular, implementation of such goals as economic development, social justice, and national independence must be placed at the top of the reconstruction agenda. Required, above all, is the participation of the people—*all* the people—in formulating a reconstruction strategy. Much might be learned from the experiences of other nations, but we must never forget that the Iranian nation needs to formulate its reconstruction strategy on the basis of its national priorities, which in turn are best understood by the Iranians (particularly the intelligentsia) themselves.

Another principle to be followed throughout the reconstruction process relates to planning and democratic centralism. This requirement is imposed by the extensive involvement of the state in the society and by the large size of the public sector in the economy. Reconstruction planning must satisfy the two criteria of comprehensiveness and self-reliance. The former criterion demands that the private sector also be brought under the planned long-term supervision of the state; the latter requires that the reconstruction be implemented largely on the basis of availability of national resources. Comprehensiveness controls for social justice, and self-reliance controls for national independence. Democratic centralism, on the other hand, is a means toward institutionalization of controlled decentralization (as opposed to anarchism) and can be implemented only if supporting organizations and procedures are fully established. Sectoral and territorial councils are examples of needed organizations; the two-way, top-down/bottom-up planning approach is an example of the required procedure;[20] and regional planning is one effective means of institutionalizing such a planning approach.

Finally, aside from the need to develop technical and legal competency in such critical areas as determination of damage, and identification of resources and their mobilization, a suitable reconstruction strategy for Iran must incorporate an integrated settlement-system philosophy and a central mechanism of permanent income and asset redistribution across different social classes and territories. Regarding the former, rural and urban planning will be directed toward the creation of a hierarchy of cities and rural centers connected by transport/communication and functional links. The latter represents the most effective means of reconciling sectoral and territorial objectives, of balancing development across territories and social classes, and of bringing into creative harmony the inherent conflict between efficiency and equity objectives. Implementation of such a mechanism hinges upon the restructuring of national ownership laws and the tax system in favor of the poverty-stricken areas and the working people.

Notes

1. The figures mentioned in this paragraph were cited by the officials of the Islamic Republic in their papers, which were presented at the International Conference on Reconstruction of the War-Damaged Areas of Iran, held at Tehran University, March 6–16, 1986. The author was among the participants. Regarding the human damage, see also *The Imposed War: Defense vs. Aggression*, vols. 1–3, War Information Headquarters, Supreme Defense Council of the Islamic Republic of Iran, Tehran (1983–1985); *Kholaseh-e Gozaresh: Baravourd-e Khasarat-e Eqtesadi-ye Jang-e Tahmili-ye Araq Aleyh-e Iran Ta Shahrivar Mah-e 1364* [Summary Report: An Estimate of the Economic Damages of the Imposed War of Iraq Against Iran Until September 1985], Ministry of Plan and Budget, Tehran, 1986; Nancy Greenberg, "The Human Toll: The Iran-Iraq War's Cost to the Iranian People," the 20th Annual Meeting of the Middle East Studies Association of North America, Boston (November 20–23, 1986); and Sekandar Amanoulahi, "The Effect of the Iran-Iraq War on the Khuzestan Refugees," mimeo, Department of Sociology and Regional Planning, University of Shiraz, 1986.

2. The author visited some of these cities in Khuzestan province in March 1986. In Haveizeh, for example, he saw only one damaged building (a mosque) still standing; the rest of the city had evidently been bulldozed by the Iraqis, who had the city under their occupation for several months before they were forced out.

3. *Kholaseh-e Gozaresh*, op. cit., pp. 165–174, 278–313.

4. This figure was quoted by Mohammad Ali Kamrava, the deputy minister of housing and urban development, in his paper presented at the International Conference on Reconstruction of War-Damaged Areas of Iran, op. cit.

5. *The Imposed War*, vol. 3, op. cit., p. 9.

6. For an estimation (actually an underestimation) of the economic damages of the war, but nevertheless an interesting analysis, see Abbas Alnasrawi, "Economic Consequences of the Iraq-Iran War," *Third World Quarterly*, vol. 8, no. 3 (July 1986), pp. 869–895.

7. This figure was quoted by Mohammad Ali Kamrava, op. cit.

8. *Gozaresh-e Eqtesadi-ye Sal-e 1363* [Economic Report of the Year 1363/1984], in two volumes, Ministry of Plan and Budget, Tehran, 1985. In particular, see vol. 2, ch. 4, pp. 1–19, and ch. 5, pp. 9–11; see also *Salnameh-e Amari*, 1363 [The Yearbook of 1363/1984], Ministry of Plan and Budget, Statistical Center, Tehran, 1984, p. 762.

9. See Hooshang Amirahmadi, "Economic Operations in Post-Revolutionary Iran: Major Impacts, Problems, and Policy Directions," paper presented at the 20th Annual Meeting of the Middle East Studies Association of North America, Boston (November 20–23, 1986).

10. An example of such sectoral strategies and policies for reconstruction is "Objectives and Strategies of the Ministry of Industries Concerning Reconstruction of Industries in the War-Damaged Areas, Approved on 10, 11, 1360 [January 1, 1981] by the Committee for Design of Strategy and Policies of Reconstruction of War-Damaged Areas," in *Barnamehha-ye Bazsazi-ye Sanaye-'a Manateq-e Jang Zadeh* [Reconstruction Plans of Industries of War-Damaged Areas], Ministry of Industries, Tehran, 1361 [1982].

11. *Kayhan* newspaper, 16 Aban 1362 [1983] p. 3.

12. Ibid.

13. *Kayhan-e Hava'i* newspaper, 19 Tir 1364 [1985], p. 9.

14. *Ettela'at* newspaper, 3 Tir 1364 [1985], p. 17.

15. *Kayhan-e Hava'i*, 19 Tir 1364 [1985], p. 9.

16. See *Barnamehha-ye*, op. cit.

17. "Report on Housing for Reconstruction and Renovation of War-Damaged Areas," Ministry of Housing and Urban Development, Tehran, September 1984.

18. Hooshang Amirahmadi (1986), op. cit.

19. These published materials include *Plan of Comprehensive Project* [for Khorramshahr] (by Mandan); *Summary of Works and Studies Performed for Reconstruction and Planning of War Inflicted Port City of Khorramshahr* (by the Iran Housing Company); *Organizational Structure, Finance, Inventory Control and Purchasing Systems for Reconstruction and Renovation of Khorramshahr* (by the Industrial Management Organization); *Brief Report of Agriculture, Cattle Breeding, and Animal Husbandry* (by the Yekan consulting engineers). All were published by the Khorramshahr's *Setad-e Mo'in* and are undated (although they were most likely produced in 1985–1986).

20. The approach combines central planning with local participation in decision-making and implementation. For further detail, see Hooshang Amirahmadi, "Regional Planning in Iran: A Survey of Problems and Policies," *Journal of Developing Areas*, vol. 20, no. 4 (July 1986), pp. 501–530.

PART THREE

Socioeconomic Transformations and Policies

9

Post-Revolutionary Demographic Trends in Iran

Akbar Aghajanian

Introduction

The 1979 Islamic Revolution was a turning point in the recent history of Iran. Starting with the political overthrow of the monarchy, the Islamic Revolution ushered in the establishment of an Islamic society. The Islamic Republic, a political system not separated from the dominant Muslim religion, has been the first step toward this goal. In his writings prior to the Revolution, Ayatollah Khomeini mentioned the government of God; and, since the success of the Revolution, he has often mentioned that all other institutions should be Islamic and function according to the rule of Islam. In the meantime, attempts have been made to set an Islamic judicial system, an Islamic legal system, an Islamic economy, an Islamic educational system, and an Islamic family system. (In most cases, however, the definition of various institutional elements described with the adjective "Islamic" is not yet clear.) However, the very dominance of the idea that not only the government but all other institutions and affairs of society should be Islamic has led to the Islamization of some institutions in post-revolutionary Iran, including some elements of the economy, the educational and legal system, and the family. The only institution eradicated was the monarchy.

Immediately following the Revolution, a large number of industries and banks were nationalized, and a significant amount of wealth was confiscated toward the goal of Islamic equality and reversal of economic corruption. Also established in the production and distribution sectors were a significant number of cooperatives, which were financed largely by the government.

The International Population Program, Cornell University, provided research facilities for this project while the author was on sabbatical leave from Shiraz University in Shiraz, Iran. The author thanks Professors Hooshang Amirahmadi and Charles Hirschman for their careful readings of an earlier version of this chapter and for their valuable suggestions.

In addition, laws regarding land reform have been approved and partially implemented.

An array of institutions have been established to provide social and public welfare. *Bonyad-e shahid* (Martyr's Foundation) provides support for families who lost members in the revolutionary protests and later in the Iraq-Iran war. *Daftar-e Imam* (Imam's Office) provides support for poor families. *Bonyad-e Omur-e Jang Zadegan* (Foundation for the Affairs of the War Inflicted) provides support for war refugee families. *Sazman-e Zamin-e Shahri* (Organization of Urban Land) distributes housing land in urban areas. The Ministry of *Jihad-e Sazandegi* (Reconstruction Crusade) has been established to improve the life of the 50 percent of the population living in about 60,000 villages. With all its activities, this ministry has opened a new horizon for the rural families ignored in the process of economic development under the Shah's regime.

Since the Revolution, both the content and the form of mass media have changed. With the establishment of Friday Prayers, large numbers of people gather in 300 cities every Friday to hear various issues discussed in very simple language. These issues, whether political, economic, or cultural, are centrally determined (by committees in Qum). Considering the low literacy rate, one can imagine the significance of transmitting issues of concern to the Islamic Republic through formal presentations on radio and television.

Radio and television are run by a council of three persons from the three divisions of government: legislative, administrative, and judicial. The function of this council is to observe the role of the mass media system in acting as "a university for the masses" and expanding "Islamic values," as defined by Ayatollah Khomeini. In pursuit of this goal, about 85 percent of the programming has been devoted to the teaching and promoting of various aspects of Islamic society.

Since the Revolution and approval of the Constitution of the Islamic Republic, it has been suggested that the laws should be changed to Islamic laws. Thus, the Family Protection Law of 1967 has been replaced by the Special Civil Law, which was approved in 1979. Legal family planning as a government policy has been dismissed, along with the policy of birth control.

The war with Iraq has profoundly influenced the fabric of Iranian society since September 1980. Thousands have been killed, and many families have lost members, their homes, and their jobs; some have sought housing under bad conditions in dorms and camps. The conditions of life for some of these refugee families has deteriorated as the war has continued. Many families depend on limited help from *Bonyad-e Mahajeran-e Jangi* (War Migrant Foundation), and there is a high rate of unemployment.

Detailed analysis of these changes and major events is indispensable to an understanding of post-revolutionary Iranian society. It is the contention of this chapter that these events and changes, and the revolutionary process and revolutionary institutions in general, have had a profound effect on the preexisting institutions of family, law, and education, and on the population in particular. That is, concurrent with various legal, economic, and social changes, major demographic changes have taken place. These changes are reflected in the trends in various indices of population dynamics. The basis for this argument is the sociological theory of social change, which suggests that an interrelationship exists among the social institutions such that changes in one institution lead to further changes in other institutions, including the structure and function of the population itself.[1]

Setting the Scene: Pre-Revolutionary Population System

The population of Iran in 1956 was approximately 19 million. By 1966 it had reached 25 million and ten years later, in 1976, it totaled 34 million. The census showed a growth rate of 3 percent per annum during the 1956–1966 period—a rate considered by government officials to be a negative influence on economic growth and employment creation. Hence, in 1967, a family-planning program was established to promote "the physical, mental, and social-economic welfare of the families." Furthermore, in view of the serious negative influence of rapid population growth on the economic development of the country, the Fifth Five-Year Socioeconomic Plan (1973–1978) proposed the goal of reducing the annual growth of the population to 1 percent within a twenty-year period.[2]

This goal proved too ambitious. Moreover, the continued pattern of uneven development, centered in Tehran (the capital city) and in a few other provincial capitals, did not provide the complementary condition for efficiency in the family-planning program. This problem was much more serious in the neglected rural areas, where the population was increasing most rapidly.

By 1976, Iran had a population of 33,704,744 that was growing at an average rate of 2.7 percent, according to the 1966–1976 intercensus. This growth rate was determined by a declining mortality, especially child mortality, and persistently high fertility (particularly in rural areas). Fertility rates in 1976 reflected the fact that women were giving birth to six children during their reproductive years (15–44).

There were rural urban differences in fertility as well as socioeconomic differences.[3] Fertility was significantly higher in rural areas, where subsistence agriculture was dominant and most farmers had access to less than 5 hectares (12.4 acres) of land. High fertility, limited access to land, and lack of development of nonagricultural activities in rural areas pushed a large number of young males to the cities, where they joined the growing poor migrant population.[4] National and provincial capitals were growing at an annual rate of 5 to 6 percent in the 1970s, and villages were depopulated as poverty and underdevelopment expanded in rural areas.

Post-Revolutionary Demographic Trends

In the years since the Islamic Revolution, the policies of the Islamic government have influenced population dynamics in Iran both directly and

TABLE 1
PROPORTION EVER-MARRIED IN THE POPULATION IN IRAN, 1976, AGE 15 AND OVER BY SEX

Age	Men	Women
15-19	6.4	65.6
20-24	39.5	78.6
25-29	77.6	99.2
30-34	92.3	99.2
35-39	96.8	98.6
40-44	98.2	99.0
45-49	98.7	99.1
50-54	98.9	99.2
55-59	99.1	99.2
60-64	98.9	99.2
65+	98.9	99.2

Source: Statistical Yearbook, Ministry of Plan and Budget, Iran Statistical Center, Tehran, 1981.

indirectly. In this section, we shall discuss the available data and speculate on the determinants and consequences of demographic factors in this post-revolutionary era. This analysis is limited by the availability of data, of course, and a full understanding of the demographic changes involved will not be possible until the results of the 1986 census are made available and more national survey data is taken.

Marriage

A major aspect of marriage in Iran is that it is universal—that is, all people marry and they marry young. The value system influenced by the social philosophy of Shi'ite Islam has always encouraged marriage. In Table 1 we can see just how universal marriage is in Iran. In 1976, 34.4 percent of females in the 15–19 year age group were never married. By age 24 only one-fifth of the female population was never married, and by age 30 all were married except for a fraction of 1 percent. Similar patterns of marriage can be seen for men, although the patterns start from age 20.

TABLE 2
NUMBER AND RATE OF MARRIAGE IN IRAN 1976--1983

Years	Numbers (000)	Crude Marriage Rate
1976	170	4.9
1977	170	5.2
1978	184	5.1
1979	302	8.1
1980	337	8.8
1981	294	8.4
1982	353	8.7
1983	410	8.9

Source: Statistical Yearbook, op. cit., 1984.

Only a very small portion of the male population 40 years and above were reportedly never married in 1976.

The number of marriages and the crude rate of marriage, as measured by the number of marriages per 1000 people, indicate that a significant increase has occurred in the post-revolutionary era. The rate of marriage was almost constant during the three years prior to the Islamic Revolution, and it did not change in 1978, the year of revolutionary protests. Yet it jumped from less than 5.1 in 1978 to 8.1 in 1979. In absolute terms, these percentage points represent an increase from 180,000 marriages to about 3,000,000 marriages in 1979. The crude marriage rate continued to increase in 1980. It declined in 1981 and has been increasing since 1982. Similar patterns can be seen by observing the absolute number of marriages. That number has been increasing since 1979, with the exception of 1981 (see Table 2).

There are several reasons for the changes noted above. Immediately after the Revolution, the legal minimum marriage age (15 for females and 18 for males) was abandoned. Since then, the minimum legal age of marriage has been ambiguous. According to the Shi'at code of action, females can get married at 9 and males at 14. These ages have not been legalized, however—perhaps because of the reservations concerning physical ability relating to pregnancy.

Marriage (specifically, early marriage) was promoted as part of the revitalization of Islamic society and the abolishment of the Western lifestyle. The Islamic value system considers marriage as both an alternative and a barrier to vices related to the sexual needs of human beings. That is, in a society where men and women marry early, there will be fewer moral problems because all desires and passion are met in the context of the family. This emphasis on family formation has been repeatedly mentioned in the Friday Prayers and by Ayatollah Montazeri, Ayatollah Khomeini's successor.

In addition to the legal ease and social promotion of marriage, the early post-revolutionary atmosphere and economic optimism about future prospects of affluence have had important positive effects on attitudes toward marriage and early marriage. Historically, temporal factors, such as war or economic cycles (expansions and depression), have influenced and tempered marriage.[5] These factors have been well observed in countries with business cycles that have experienced war. The 1981 drop in the marriage rate, we believe, was the effect of the Iraq-Iran war on Iranian society. The sudden attack by Iraq took many Iranians by surprise and dashed their optimism. In addition, following the penetration of Iraqi forces and their takeover of Khurramshahr port, the religious and secular community turned its attention from family-formation issues to the vital issue of war. However, as the war continued, the religious community shifted its attention back to the marriage issue, arguing that fighting for Islam should not entail the postponement of marriage. After all, Islam needs Muslim soldiers in order to further its cause, and this can be accomplished only through marriage. On several occasions, it was reported that many men married before going to war. The simultaneous promotion of marriage and fighting for Islam was an important factor in contributing to the increased marriage rate in later years of the war. Although some families postponed marriage until after the war, it soon became clear that there would be no quick ending to the war, and they began to form families, too.

Polygyny is another issue. Although there is no hard data to substantiate that it actually increased, two factors may b responsible for having encouraged polygyny in recent years. First, the 1967 Family Protection Law, which prohibited men from taking a second wife without the permission of the first wife, was eliminated after the Revolution. According to the Shi'ite code of action, a man could be married to four wives at the same time with a formal contract. Second, as the war continued and casualties increased, the number of young widows also increased. To avoid various social problems, polygyny was encouraged. The widows were urged to marry again by Ayatollah Khomeini himself[6] (in the Friday Prayers) as well as by Ayatollah Montazeri in many of his speeches. Thus, in the middle years of the war, 1981 and 1982 in particular, the number of marriages increased significantly. It is plausible that a large number of these marriages were remarriages of widows.

TABLE 3
NUMBER OF DIVORCES AND CRUDE DIVORCE RATE

Year	Number (000)	Crude Divorce Rates
1976	18	107
1977	17	94
1978	15	81
1979	21	74
1980	23	64
1981	24	81
1982	32	87
1983	33	89

Source: Statistical Yearbook, op. cit., 1981, 1982, 1983.

Divorce and Family Instability

The rate of divorce was 94 per 1,000 marriages in 1977, the year preceding the revolutionary protests. It fell to 81 in 1978 and then to 64 in 1980 (see Table 3). This marked the end of the decline in the divorce rate during the post-revolutionary era. It has been increasing since then. By 1982 the rate was back up to 87 per 1,000 marriages, and the trend seems to be continuing.

How can the declining and then increasing divorce rate be explained? During the revolutionary fever of 1978, the Family Protection Court, like many other public institutions, was not functioning regularly and was disbanded after the Revolution. As a result, many applications for divorce were not processed. It is also possible that the excitement of the revolutionary situation had a favorable impact on family problems, leading to temporary relief of tensions. Economic optimism and hopeful prospects further helped the situation, as reflected in the declining divorce rate of the immediate post-revolutionary years.

In 1979, a Special Civil Court (Dadegah-e Madani-ye Khas) was established to replace the old regime's Family Protection Court. The Special Civil Court draws its rules from Islamic law, which is based on the Quran and other religious sources. The judges in this court are *ulama*, who possess knowledge of the Islamic code of action. The Islamic judge plays an important role in protecting the family from disintegration by trying to convince husbands and wives to reconcile. It is only after the judge and the social workers have worked for reconciliation that the court steps in to investigate the file and make a decision concerning divorce. Some 65 percent of the cases are reportedly reconciled.[7]

However, the new law also allows couples who have mutually agreed to divorce to go to the office of a notary public (*mahzar*) and register their divorce before two male witnesses. It is this category of divorces (cases not brought to the court) that has exhibited an increased since 1980.[8] What makes divorce easier under this new law may also increase the possibility of abuse of the "mutual consent" aspect of the law. In a society with a strong patriarchal family structure, the wife's "consent" may not be difficult to secure: A wife may be forced to consent by her husband and his immediate family. In addition to economic deprivation and perpetuation of ignorance, beating is often a method of securing "consent."[9]

There are demographic reasons as well for the increased divorce rate after 1980. First, there were more marriages following the Revolution and, hence, a larger married population at risk of divorce. It may be that many of the couples were inadequately prepared for family responsibility and too optimistic about the economy; in subsequent years, economic strain resulted in family problems and led to more divorces. In addition, the Iraqi war has influenced the social fabric of Iranian society and disturbed the daily life of families and individuals. This has been especially true for refugee families from the southern and southwestern areas, where families have lost their homes and jobs and are settled in highly crowded camps and dorms. Adjustment to this new life has been difficult for the war refugee families and may have contributed to family breakups.

Another indirect effect of the war on the divorce rate may be related to the remarriage of war widows, especially those married as the second wife in polygynous marriages. In other words, such marriages may well be more vulnerable to divorce.

A possible cause of family instability in the years immediately following the Revolution has been the instability of the urban middle class, which has been readjusting its life according to the Islamic value system. Such readjustment has been particularly difficult for the Iranian middle- and upper-class women who were deeply affected by the Western influence propagated by the old regime. Family tension may have increased as a result of their inability to readjust.

Fertility Levels and Trends

At the dawn of the Islamic Revolution, fertility levels were relatively high in Iran in comparison to the industrialized and semi-industrialized nations, or even in comparison to some Asian countries such as Sri Lanka or Malaysia.[10] In 1976 the crude birth rate was estimated to be 41.5 per 1,000 people.[11] The data available suggest that during the post-revolutionary era a significant increase has occurred in the number of births and the birth rate in Iran. In 1975, the birth rate was 45 per 1,000, and by 1980 it had

TABLE 4
NUMBER OF BIRTHS AND CRUDE BIRTH RATE

Year	Number (mid-year)	Crude Birth Rate
1976	1,402	41.2
1977	1,409	40.5
1978	1,338	38.0
1979	1,689	45.0
1980	2,450	63.0
1981	2,421	61.0
1982	2,101	51.5
1983	2,128	51.1

Source: Mid-year populations are from the United Nations, World Population Statistics; birth rate are from the Statistical Yearbook, op. cit., 1980, 1983.

increased to 63.0. The birth rate has remained above 50 births per 1,000 people since 1982.

In 1978, the year of revolutionary protest, the birth rate fell, probably because the decision for having children is usually postponed in such situations. Later, in 1979, there was an increase in the number of marriages, and, as a result, the number of births increased in subsequent years (see Table 4). Other factors played a major role as well. These include economic optimism and hopeful prospects, promotion of procreation, and the dismissal of a family-planning policy as an imperialistic plot. Women were encouraged to have additional children so as to contribute to the victory of Islam and, later, to increase the number of soldiers of Islam.

Although in theory all family-planning services were placed under the sole jurisdiction of the Ministry of Health, in practice the Islamic government has made no serious effort to provide such services. In fact, the government does not have any policy for reducing the birth rate. The discontinuation of such services has neutralized the effects of the Shah's family-planning program on reducing the birth rate.

In general, the continued high rate of marriage and the promotion of childbearing, the lack of any policy of birth control and of family-planning

TABLE 5
MEASURES OF MORTALITY IN IRAN, 1966, 1976

Measure	1966	1976
Life Expectancy at Birth:		
Male	48.3	55.8
Female	47.7	55.0
Infant Mortality	184	112

Source: Statistical Yearbook, 1982.

services for older women, and the large number of women in their reproductive years will keep the birth rate high in post-revolutionary Iran. Although the fertility rate among educated parents is lower, the proportion of such parents is not large enough to affect the average behavior of the population.

Mortality Levels and Trends

It is evident from the data in Table 5 that during the period 1966–1976, mortality rates declined in Iran. The Iranian mortality rate was among the highest in the world in 1956; life expectancy at birth was 48.3 years for males and 47.7 years for females. By 1976 these figures had increased to 55.1 and 56.3 for males and females, respectively. The infant mortality rate, which was estimated at about 184 per 1,000 live births during the 1956–1966 period, decreased to 112 per 1,000 live births in 1976. Yet one must note that, with the increasing oil revenues and the significant growth in the economy, a greater reduction in the mortality level was expected, especially at ages below one year.

Since the Revolution, little data on mortality has been gathered. Only the number of deaths per year is available, and even that is highly underreported. Nevertheless, an increasing trend is observable in the mortality level in Iran during this post-revolutionary era (see Table 6). Four factors have been largely responsible for this increasing trend: (1) deaths during revolutionary clashes and the executions of people associated with the previous regime or opposition groups; (2) killing, by opposition political groups, of supporters of the Islamic Republic; (3) the impact of the Iran-Iraq war during more recent years; and (4) the reduction in the quality and quantity of health services. This last factor has been particularly damaging. As a result of

TABLE 6
NUMBER OF DEATHS IN IRAN IN VARIOUS YEARS*

Year	Number of Deaths
1978	127,857
1979	142,420
1980	162,176
1981	178,099
1982	200,614
1983	207,228

*year of registration

Source: Statistical Yearbook, op. cit., 1983, 1984.

the war, the closure of universities, and the flight of a large number of medical personnel after the Revolution, health services have suffered tremendously. With the continuation of the war, most hospital beds were devoted to wounded soldiers and volunteers of the war, thus placing heavy pressure on medical supplies, personnel, and services. As time passed, the more specialized doctors left the country, and there was greater inefficiency in the supply and distribution of drugs by government agencies. All of these new limitations had a depressing effect on the quality of health care and hence mortality. Despite the government's efforts to improve the situation, the quality and quantity of health care remain low for the majority of people. A further increase in the mortality rate, especially infant mortality, should be expected in the near future. This situation is imminent, now that the economy is declining and the nutrition of low-income families is deteriorating as a result of high inflation. The problem is exacerbated by the fact that low-income families bear the largest number of children.

Rural-Urban Migration

The process of rural-urban migration is not a recent phenomenon in Iran. In fact, migration to the city dates back to the 1950s, with a major exodus during the 1960s and 1970s. During the 1956–1966 period, the urban population of Iran increased at an average annual rate of 5.1 percent, compared to 2.1 percent for rural areas. The latter have lost population through the process of rural-to-urban migration. In the pre-revolutionary decade, the annual rate of rural-to-urban migration was about 4.6 percent per year, and males from 15 to 24 years of age have been moving out of villages at a rate between 15 and 18 percent per year.[12] In terms of numbers, in the 1966–1976 decade, about 2,111,000 villagers left their homes to go to cities, particularly to Tehran and other provincial capitals.[13]

In analyzing the determinants of this heavy rural-urban migration, Kazemi[14] uses the push-pull model of migration and considers the failure of land reform and the deterioration of agriculture as the "push" factors and the higher income in the cities as the "pull" factor. He also speculates that literacy and education have been significant factors in the movement from village to city. Although agricultural deterioration has undoubtedly been a factor in the high rate of rural-urban migration, there is a need for further research on the question of rural poverty and rural/urban uneven development. In fact, rural-urban migration can be explained as a function of rural periphery and urban centralization in the history of economic development in Iran.[15]

In determining the post-revolutionary trend in rural-urban migration, we can consider only those policies that have had either direct or indirect effects on the motivation to move from village to city. One of the most important of these policies concerned the distribution of land for housing in cities among the Mustazafan (poor) in the first year after the Revolution. The policy was intended to improve housing for urban squatters and to stop the land speculation market, which had been an important factor in increasing the price of land. At one point, the head of the Housing Foundation announced that "we are going to provide housing for all the poor in six months." Of course, at that time, housing for the poor was considered a hot issue—and one on which the Islamic Republic hoped to capitalize in the interests of its own advancement and consolidation. However, in practice, provision of land and building houses to the extent needed entailed work beyond six months, or even several years' time. But the expectation of getting a piece of city land motivated many villagers to leave their villages and register as residents of cities. Some did actually acquire land very quickly. However, as time passed, there were more and more villagers coming to the cities and less and less land to distribute.

The Iran-Iraq war forced a large number of rural families from the southern and southwestern villages to such cities as Shiraz, Isfahan, and Tehran—even to small cities like Marvdasht. These families were first taken to camps, but the refugees soon moved out in pursuit of better housing. There is no indication that they will return to the villages, even if the war ends.

With the continuation of the war and the emergence of a black market economy in the cities, street sellers have had the opportunity to earn a reasonable living. This opportunity has been an incentive for pulling migrants from the villages. The migrants can easily earn much more through sales of black market items such as corn oil or cosmetic items than through hard work in the villages.

There is no doubt that migration has intensified during the post-revolutionary era. The data regarding the size of cities in 1976 and 1982 provide a good basis for this argument (see Table 7). For example, Shiraz had a population of 425,000 in 1976. By 1982 this figure had increased to about 800,000, reflecting an annual growth rate of 10 percent. Other cities, such as Tehran and Isfahan, have also grown at a significantly high rate.

Not only the migration of war refugees to cities, but also rural-to-urban migration has contributed to the growth of these cities. This trend will continue in the future, given Iran's urban-based commercial economy and the deprived agricultural sector. However, one has to consider the role of revolutionary institutions, such as the Ministry of Construction Crusade (Jihad-e Sazandegi) and the Council on Redistribution of Agriculture Land, in slowing the rate of migration from villages. The government has made a significant effort to provide amenities for the villages, and land has been distributed in some areas. Nevertheless, given the current rate of fertility in villages, some of the growing population will need to be absorbed in the nonagricultural sector. The Islamic Republic needs to create such jobs in the rural areas if the high rate of rural-urban migration and its consequences are to be avoided.

Conclusion

In 1976 the census of population and housing in Iran revealed a population of almost 34 million. This figure represented a 27 percent increase over the 1966 population. By 1978 the population had increased to 36 million and, by 1986, to about 45 million. The age structure of the population is very young. In 1976, 44.5 percent of the population were between 0 and 14 years of age. This age structure, along with high fertility levels, youthful marriages, and a lack of any serious family-planning services provide a clear prospect for significant population and labor force growth in the coming years. Given a growth rate of 3.1 percent, as assumed in the first socio-economic plan of the Islamic Republic, the population will double in twenty-five years (see Introduction, note 2).

The social and economic consequences of such population dynamics are not consistent with the ideal goals of improving the welfare and well-being of the population. This growing population needs to be fed, educated, and provided with jobs. The creation of at least 500,000 jobs each year, the minimum required in the face of such a high rate of growth in the labor force, calls for the investment of large amounts of limited oil revenues in productive activities and capital investment, as opposed to the use of available resources for feeding, clothing, and housing the increasing population. The economic growth of the Islamic Republic is not consistent with such a high rate of population growth. In the near future the government must develop a policy that ensures limited population growth, better income distribution, improvement of agriculture, and decentralization of manufacturing, all of which should be directed toward the poor. The government must also accept the fact that the problem of poverty in Iran is the result not only of inequality but also of the low levels of production and income. Indeed, the mitigation

TABLE 7
POPULATION SIZE AND GROWTH RATE OF CITIES* IN IRAN

City*	1976 (000)	1982 (000)	Growth Rate Per Year
Tehran	4530	5734	4.3
Mashhad	667	1119	9.4
Isfahan	661	926	6.1
Tabriz	425	852	6.4
Shiraz	425	800	11.5
Ahwaz	334	470	6.2
Bakhtaran	290	531	11.0
Qum	247	424	9.8
Rasht	188	259	5.8
Hamadan	165	234	6.3
Rezayh	164	262	8.5
Ardabil	147	221	7.4
Kerman	140	238	9.6
Ghazvin	139	244	10.2
Yazd	135	193	6.4
Dezful	121	140	2.7
Arak	116	209	10.7
Khoram-abad	104	199	11.7
Boroojerd	101	177	10.2
Zangan	100	175	10.1

*Cities of 100,000 and more population in 1976.

Source: Statistical Yearbook, op. cit., 1980, 1983.

of such absolute poverty will require careful population planning so as to control the growth of population and improve its quality of life.

Notes

1. C. Goldschneider, *Population, Modernization, and Social Structure* (Boston: Little, Brown, 1971).

2. *Draft of the Fifth Five-Year Plan of Iran* (Tehran: Plan and Budget Organization, 1973) (in English).

3. Several fragmentary studies have corrolated fertility levels by socioeconomic status in the 1970s. See, for example, A. Paydarfar, "Socioeconomic Differentials in Fertility in Shiraz," *Journal of Marriage and the Family* (1970); A. Aghajanian, "Income, Consumption of Modern Goods, and Fertility: A Study Among Working Class Families in Iran," *Journal of Bio-Social Science* (1979); and A. Aghajanian, "Community Characteristics, Socioeconomic Status, and Fertility in the Iranian Rural Communities," *Genus* (1981).

4. F. Kazemi, *Poverty and Revolution in Iran* (New York: New York University Press, 1983).

5. D. J. Bogue, *Principles of Demography* (New York: Wiley, 1969).

6. Khomeini was quoted as saying, "I give my sincere and fatherly advice to these young men and to women who have lost their husbands to consider marriage, this divine and valuable tradition, and to leave behind children to preserve like themselves" (*Los Angeles Times*, April 16, 1982, p. 20).

7. *Rooz-nameh Khabar* (Shiraz, 1361) [1982].

8. *Rooz-nameh Keyhan* (Tehran, 1361) [1982].

9. Although no systematic studies have been made of wife beating in Iran, casual observation suggests that this is a very common problem.

10. Economic and Social Committee on Asia and Pacific (ESCAP), *Population Data Sheet for Asia and the Pacific* (Bangkok, Thailand, 1977).

11. *Rushd-e Jam-eyat-e Iran, 1353* [Growth of Iranian Population] (Tehran: Plan and Budget Organization, Statistical Center, 1356 [1977]).

12. Ibid.

13. *Motale'ah-e Rushd-e Mohajerat dar Iran* [A Study of the Migration Growth in Iran] (Tehran: Plan and Budget Organization, 1361 [1982]).

14. Kazemi, op. cit.

15. A. Aghajanian, "Uneven Development and Urbanization in Iran, 1966–1976," Mimeo (International Population Program, Cornell University, 1985).

10

A Comparison of Land Tenure in Iran Under Monarchy and Under the Islamic Republic

Manoucher Parvin and Majid Taghavi

Introduction

The history of peasant struggle in Iran, like many other such struggles, is a sad and gloomy one. Regionally differentiated crop-sharing agreements, chronic indebtedness, and subsistence income have been the lot of the tillers of the land. Peasants have made a few sporadic efforts since the beginning of this century to loosen the hold of the landlords, but they were systematically suppressed by the ruling regimes, who represented the interests of the landlords.[1] They survived the political repression and toiled at odd jobs, which they had to accept just to make ends meet, and bore the whims of the landlords. Then the regime of the Shah and, later, that of Ayatollah Khomeini stated their intentions to change this condition for the better through their land reform programs (LRPs).

At the initial point of the land reform (about 1962), the rural population of Iran constituted approximately 67 percent of the total population. Thus, the reform was of great economic, political, and social importance in the lives of a large number of people.

The historical and analytical overview in this chapter compares the conditions of peasants and lands under the constitutional monarchy and the Islamic Republic. The focus is on the land reform programs of the two regimes. The comparative analysis of these LRPs, specifically of their "land reform" content, necessitates an overview as more detailed studies of specific issues and periods of each are available elsewhere.[2]

Although this chapter makes extensive use of previous research, it also diverges from that research in three essential ways: (1) From a historical perspective, it synthesizes and generalizes the previous work, extending it to the present; (2) it compares the LRPs of the two regimes from the viewpoint of political economy and ideology; and (3) from a methodological standpoint, it utilizes the relevant aspects of Marxist analysis.

The transformation of an economy based on agriculture to one based primarily on industry and service sectors requires a complex metamorphosis in the technology of production, in the composition of demand, in physical and human capital structure, in social and political institutions, and in attitudes.

There exists more than one developmental path from an agricultural economy to an industrial one: Even though production techniques (e.g., input-output tables) at the initial and end points of two different paths may be similar, production relations that depend on the ownership and control of the means of production may not be. From an equity viewpoint, some critical questions related to economic growth arise; concerning which classes or groups have gained most from the development and why, and, in the process, what fate has befallen private ownership in general and land ownership in particular.

Accordingly, the nature and degree of land reform, if it happens, and its substitutes, if it does not, provide vital clues regarding the political economy of development and its potential.[3] *Land reform* is defined here as the redistribution of land or associated rights in land from large holdings to smaller holdings, and/or from those who do not till to those who do. Land reforms differ according to the emphasis placed on the dual goals of efficiency and equity, on the method and extent of compensation paid, if any, and on other institutional measures to support or frustrate the stated goals. *Agricultural reform* refers collectively to those economic policies whose aims are primarily to increase productivity without changing the status of ownership.[4] If land reform and agricultural reform are undertaken simultaneously, the process is usually called a *land reform program*, meaning redistribution and support for an increase in productivity. Land reform and agricultural reform as organic parts of an LRP are independently interrelated, inasmuch as land reform has efficiency implications due to the incentives of peasants to cultivate their own land, and agricultural reform has equity consequences due to the assistance and subsidy of the government, which in general is not uniform. In general, land reform may diminish the political power of the landlords, or transform them into members of the modern merchant or capitalist classes with new bases of power; by contrast, agricultural reform may enhance it.

The Shah's Land Reform Programs

The Real Objectives

The Shah's reforms must be studied within the framework of a dynamic world-monopoly capitalism and its reflection in Iran: the growth of a dependent industrial bourgeoisie. The traditional agricultural sector of Iran was of little interest to an emerging industrial bourgeoisie and world capitalism. In fact, due to the following reasons, it proved an obstacle: (1) It deployed the majority of the labor force in agriculture, a labor force that could otherwise have been employed in factories; (2) the sectoral consumption was largely restricted to commodities with limited money transactions, implying the near closure of village markets to capitalist products; (3) the agricultural sector did not produce standardized foodstuffs and raw materials for world markets dominated by monopoly capital; and (4) the existing land tenure system, based on an unskilled labor force, presented difficult conditions for the investment and organization of a capitalist mode of production. To overcome all of these obstacles, nothing could have worked better than a limited land reform and a still more limited agricultural reform.[5]

The LRP was conceived in 1961 and put into effect in 1962; later, it became an important part of the "White Revolution." The program was to have a fundamental socioeconomic impact on the lives of millions of Iranians. It promised peasants an end to the injustice of centuries; it promised improved irrigation, better seed, mechanization, adequate credit, technical assistance, and, above all, secure ownership. By breaking up large estates made of several villages, the land reform was to break the hold of landlords on the peasants' lives and on the political and economic institutions of the country. Thus, the LRP of the Shah was to combine land and agricultural reform in one package.

But there was more to the program than was announced. The real purpose of the reform was to develop a new system out of the old one, so as to best serve the interests of the growing domestic dependent bourgeoisie and Western monopoly capital. The Shah was to function as a link by integrating the Iranian agricultural sector into the national and world economies, by facilitating growth of agribusiness, and by transmuting the dislodged and excess peasants into both a lumpenproletariat and a group of industrial workers. The LRP also intended to divide peasants politically into those with land and those without land, thus diminishing the chances that peasants would unite and spark an agrarian revolution. Many people assumed that the land reform would create a solid and stable, if partial, support of the peasantry for the Shah.

Stages of the LRP and Its Impact

Initially, private land was held by either petty or big landlords. The latter, for the most part, were absentee owners living in the towns and cities; their representatives, who lived in the villages, were in charge of collecting rents from the peasants and tenants. Land not privately held consisted of the Crown Lands, the Public Domain land, and that of religious trusts and foundations. By the year 1960, the Crown Lands totaled nearly 200,000 hectares (494,000 acres) and consisted of 3,000 villages (nearly 7 percent of the total).[6] A total of 500,000 hectares (1,235,000 acres) consisting of 4,800 villages (12 percent of the total), belongs to religious foundations.[7] In Turkman Sahra, the scene of eventual violent confrontations, the Shah and his associates owned approximately 95 percent of the most cultivated and developed lands.[8] Table 1 shows the distribution of Iran's villages among different economic classes prior to the LRP.

TABLE 1
SHARE OF EACH ECONOMIC CLASS FROM
TOTAL NUMBER OF VILLAGES IN IRAN

Land Owners	% Share of Total Villages
Big Landlords, including Shah	38
Medium size Landlords	14
Religious Foundations	12
State Owned	6
Petty Landlords	30

Source: D. Domin, Contemporary Farming in Iran, Moscow, 1965, p. 18.

There were several stages of land reform under the Shah. The first resulted in the actual redistribution of some land; the second stage started well but faded soon due to the implementation of additional legislative articles promoted by interests other than the peasants, giving rise to discontent during the 1967–1968 period. The third stage, initiated in 1969, was not intended as a land reform—and, in fact, did not become one. It consisted of regulations designed to establish farm corporations by landlords and peasants and to terminate tenancies that had been left unenforced by sales of the land to peasants.

Worse yet, the "agricultural reform" aspect of the LRP package was weak. There was little of the promised institutional support for the new owners, irrigation problems remained unsolved, soil erosion continued, seed improvements were limited, and roads that were to be constructed remained on the drawing boards. Such results were not surprising inasmuch as a small portion of the planning programs' budget was allocated to agricultural reform.[9]

By 1966, 1 million peasant households (30 percent) acquired land averaging 3 to 10 hectares (7.4 to 24.7 acres) each. About 1.4 million households (44 percent) became tenants, and more than 2.5 percent acquired shares in the new agricultural units. More than 20 percent of the remaining rural households were untouched by the land reform. Indeed, a million landless household owners, who by definition were not considered farmers to begin with, were kept out of the program altogether.[10] In addition, an undetermined but large number of peasants were forced off the land because landlords, using the pretext of mechanization, evicted them in order to bypass the LRP provisions for redistribution. The local courts then became flooded with disputes, which the landlords generally managed to turn in their favor. Accordingly, some peasants emigrated to the Gulf states, some migrated to the oilfields for seasonal or permanent work, and some were proletarianized and joined workers in the towns and cities. A handful of smaller and medium-sized landlords who did not or could not adapt to the necessary changes were forced out of the scene as well.

Even nomadic tribes and herdsmen were affected adversely by the "White Revolution." With the nationalization of pasture lands, the nomadic population was deprived of grazing grounds and forced to migrate to the cities.[11] The dislocation of nomads from pasture land without compensation brought about a catastrophic reduction in the production of meat. As a consequence of production setbacks and increases in demand due to income and population growth, meat imports increased dramatically and a new dependency, which could be described as a "national protein dependency," was developed.[12]

This trend was not unexpected. As a consequence of the LRP, the rapid increase in population, and the subsidized imports, Iran was no longer generally self-sufficient in food products. Iran became a large importer of staple food, using its oil revenues as payment.[13] It imported meat from Australia and New Zealand, rice and wheat from the United States, potatoes from Pakistan, citrus fruits from Israel and Lebanon, and cheese and butter from the Netherlands and Greece.

Large commercial farms (mostly in Gurgan, Khurasan, and Khuzistan) spread and began exploiting the peasants, especially by hiring cheap Afghan laborers, and thus forcing wages down. Agribusiness and government-run cooperatives constituted the other large landholders. None of the remaining or new large holdings met the basic needs of the peasants in terms of work security and reasonable income; they were also irrelevant to the national economy. Various new kinds of absentee landlords sprang up, some of whom encircled the cities as speculators in farmlands.[14]

With the expansion of the oil sector and the assembly-line industries on the one hand, and the LRP shortcomings on the other, the share of agriculture in the GDP declined very sharply. It dropped from 35.2 percent in 1955 to 24.5 percent in 1967. It decreased even further, to 18 percent of the GDP, in 1972. With the worsening of economic conditions, the agricultural share declined drastically to as little as 9 percent of the GDP in 1977.[15]

From the standpoint of efficiency, it appears that the medium-sized plots became more productive than the large holdings.[16] The lack of institutional support for new farmers stagmated productivity, and government price and subsidy policies proved destructive.[17]

The LRP, along with other programs in the "White Revolution," prepared the groundwork for transforming Iran into a dependent capitalist state. It prodded a shift from the traditional mode of production to the national market and turned the national market into a world market. The incentives were of historical dimension, inasmuch as the contrived process created a domestic market for consumption (whereby intermediate and capital goods were imported from the West) and expanded the production of domestic primary goods for export.[18] In 1967, for example, 22.8 percent of Iran's imports were devoted to consumer goods, 23.8 percent to capital goods, and the remaining 53.4 percent to intermediate goods. These figures, especially the last one, indicate the extent to which the Iranian economy was absorbed into the world capitalist market.[19]

By the early 1970s, some of the former landlords had been transformed into members of the bourgeoisie. The Shah, his family members, and his associates, who were the largest landholders, eventually formed the largest bureaucracy and comprador bourgeoisie of Iran.[20]

The proletarianization of a large proportion of the peasants, when combined with the existing population of industrial workers, led to grave economic hardships—a grievance that contributed to the upcoming Revolution. In late 1977 and throughout 1978, continuous demonstrations and strikes on a wide scale led to the overthrow of the Shah in February 1979. The cause of the Revolution was not solely economic, but economic deterioration did play an important role—perhaps even a critical one—along with other political, social, and religious grievances.

By now, a large number of articles and books on the Iranian Revolution have appeared on the scene.[21] Our purpose here is neither to report on the Revolution nor to summarize the literature about it. If we are to understand the predicaments of the next regime with respect to the LRP, however, we must briefly discuss the class origins of the major revolutionary groups.

The peasants (some of whom were part-time city dwellers) and the laborers, their political consciousness heightened by the clergy, radical revolutionaries, students, and other progressive elements, became a significant force in the Revolution. Bazaar merchants, ex-landlords, and certain wealthy and powerful religious leaders had no choice but to identify with the revolutionary movement. In the absence of any competition from other widely based organizations, the clergy, which was well organized, managed to seize the leadership and establish the Islamic Republican Regime (IRR).

The LRP Under the Islamic Republic

Period of Indecision (1979–1985)

Since its inception, the Islamic Republican Regime has prided itself on representing the interests of the "dispossessed." This disadvantaged group consists of the petty bourgeoisie, the workers, the peasants, and, generally, the poor and powerless. However, the IRR's policies and actions do not quite support its claims.

After several years of absolute rule, the IRR (whether by intention or not) has failed to halt the deteriorating economic conditions—in both absolute and relative terms—of the workers and peasants.[22] The fact that the LRP has remained stagnant until recently (see the last section of this chapter) while enormous political and economic resources have been wasted on a never-ending war or other foreign ventures, constitutes a historical example of unfulfilled promises.

The stated reasons for the IRR land reform bill were to bring about Islamic justice, to increase output, and to free the nation from foreign dependence on food supplies. The land reform bill, which was approved by the revolutionary council in June 1979 and eventually passed by the Majles (Parliament) was still not law as of 1985 because it was vetoed by the Council of Guardians. The law consists of four provisions. The first, *band-e alef*, calls for the distribution of uncultivated lands (*mawat*) and grazing lands (*marateh*). The second provision, *band-e be*, deals with the redistribution of the cultivated lands confiscated by the revolutionary courts. The third, *band-e jim*, calls for the redistribution of the large unutilized holdings. And, finally, the fourth provision, *band-e dal*, calls upon the large or medium-sized landowners to divide and distribute their cultivated lands among the peasants as determined by the local courts. The implementation of the first two provisions is under way, but no reliable information exists concerning the extent of their success.

Problems of Indecision

The first confrontation over the third and fourth provisions, *band-e jim* and *band-e dal*, took place in Turkman Sahra. In late 1979 the Turkmans in the northeast of Iran, in reviving their old claims, organized their village councils. These councils were to divide and distribute those lands left behind by the big landlords, who had already fled the country.

The reaction of the regime was very harsh. The Army and the Revolutionary Guards were sent to the area to dismantle the councils and exterminate the leadership cadres. They did so both promptly and violently. Soon after the regime's victory over the Turkmans' progressive peasant movement, Ayatollah Khomeini appeared on television and declared, "We do not represent a Marxist government and we are against any un-Islamic distribution of land. We urge the Majles to stop approval of 'band-e jim' and 'bande dal' for the time being."[23]

Thus, until 1985, the circumstances of the peasants did not change with the Revolution. It is thus no surprise that the regime began to rely more and more on subsidies from oil revenues, on thought control and coercion to enforce involuntary compliance of the disadvantaged it claimed to protect, and on authority over the very Muslim subjects it purported to represent.[24] It would have been unthinkable in terms of efficiency to have used all these coercive resources just to keep the disgruntled intellectuals and bureaucrats in line. It is the disgruntled, disadvantaged workers and peasants who constitute the major concern of the regime.

The approval of these last two provisions was delayed because of the emergence of residual landlord profiteers and new *de facto* owners who managed to enter into the government as aides, associates, ministers, and members of Parliament. The political rationales offered for the delay of the land reform were (and continue to be) the U.S. hostage crisis, the Iran-Iraq war, and the existence of counterrevolutionary forces. The official ideological justification is the sanctity of private property in Islam.[25]

The conservative twelve-member Council of Guardians appointed by Ayatollah Khomeini to oversee the Parliament has rejected a large number of bills passed by the Parliament. The council's purpose, according to the regime, is to enforce the Islamic Constitution and therefore to reject any bills inconsistent with the Islamic laws. In fact, despite the regime's claim, this council was formed to create a balance in favor of the conservative wing of the Parliament against the radical adherents of the Imam's line. The Council of Guardians has been very important in counterweighting the imbalance in the Parliament.[26] For example, after months of debate, the Parliament approved the land reform bill in August 1981. But the bill was immediately overruled by the council for being un-Islamic and inconsistent with the Constitution. This bill was one of the first of many victims of the council's veto power.

The radical wing stresses the necessity of state intervention for social and political reforms. Agrarian reform is one of the goals of this group. On the other hand, the more conservative groups believe more in a private-enterprise approach and consider the end to the Iran-Iraq war to be the first step toward the restoration of economic stability and recovery. For this reason, these conservative groups have made little progress in implementing the land reform, and they have rejected altogether the last two provisions of the land bill.

Despite all disagreements, both the radical and conservative wings have been hesitant thus far to initiate any direct confrontation; they seem to be following the advice of Ayatollah Khomeini to forget their differences and try to establish a peaceful environment. After all, both groups have learned from experiences that it is advisable, at least for the time being, to follow this advice and to uphold inaction on the land reform bill rather than to pursuing their group interests in more specific and concrete terms.

De Facto Ownership

Even though the land reform bill remains dormant, the land itself is not. This situation is only one of the contradictions of the regime, whose stated policy and implemented policy diverge drastically. In brief, Iran has experienced a post-revolutionary selective land confiscation that has resulted in a chaotic *de facto* land redistribution. While the land reform bill is being debated, voted on by the Majles, and rejected by the Council of Guardians—and as the problem is solved and re-solved and conflicts are dissolved—an *ad hoc* committee of the regime in each state, with representatives from the office of Ayatollah Khomeini, the government, the Parliament, the local courts, and the religious leadership, has put the seal of approval on some of the confiscations, has agreed with some of the *de facto* redistributions or ordered adjustment, and has even issued certifications of new ownership, thus legitimizing at the local (micro) level what the Islamic Republic has refused to legalize at the national (macro) level.

The nation and its scholars are thus kept in the dark about whether it is Islamic or un-Islamic to seize land, and if it is allowed, then when, where, and under what circumstances. This deliberate ambiguity provides the best chance for arbitrariness to the warlords of the IRR. In this regard, they can do as they please in regard to both the land and the peasants.

A simple question of whose class interest the IRR represents cannot find a convincing answer based on hard facts at present. One can speculate about the application of the Marxian parasitic state, where the state is able to manipulate the working class and bourgeoisie for a period of time and remain independent of both.[27] The IRR is more complicated here. The existence of a large income flow with very little labor content in the form of oil rent and the use of religious symbols and resources by a monopolized mass media seem to give more power and durability to the IRR than Marx would have expected from a parasitic state. However, time has a way of unraveling mysteries. The unapproved land reform bill, the suppression of peasant cooperatives at Turkman Sahra and elsewhere, and the repression of the workers' councils indicate the tilting of the IRR toward the petty bourgeoisie, which, with state aid and the adoption of a residual bourgeoisie from the old regime, is evolving into a new bourgeois ruling class in Iran.

There are some conservative writers who consider the IRR a socialist regime because of specific nationalizations of business enterprises and sporadic confiscations of private property. But such evidence is not sufficient. We must look at the ownership and control of all means of production and production relations to understand the nature of the IRR. In a non-Marxian examination of the question, one can simply look at absolute and relative income distributions of different groups and classes and draw the appropriate conclusions.[28]

Agricultural Output

Despite the disarray over the question of land, the regime's propaganda machinery has been working hard to present its claims of growth and development in agriculture, supported with its own statistics. However, according to the figures set out in the first five-year development plan (which was never put into operation), the GDP in real terms would not exceed that in 1979–1980 until 1985–1986, when GDP was predicted to reach $142 billion (in constant prices equal to those of 1982–1983). In 1979, the economy was predicted to grow at the rate of 9 percent per year in real terms. In Table 2, it is claimed that the share of agriculture in the GDP has been growing over the period 1979–1980 to 1981–1982, followed by smaller rates for 1982–1983 and 1983–1984. It is further claimed that the share of the oil sector has been kept well below one-fourth of the GDP. The five-year economic plan, with its optimistic calculations, claims to be able to allocate relatively large shares of investment to agriculture. As is shown in Table 3, the regime envisaged allocating as much as 13.8 percent of the total investment for 1983–1984 to agriculture, raising it to nearly 17 percent by the end of the development plan period.[29]

TABLE 2
PROPORTIONAL SHARES OF MAJOR SECTORS IN GDP (IN PERCENTAGES)
(constant 1982--1883 prices)

	1979-80	1980-81	1981-82	1982-83	1983-84
Agriculture	12.2	16.3	16.4	15.5	15.3
Oil	35.6	12.9	14.6	18.9	20.3
Industry & Mining	13.7	16.5	16.1	17.3	18.5
Services	38.5	54.3	52.9	48.3	45.9
Total GDP	100.0	100.0	100.0	100.0	100.0

Sources: Bank Markazi Iran, Annual Reports, 1979--1980; First Five-Year Plan of the Islamic Republic of Iran.

TABLE 3
PROPORTIONAL SHARES OF MAJOR SECTORS FROM TOTAL INVESTMENT
(in percentages) (constant 1982--1983 prices)

	1983-84	1984-85	1985-86	1986-87	1987-88
Agriculture	13.8	14.5	15.3	16.0	16.7
Oil	4.3	4.8	4.6	5.4	6.4
Industry & Mining	54.7	53.7	52.6	51.5	50.3
Services	27.2	30.0	27.5	27.1	24.6
Total GDP	100.0	100.0	100.0	100.0	100.0

Source: Five Year Plan, op. cit.

We cannot know for certain how these statistics and forecasts were obtained, but it is clear that there are a number of obstacles in the way to Iranian agricultural development. Lack of water and irrigation systems, lack of seeds and fertilizers, increasing rural-urban migration, improper allocation of investments and loans, and depletion of expertise and managerial resources through self-exile constitute some of the difficulties of the LRP of the Islamic Republic. Above all, the fuzziness of *de jure* ownership in general and the riskiness of *de facto* ownership in particular have created an overall pall of uncertainty, which in turn has inhibited investment and other forms of commitment to development. (Further elaboration of these points is beyond the scope of this paper, however.)

Summary Comparisons up to 1985

The lack of reliable data prohibits a conclusive statement concerning the efficiency and equity characteristics of the LRP under the Islamic Republic. But there are some signs (amidst the confusion). We know very little about the extent or nature of *de facto* land redistribution and output changes, although we can see that the all-important goal of national food self-sufficiency is now further away from realization than ever. So long as the question of land reform remains unresolved, high rates of growth and development in agriculture are highly unlikely. Ownership uncertainty inhibits investment and other forms of commitment. Moreover, it is hard to believe that the leaders of the IRR would sacrifice their very basic interests and allow even its own version of land reform to be put into effect.

For instance, in Zavar and Bazminan, in Gillan province, where the government had claimed an increase in rice output of 30 percent, villagers contradicted the account, saying that due to lack of water and government aid, output was actually reduced by 65 percent.[30] Denied the promised loans and other aid, the peasants of Latak and Kolahchai villages of Mazanderan took the initiative and formed their own cooperatives. Soon, the revolutionary guards, at the instigation of the former landlords, managed to dismantle the cooperatives.[31] There are many more examples that would strongly overrule the regime's optimistic claims and predictions. Not a day passes without numerous letters of complaint or demands from farmers in Tehran's daily papers. One cannot draw statistical conclusions from such evidence, but the constant flow of distress signals by the peasants cannot be ignored.

Industrial policy is also in a state of paralysis. Whether the IRR is heading toward a mixed (dependent) capitalist economy or a dependent state capitalism is not clear. Even though the Islamic Republic is committed to diminishing the dependence on imports of industrial and agricultural goods, no major trend toward success has yet been observed.

The Shah's land reform aimed at weakening the landlords' political and economic power in favor of a growing (dependent) capitalist system; although it partially achieved its goal, it also caused lasting stagnation in the agricultural sector by doing poorly in the agricultural part of the LRP package. Such failure contributed to political discontent, unrest, and revolution.

The Shah attempted to impose a Western culture stripped of its essential ingredients of self-reliance, scientific objectivity, and bourgeois democracy on peasants, workers, and petty bourgeoisie who were still imbued with Islamic tradition. Meanwhile, he also tried to industrialize the country and to benefit from it personally. The contradictions were too many, and he failed.

Less than twenty years after the implementation of the Shah's LRP, we are witnessing the emergence and consolidation of a theocracy. In this historical process, the IRR leaders substitute for the landlords. The *welayat-e-faqih* (government of the jurist) is now imposing an Islamic rule stripped of its essential ingredient of consensus democracy on a westernized middle class, but it is unable to win a war and industrialize at the same time. A large number of professionals with techno-managerial skills have left the country in self-exile, whereas the children of the peasants are being sent to the battle zones. The contradictions are too many and too unmanageable here, too. To survive, the IRR must dramatically mend its ways. The lack of equity and low efficiency in agriculture are the links between the failings of the two regimes and their similarities. One important difference is the halt in growth of foreign-owned or controlled agribusiness in Iran. We hesitate to speculate as to what might have happened in this connection if the Revolution had not occurred.

Rafsanjani, the speaker of the Majles, has once more raised the issue of land reform. In a recent speech, he alluded to the ideal of "land to the tillers" while also asserting the Islamic sanctity of private ownership. Ali Meshkini, the Friday Imam of Qum, has been more specific. He suggests the distribution of only uncultivated land (*mawat*) to those who would put it into good use.[32]

A Period of Decisiveness

The alarming deterioration of the agricultural sector finally promoted two important LRP legislations. These merit some discussion because they could affect both the equity in and efficiency of the agricultural sector under the Islamic Republic.

The first legislation occurred on May 19, 1985, when a new land reform law cleared the Parliament. This law simply transformed the *de facto* ownership created after the Revolution into *de jure* ownership. The amount of land involved is said to be about 800,000 hectares (1,976,000 acres).[33]

Some of these lands are now in the hands of revolutionary institutions and, in fact, were already meted out in the 1980–1981 period by committees of seven for temporary use. The enforcement of this law, which is designed to eliminate ownership uncertainty, increase investment, and improve productivity, has faced problems due to the claims and counterclaims of new owners. Nevertheless, after years of indecision, the enactment of this law implies greater confidence of the regime in its own stability and ability to take major steps toward stabilizing land ownership.

The second law, enacted in the last month of 1985, basically amounts to "nationalization" of all *mawat* land outside urban boundaries. Ideologically and politically, this is an important step inasmuch as the law nullifies all existing deeds of such lands and released them for public use. The ideological justification is simple enough. Before the Absent Imam resurrection, all *mawat* land in effect belonged to the Islamic commonwealth. But if *mawat* property is brought under cultivation with the permission of a religious authority, then ownership can rightfully be claimed and must be awarded. However, all such land brought under cultivation before the change of regimes must be confiscated because no religious authority could have sanctioned their cultivation during the previous regime. It is this last exception that will cause problems for the courts, according to the representatives who voted against the new law.

These two laws bring the comparison of LRPs under the two regimes up to date and into sharper contrast. Certainly, the Islamic Republic has finally moved beyond the monarchy in terms of improving equity and increasing the state role in the agricultural sector and public ownership of land. Although slow in coming, the recent LRP laws are daring. They have obviously solved some problems, but they will also create some undesired side effects due to ambiguities or problems of enforcement. At present, it is too early to determine the net impact these laws will have on efficiency in the agricultural sector. However, as pointed out before, these laws indicate a new trend toward decisiveness on the part of the regime.

How would these LRP laws affect the cherished goal of the regime to decrease food dependency? Again, there is no certain answer at this time. But in broader terms, one could ask: Is emerging land tenureship superior to cooperatives or collective ownership from the viewpoint of efficiency? For example, how are chronic problems of water shortage and management, capital improvements, and transportation to be overcome by this new structure of land tenureship and ownership? These are some of the interesting and important questions that need to be dealt with soon.

Notes

1. For historical examples of these struggles, see Eric J. Hooglund, *Land and Revolution in Iran, 1960–1980* (Austin, Tex.: University of Texas Press, 1982); E. H. Jacoby, *Agrarian Unrest in South East Asia*, 2nd edition (: Asia Publishing House, 1961); F. Kazemi, *Poverty and Revolution in Iran* (New York: New York University Press, 1980); and A.K.S. Lambton, *The Persian Land Reform* (Oxford: Oxford University Press, 1969). For a history of peasant-landlord relationships and their local variations, see G. G. Gilber, "Persian Agriculture in the Last Qajar Period, 1860–1906: Some Economic and Social Aspects," *Asian and African Studies*, vol. 21, no. 3 (1979).

2. A. Ashraf, "Peasants, Land and the Revolution," in *Peasantry and the Agrarian Question* (Tehran: Agah Publishing Co., 1982) (in Farsi); A. Ashraf, "Historical Obstacles to the Development of a Bourgeoisie in Iran," *Iranian Studies*, vol. 2, nos. 2–3 (Spring–Summer 1969); M. A. Katouzian, "Land Reform in Iran: A Study of the Political Economy of Social Engineering," *Journal of Peasant Studies* (January 1974); M. Katouzian, "Oil Versus Agriculture: A Case Study of Dual Resource Depletion in Iran," *Journal of Peasant Studies* (April 1978); and L. Rey, "Persia in Perspective," *New Left Review* (1963). Katouzian's article (1974) gives a Wittfogolian interpretation of Iran's recent history. See also A.K.S. Lambton, "Land Reform and Rural Cooperative Societies in Persia," *Royal Central Asian Journal*, vol. 56 (1969).

3. M. Parvin and M. Hic, "Land Reform Vs. Agricultural Reform: Turkish Miracle or Catastrophe Delayed?" *International Journal of Middle Eastern Studies*, vol. 16,

no. 2 (May 1984), pp. 207–232. The political economy that resulted from the elite's substitution of agricultural reform for land reform is examined here. Debate on the subject has continued since the establishment of the Republic by Ataturk in 1923. The Islamic Republic's debate on and sidestepping of land reform are similar to related events in Turkey.

4. M. Parvin and L. Putterman, "Population and Food Dynamics: A Caloric Measurement in Egypt," *International Journal of Middle Eastern Studies* (December 1980). Examined here is the question of productivity change in the agricultural sector in conjunction with food self-sufficiency; one conclusion drawn is that national food sufficiency may not be an optimal economic goal. One of the stated goals of the Islamic Republic is self-sufficiency in food as an ideological, political commitment—not as a function of economic calculation concerning the best use of land for cash crops or food grains in various regions.

5. M. Parvin and A. N. Zamani, "Political Economy of Growth and Destruction: A Statistical Interpretation of the Iranian Case," *Iranian Studies*, vol. 12, nos. 1–2 (Winter–Spring 1979). In this work the postwar growth of dependent capitalism in Iran is elaborated. For a historical review of the development of the dependent bourgeoisie, see Ashraf (1969), op. cit. See also M. H. Pesaran, "The System of Dependent Capitalism in Pre- and Post-Revolutionary Iran," *International Journal of Middle East Studies*, vol. 14 (1982), pp. 501–522; and M. H. Pesaran and F. Gahvary, "Growth and Income Distribution in Iran," in R. Stone and W. Peterson (eds.), *Econometric Contributions to Public Policy* (London: Macmillan, 1976), pp. 231–248.

6. *Tehran Economist*, no. 427 (1960), p. 5.

7. Ibid., p. 12.

8. *Imperialistic Land Reform and Class Conflict in Iran* (Tehran: Iran's Communist Society, 1980), p. 74.

9. Kazemi (1980), op. cit.

10. Parvin and Zamani (1979), op. cit., p. 51.

11. *Imperialistic Land Reform and Class Conflict in Iran*, op. cit., p. 65.

12. For details, see *Kayhan* (Tehran's daily paper), August 2, 1971, September 8, 1972, and November 25, 1972.

13. See Katouzian (1980), op. cit.

14. See Hooglund, op. cit.

15. See *Balance Sheet*, Central Bank of Iran, various years.

16. Parvin and Zamani (1979), op. cit.

17. See Katouzian (1978), op. cit.

18. See M. Taghavi, "Production Functions in Iranian Manufacturing Industries," Ch. 4 (Ph.D. thesis, University of Exeter, 1983).

19. See Parvin and Zamani (1979), op. cit.

20. There are no official data regarding the economic involvement of the Shah and his associates after the land reform, but it is believed that they had big shares in a majority of large-scale industries, agri-businesses, and so on.

21. See *Iranian Revolution in Perspective*, a special issue of *Iranian Studies*, vol. 13, nos. 1–4 (1980). In this issue, the Revolution is viewed by many authors from different perspectives. The issue also contains an extensive bibliography relating to the Iranian Revolution.

22. See M. Karshenas and M. H. Pesaran, "Islamic Government and the Iranian Economy," 17th Annual Meeting of the Middle East Studies Association of North America (MESA), Chicago, November 3–6, 1983. The authors conclude that the present economic condition is bleak and that its future is hopeless. See also D. Salehi-Isfahani, "The Economic Consequences of the Islamic Revolution in Iran,"

presented at the 15th Annual Meeting of MESA, Seattle, Washington, November 4–7, 1981.

23. *Kayhan*, October 28, 1979.

24. M. Parvin, "Economic Determinants of Political Unrest: An Econometric Approach," *Journal of Conflict Resolution*, vol. 17, no. 2 (June 1973). The author establishes a link between relative and absolute deprivation and discontent on the one hand, and latent and manifest unrest on the other. The greater the plight, the greater must be the means of enforcing compliance and maintaining authority. For example, as the IRR's broad base of power shrinks in scope and softens in intensity, it has to resort to more propaganda, repression, and coercion to maintain authority.

25. Islam alludes to possible collective ownership of land and water, which were the most important means of production in the Prophet's time. See Parvin and Hic (1984) for a discussion of the relevance of this factor in delaying land reform in Turkey.

26. In an interview with the Tehran daily paper *Ettela'at* on January 21, 1982, the speaker of the Majles, Hashemi-Rafsanjani, said, "Unfortunately, the views and perceptions of the Council of Guardians on certain matters do not comply with that of the majority of the Majles. This has brought to a halt the deliberations on a number of important bills such as [those] of land and nationalization of foreign trade."

27. K. Marx, "The Eighteenth Brumaire of Louis Bonaparte," in K. Marx and F. Engels, *Selected Works*, vol. 1 (New York: International Publishers, 1980).

28. In June 1982, when Abbas Ali Zalli, the deputy minister of agriculture, was asked by *Kayhan* about agricultural development, he stressed that Iran would be largely self-sufficient in wheat, rice, and meat by the end of the century. He also claimed that an annual average growth rate of 7 percent in agriculture had already been achieved.

29. See Karshenas and Pesaran (1983), op. cit.

30. *Kayhan*, June 8, 1980.

31. *Ettela'at*, July 12, 1980.

32. *Iran Times*, June 1, 1984.

33. *Ettela'at*, May 18, 1985.

11

Determinants of the Islamic Republic's Oil Policies: Iranian Revenue Needs, the Gulf War, and the Transformation of the World Oil Market

Michael G. Renner

Introduction

This chapter represents an attempt to understand the determinants of the current oil policies of the Islamic Republic. It is intended to show how and to what extent Iran remains dependent on the world market even after a revolution that has emphasized breaking all dependencies. To this end, I will discuss those factors that have had a profound impact on Iranian oil pricing and marketing: the state of the Iranian economy, the war with Iraq, the state of the contemporary oil market, and Iran's adversarial relationship with Saudi Arabia and OPEC.

The approach chosen here is rooted in the political economy of the contemporary world oil market.[1] Its basic premise is that, without an invigorated domestic economy, Iran will remain dependent on the vagaries of the global oil market, over which it has no substantial measure of control. Post-revolutionary Iran has experienced large fluctuations in oil production and in revenues earned. A rapidly changing world oil scene has underscored the necessity for Iran to diversify its oil-dominated economy.[2] In order to make the domestic economy less dependent on the influx of oil money and, hence, to give the country greater leeway in its oil pricing, production, and export policies, measures that will stimulate and strengthen the nonoil components of the local economy are needed. The Islamic Republic has thus far been unable to devise and implement a coherent policy to that end. Although Iran has attempted—with some success—to attain a higher degree of self-reliance in its oil operations and to replace traditional Western customers with oil buyers in the Third World and the Soviet bloc, it has been unable to cut loose from its dependence on oil revenues and, by extension, from the Western-dominated price-setting mechanism of the world market.

Most authors who have covered Iranian oil policies have done so primarily with an eye toward the country's internal development and industrialization strategy; that is, they have analyzed the use of oil revenues in the emerging modern economic sector. F. Fesharaki and B. Mossavar-Rahmani[3] have focused primarily on the Shah's policies, but they have also written about the first two or three years of the Islamic Republic's experience. L. Turner and J. Bedore, on the other hand, have compared Iranian and Saudi industrialization policies.[4] Fesharaki and Mossavar-Rahmani place less emphasis than this chapter does on the international oil market, although they are no doubt aware of its impact on Iran's policies. Mossavar, in particular, is much more concerned with domestic energy strategies and the formulation of a national energy plan than with an analysis of the external factors. Yet, this chapter starts with the same premise as that in Mossavar's book—namely, with the idea that the initial policy direction taken after the Revolution was one geared toward a viable self-reliant course. Mossavar attempts to spell out the domestic measures needed to bring about such a policy, whereas the present chapter is concerned with an analysis of the factors inhibiting implementation of such a policy.

In general, many of the existing studies have a great deal more to say about the Shah's oil policies than about those of the Islamic Republic. At their respective times of writing, too little reliable information was available about the latter—a problem that persists even now. Nevertheless, this chapter attempts to give an updated presentation of the Islamic Republic's oil policies, utilizing information drawn primarily from secondary literature: specialized oil publications, the business press, and publications specializing on the Middle East.

Among the growing literature on the Iran-Iraq war, D. E. Long[5] has sought to assess the impact of the war both on the world oil market and on Iran. He does not, however, provide a detailed analysis of how the changing war fortunes have affected Iran's policies.

The difference between these studies and the present chapter is thus primarily one of emphasis. This chapter attempts to relate all the major factors—the economy, the war, the oil market, and OPEC—to Iranian decision-making, whereas most of the existing literature is concerned with one of these aspects in particular. In an effort to interpret the Islamic Republic's oil policies in a *broad* framework, this chapter probably comes closest to S. Bakhash's 1982 study.[6] However, whereas Bakhash's study centers more on Iran's internal debt and decision-making processes (particularly on the ideological factors that determined the change of direction after the Revolution), the present chapter places more emphasis on how external factors have influenced Iran's policies and brought about several turning points.

After the Revolution: Hopes for a New Direction

After the Shah's overthrow, there seemed to be a unique opportunity to revise Iran's oil policies fundamentally. Foreign-exchange reserves of more than $10 billion on the eve of the Revolution, and further improvements in the balance-of-payments position until early 1980, seemed to bolster a radically different orientation predicated upon low export volumes (with product exports progressively replacing sales of crude oil) and steadily higher prices of oil. Abolhassan Bani-Sadr, revolutionary Iran's first president, was one of the leading thinkers propagating a new oil policy. During the first months after the Revolution, virtually all factions in the country were in favor of significantly lower levels of production and exports of oil. There also was broad, though not total, consensus that the operations of international oil companies in Iran should be terminated or at least sharply curtailed. Oil operations under the Shah's regime were believed to be sustaining corruption and wasteful expenditures and were considered a sellout to Western interests.[7]

Estimates of future revenue needs were revised sharply downward, as arms purchases were to be cut drastically and expensive civilian showcase projects eliminated. The alarmingly low lifespan of Iran's remaining oil reserves—29 years in 1975—offered additional grounds for a policy turnaround (indeed, the lifespan in 1984 was some fifty years). The proposal to create an "oil-free" economy in the long run gained wide currency. Physical and technical problems—foreign advisers were dismissed (an estimated 18,000 expatriate employees in the oil industry departed Iran) and technical staff in the oilfields were purged or fled the country—would have impeded any return to pre-revolutionary production levels anyway. Because of these developments, Iran's oil production capacity after the Revolution was reduced to about 3 million barrels per day (mb/d).[8]

The hunger for revenue turned out to be much greater than anticipated in the euphoric atmosphere prevalent after the Shah's ouster. A wide range of government spending programs and, most important, the war against Iraq strained the Islamic Republic's finances and repeatedly created balance-of-payments crises. To put Iran's development on a solid footing and to make the country less vulnerable to pressures exerted by the world oil market, its reliance on oil had to be reduced. Iran certainly possesses the means to develop the nonoil sectors of its economy: a large population and on internal market, a wealth of traditional skills and trades, and considerable natural resources other than oil (such as copper, iron ore, phosphates, and coal). Yet the Islamic Republic has had to cope with a rapidly deteriorating economic situation—the heritage of the Shah's policies and the result of revolutionary dislocation. That problem has been compounded by the government's inability to devise policies to activate and utilize the nonoil sectors of the Iranian economy.

We now turn to the factors that have prevented Iran from implementing a policy of reduced reliance on oil.

TABLE 1
IRAN'S FOREIGN EXCHANGE RECEIPTS AND PAYMENTS (IN $ BILLION)

	1979-80	1980-81	1981-82	1982-83	1983-84
Export Earnings	19.8	12.2	12.9	22.1	18.1
Imports	11.5	15.7	15.3	15.8	22.0
Balance of Trade	+ 8.3	- 3.5	- 2.4	+ 6.3	- 3.9
Net Service Costs	- 2.2	- 1.3	- 0.3	- 0.4	- 0.4
Net Capital Transfers	- 0.1	- 0.3	+ 0.5	- 7.7	- 0.5
Balance of Payments	+ 6.0	- 5.1	- 2.2	- 1.8	- 4.8

Source: "Khomeini's Other Crisis,'' Financial Times, July 3, 1984.

The Iranian Economy and Balance of Payments

Purges of professional and managerial staff after the Revolution, as well as shortages of raw materials and spare parts in industry and agriculture, led to considerable disruption of economic activities. Most factories are still operating at only 60 percent of capacity or less, more than 5 million people are unemployed.[9] Work on petrochemical, steel, and copper complexes under construction has been stalled. Despite higher producer prices, agricultural output has declined for all major crops.[10] It was not until 1985 that a land reform bill passed Parliament. The ballooning world oil surplus of 1980 and 1981 caused considerable deterioration in Iran's balance-of-payments situation. Export revenues dropped precipitously from $19.8 billion in 1979–1980 to $12.5 billion in 1980–1981, and $12.8 billion in 1981–1982 (see Table 1).

On the other hand, government expenditures rose rapidly to sustain failing industries, subsidize food imports, alleviate widespread unemployment, provide various public services, and allocate vast funds to the swelling revolutionary organizations.[11] To secure its rule, the Khomeini regime built up a massive repressive apparatus that has absorbed tremendous amounts of resources. To finance the vast array of government programs and the soaring import bill ($10.5 billion in 1978–1979; $15.7 billion in 1980–1981), the government first drew on its foreign-exchange reserves (which were reduced by some $8 billion in 1980–1981)[12], then resorted to massive deficit spending. In 1980–1981, the budget deficit amounted to $11 billion, or one-third of the entire government budget. The country was in dire need of foreign exchange.[13]

It was in this situation that the Raja'i government moved away from one of the Revolution's early premises—namely, that oil production levels should be kept much lower than they had been under the Shah's rule. Indeed, the newspaper *Kayhan* stated flatly that "oil is the lifeblood of this revolution."[14] In the hope of stimulating the flagging economy, the government submitted an ambitious budget to the Majles, calling for $41.3 billion in overall expenditures for 1981–1982, with $13.8 billion slated for development spending. The budget was predicated on assumed oil revenues of more than $30 billion—more than two and one-half times the actual income of the previous year. Members of Parliament and opposition groups sharply criticized the budget proposal, which would have necessitated oil exports of about 2.5 mb/d. The government was forced to reduce its oil revenue projections to $18.7 billion, which translated into exports of some 1.5 mb/d. Actual exports for the year—at below 1 mb/d—fell far short of even this more moderate goal.

Despite maverick oil-peddling tactics (e.g., the underselling of OPEC) Iran's foreign-exchange crisis has continued unabated. Although it managed to build up its foreign-exchange reserves (to some $13 billion in October 1982)[15] through its aggressive marketing strategy, the Islamic Republic soon plunged back into precarious financial straits.

In 1983–1984, the government launched an ambitious $170 billion five-year development program. Imports in that year jumped 40 percent to a post-revolutionary record of $22 billion, whereas foreign-exchange receipts came to only $18 billion; the country's foreign-currency reserves dropped to an estimated $3–4 billion, and short-term trade debts ballooned to about $6 billion. Again, the government's extensive deficit spending was severely criticized by the Majles.[16]

In 1983–1984, Parliament chopped $8 billion from $48 billion in overall spending and once again revised downward the inflated oil export revenue projections of the Moussavi government from $21.1 billion to $19.4 billion. Due to a drastic fall off in oil sales in May and June 1984, actual income came to only $14.7 billion.[17] In 1985–1986, oil income again fell below the budget estimate of $22.1 billion.[18] The government has repeatedly circumvented the Parliament's budget-pruning by spending beyond allocation levels and thereafter presenting "supplementary" budgets for approval as *faits accomplis*. Budget deficits, according to official figures reported in *Ettela'at*, grew six-fold between 1983–1984 and 1985–1986, to an estimated $30 billion.[19] By 1984–1985, 50 percent of government expenditures was financed by deficit spending. In the absence of significant international credit flows, then, the government had to accelerate its money printing and, hence, inflation.[20]

Because the Islamic Republic desires to be financially independent, the Majles has expressly forbidden the government to borrow new money abroad. Iran has reportedly reduced its foreign loans from more than $10 billion before the Revolution to about $1 billion at present. However, the country's foreign-exchange reserves have shrunk to no more than $500 million, according to the National Westminster Bank.[21] Iran's Central Bank has been forced to restrict letters of credit to the most essential imports; everything else must now be financed out of countertrade receipts.

Projections (see Table 2) reveal that even under optimistic assumptions for future oil revenues, Iran's balance-of-payments position is likely to continue

TABLE 2
IRAN'S PROJECTED BALANCE OF PAYMENTS (IN $ MILLION)

	1984-85	1985-86	1986-87	1987-88	1988-89	1989-90
Projected Merchandise Export	16.2	18.6	20.0	24.1	27.2	28.4
Projected Balance of Payments	- 2.4	- 2.8	- 2.6	- 0.4	- 0.6	- 1.2
Projected Oil Exports (in m b/d)	1.60	1.80	1.84	1.98	2.07	2.04

Source: "Oil Export Shortfall Financially Pinching Iraq and Iran,'' Petroleum Intelligence Weekly, August 13, 1984, p. 4.

to be negative. More moderate spending policies therefore seem inevitable. Austerity measures proposed by members of the Majles call for a removal of subsidies on food and essential goods.[22]

The oil price collapse of the winter and spring of 1986 brought matters to a head: Although the government stubbornly published totally inflated income projections—$45.7 billion for the 1986–1987 budget year, with $16.5 billion supposedly generated by oil sales—a realistic estimate puts oil export revenues at no more than $5–6 million.[23]

Iran's dependence on oil as its primary source of income has been greatly augmented by the deadlock over nonoil government revenues, particularly the new tax system proposed by the government. This bill has met stiff opposition from conservative clerics defending the interests of those landowners and business managers who have failed to pay their taxes. Only 30 percent of taxes due since 1982 have actually been collected, according to a special ministerial team investigating the tax system. Programs designed to rationalize the economy—involving land distribution, ownership of enterprises, and foreign trade—have been held up by the Majles and the Council of Guardians for several years.[24]

Government attempts to open up industry to the private sector, to draw business people into activity again, and to tempt back to Iran the many professionals and technicians who left the country after the Revolution have met with resistance from fundamentalists. The latter have appealed to popular dissatisfaction over falling living standards, the housing crisis, and the rationing system, as well as to the growing resentment over the prosperity of some business people. Meanwhile, the government is still expending more political energy on internecine squabbles than on breaking the deadlock between these pressing social and economic issues.

The War with Iraq

The war continues to have a number of effects on Iran and its oil policy. The conflict, now in its eighth year, has imposed an extreme burden on the already fragile economy and has wrought large-scale damage on Iran's cities and infrastructure.[25] It has increased the need for oil revenues to finance the war at the very time that Iraqi assaults have impeded Tehran's ability to maintain the level of oil exports.

After the Iranian Revolution, the Islamic Revolutionary Council decided to prune the country's military budget by 50 percent and to cancel most of the Shah's orders for new military equipment. The outbreak of the war with Iraq quickly reversed that new policy. Iran now again ranks among the world's ten largest arms importers.[26] Financing the war effort absorbs about 40 percent of the Islamic Republic's government budget. Iran and Iraq are spending about $1 billion per month each to continue the fighting.[27] The extent to which the financing of the war effort depends on the inflow of oil revenues is illustrated by the fact that Tehran, in 1983, spent the equivalent of 70 percent of its annual oil income for military purposes.[28]

Both combatants have sought to cut their opponent's economic lifeline—namely, oil exports. Iranian oil sales came to a grinding halt in October 1980 and in 1981 were at their lowest level since the Revolution. Iraq's Basrah facilities and about 60 percent of Iran's refining capacity (at Abadan) were destroyed at the outset of the war.

Throughout the war, Iraq has attacked Iran's main oil terminal on Kharg Island—through which about 90 percent of Iran's oil exports pass—and numerous oil tankers heading toward Kharg. Major Iraqi assaults occurred in May–June 1984, in January 1985, and from August 1985 to January 1986. Any flare-up in the "tanker war" is immediately translated into higher insurance rates and thus into increased transport costs.[29] Frequently, traders have suspended liftings either because the war risk seemed too great or because they were waiting for Iran to announce new rebates that would foot the extra costs. Iran's oil export revenues thus fell dramatically after each successful attack. In response, the Islamic Republic has been offering compensatory price discounts to keep the oil flowing.[30] In addition to these "war-risk premiums" Iran appears to be offering other discounts, on a regular as well as an *ad hoc* basis. In practice, all of these rebates are indistinguishable. War-related premiums may go beyond what is necessary to cover additional costs.

To safeguard its oil exports and to counter the threat of economic attrition, Iran has shifted its export operations farther and farther into the south end of the Gulf. Stepped-up Iraqi air strikes since August 1985 (which severely damaged the Kharg Island facilities and reduced Iran's oil exports to 0.2 mb/d in late 1985) made it imperative for Iran to take the following steps:

1. Since early February 1985, Iran is "shuttling" its oil to the Sirri Island terminal in the southern Gulf.

2. Iran is expanding its storage capacity on Lavan Island in the southern Gulf. With Kharg facilities badly hit, Iran started work in late 1985 on two new offshore terminals in the Gulf to replace Kharg for the duration of the war. A new onshore terminal at Asaluyeh is scheduled for completion in 1987.
3. Iran is planning to build export pipelines to Jask (circumventing the Strait of Hormuz), to Bandar Taheri (in the Gulf, 280 miles south of Kharg), and to either a Black Sea or a Mediterranean port (via Turkey).[31]

These moves were designed to avoid the trap of war discounts becoming a permanent feature of Iranian oil policies. Sirri and Lavan liftings do not necessitate any war rebates. The Sirri terminal was widely regarded as beyond the reach of Iraqi jet fighters. With the help of a newly acquired in-flight refueling capability, however, Iraq struck Sirri Island in August 1986 in what signaled a significant escalation of the conflict. A makeshift terminal on Larak Island, located even farther south, was hit in November.

Ending the war would, of course, make these costly operations unnecessary and end the immense human and economic devastation.[32] It would also allow the Islamic Republic to develop a rational oil policy and to utilize the proceeds from oil exports for constructive purposes. Even while at war, both countries are preparing to maximize their oil sales. Both have demanded higher OPEC production quotas and have recently produced more than has been allotted to them under OPEC's production-sharing plan. Iraq plans to almost double its present output to 2.4 mb/d.

Saudi Arabia's regional and oil policies have also impacted on Iran and its oil policy. In addition to financing Iraq's war effort, the kingdom had dramatically boosted its oil output to about 10 mb/d, both at the outbreak of the Iranian Revolution and again when Iraq invaded Iran. The Saudis' actions were clearly designed to displace Iranian oil, to depress world oil prices deliberately through overproduction, and to cripple the Islamic regime economically.[33] Saudi Arabia's policies contributed greatly to the Islamic Republic's later intransigence in cooperating with OPEC efforts to master the global oil surplus in the 1980s. The war and Saudi support for Iraq have made Iran more inclined to seek higher production levels through independent action.

Transformation of the World Oil Market

The deterioration of Iran's nonoil economy has given the oil sector added significance for meeting foreign-currency requirements to finance government operations, pay the growing import bill, and sustain the war effort. Iran has therefore been increasingly exposed to the uncertainty and instability of the world oil market. Over the past five years, the transformation of the global oil market has exerted considerable downward pressure on both oil prices and (OPEC) production. To maximize its oil revenue under such conditions of volatility, the Islamic Republic has displayed considerable pragmatism,

TABLE 3
OPEC AND NON-OPEC OIL PRODUCTION

	1973	1978	1979	1980	1981	1982	1983	1984	1985
a. In million barrels/day									
OPEC	31.3	30.3	31.5	27.5	23.3	19.9	18.3	18.5	17.1
Non-OPEC	17.1	18.7	19.9	20.6	21.2	22.1	23.0	24.1	25.2
Capitalist World	48.3	49.0	51.4	48.1	44.5	42.1	41.3	42.7	42.3
Total World	58.5	63.1	65.8	62.8	59.2	57.0	56.4	57.2	56.4
b. In percent of capitalist world production									
OPEC	64.8	61.8	61.3	57.2	52.3	47.3	44.3	43.3	40.4
Non-OPEC	35.2	38.2	38.7	42.8	47.7	52.7	55.7	56.7	59.6

Sources: a. BP Statistical Review of World Energy, June 1986, p. 5.

b. Petroleum Intelligence Weekly, February 18, 1985, p. 6; February 17, 1986, p. 10.

even opportunism, in its oil policies. These policies, combined with Iran's antagonism toward Saudi Arabia, have strained Iran's relationship with OPEC.

Since 1981, Iran and its colleagues in OPEC have faced a prolonged crisis that has shaken the cohesion of the organization and led to the collapse of world oil prices in the winter of 1985–1986. As a consequence of a global oil surplus, OPEC's output has declined from a peak of 31.7 mb/d in 1977 to less than 20 mb/d at present (see Table 3). Shrinking production and declining prices (prices close to $40 a barrel in 1979–1980 fell to below $15 in early 1986) have led to a considerable contraction in oil income. From a record $281 billion in 1980, OPEC revenues declined 43 percent to about $163 billion in 1983 and $159 billion in 1984.[34] Red ink splashed over the current-account balance sheets of most member countries, throwing their economies and development programs into disarray. And Iran itself has run up a negative balance in all but one year (1979–1980) since the Revolution.[35]

A combination of factors has transformed the world oil market and underscored OPEC's lack of control over the international price setting mechanism.[36] First, the higher price level prevalent in the 1970s made production in various high-cost areas around the globe competitive. The resulting rise of non-OPEC producers (Britain, Norway, China, India, Malaysia, Mexico, Peru, Colombia, Egypt, and Oman, among others) has been the most important factor in diminishing OPEC's role. Oil output in the capitalist world outside OPEC rose from 16.8 mb/d in 1973 to 23.3 mb/d in 1983 and 24.1 mb/d in 1984.[37] The new producers were charging the highest prices in the world market throughout the 1970s.[38] Yet, to reduce OPEC's influence and to increase supply security, Western oil firms and traders were inclined to purchase oil from non-OPEC rather than OPEC exporters. When oil prices began to decline, the former moved swiftly to undercut OPEC; at the prevailing prices in the early 1980s, even higher-cost producers could slash their prices and still operate profitably.

A second factor has been the shrinkage of the world market. Oil consumption in the non-Communist world dropped 13 percent between 1979 and 1983.[39] The new exporters were propelled to prominence, but the scramble for market shares among all producers also reached a high pitch. OPEC countries are left with the responsibility for "price administration" (i.e., with the responsibility for averting a price collapse) while other exporters continue to penetrate world markets without contributing to longer-term price stability. And Iran, in its turn, has paid lip-service to the goal of stabilizing prices while undercutting its fellow OPEC producers.

A third factor contributing to the destabilization of OPEC's position and the reduction oil price stability has been the rise of short-term trading on spot and futures markets. The spot market has risen like a Phoenix from its ashes. In 1979, merely 5 percent of the world's oil was sold on the spot market; by 1982–1983, this share had grown to 20–30 percent, and it is now estimated at 45–50 percent.[40] Helped by the surplus of oil, spot quotations have been below official prices since 1980. Spot transactions have become an effective instrument to manipulate oil prices and thereby to wrest control over the world oil market from OPEC. What appeared to be control over the market when Iran and other exporters followed spot prices upward was revealed to be dependence on the market when spot prices moved down.

OPEC prices are being further destabilized by the highly speculative futures market.[41] Futures contracts signal what oil traders are prepared to pay, influence spot price developments, and exert tremendous pressure on exporters to offer prices that are more to the liking of Western customers and profiteers.

Finally, erratic buildups and drawdowns of company-owned oil stocks have had an overwhelming impact on price movements. For example, destockings in January and February 1983 (which were equivalent to 40 percent of OPEC oil output) precipitated OPEC's March 1983 price cut; similarly, destocking in the fourth quarter of 1984 (equivalent to between 10 and 20 percent of OPEC production) precipitated OPEC's January 1985 price cut.[42]

Iran and Saudi Arabia

OPEC's response to the continued global oil surplus has been piecemeal in nature. OPEC has concentrated primarily on cutbacks in output (an overall

TABLE 4
IRANIAN AND SAUDI CRUDE OIL PRODUCTION AS A SHARE OF OPEC OUTPUT

	1978	1979	1980	1981	1982	1983	1984	1986
Iran's Oil Production (million barrels/day)	5.27	3.17	1.48	1.32	2.41	2.53	2.19	2.25
Iran's Share of Total OPEC Production (%)	17.4	10.0	5.4	5.7	12.1	13.8	12.5	13.2
Saudi Share of Total OPEC Production (%)	28.2	32.5	37.3	43.7	34.5	30.2	26.6	21.1

Source: BP Statistical Review of World Energy, June 1985, p. 16. Nicolas Sarkis, "OPEC: Securing a Fair Market Share, But at What Price?,'' _AfricAsia_, January 1986, p. 40.

ceiling of 16 mb/d was adopted in October 1984) and the assignment of individual quotas to member states. A more far-reaching proposal to break the power of the spot market (creating a central agency with the power to acquire any OPEC crude oil sold in the spot market and to resell it on a contractual basis) was opposed by, among others, Iran and Iraq.[43] Most of the organization's members have been reluctant to cut their official prices, although many of them granted hidden discounts. Iran, along with Algeria, Libya, and Nigeria, has consistently demanded that the richer OPEC members—Saudi Arabia and its Gulf allies—bear the brunt of reduced oil demand. In Iran's view, this outcome would not only prop up prices but would also reduce the Saudis' influence over OPEC policy, their ability to finance Iraq's war against the Islamic Republic, and "make up" for Saudi overproduction snatched from Iran during the Revolution (see Table 4). As exemplified by their alignment in the Iran-Iraq war, the deep antagonism between the rulers of the Islamic Republic and those of the conservative, pro-Western monarchies on the opposite side of the Gulf represents a danger more serious than purely economic competition.

Saudi Arabia, which held onto its official price until the fall of 1985, was among those OPEC countries that saw their exports shrink while other members of the organization produced at or above their assigned quotas. Through most of 1985, Saudi production was at historical lows—both in absolute terms and relative to overall OPEC production. Along with this decline in production, Saudi influence within the organization has also decreased. Toward the end of 1985, however, the kingdom decided to end its role as OPEC's swing producer (i.e., as the seller of last resort). At its reduced production rate, the kingdom had to draw down its foreign-currency reserves at a rate of $20 billion per year. Through attractively priced "netback" deals,[44] Saudi Arabia's oil exports rose rapidly from 2.5 mb/d in the fall of 1985 to 4.5 mb/d in early 1986 and close to 6 mb/d in the summer of 1986. This upsurge was instrumental in sending spot oil prices tumbling. From just under $30 per barrel in October 1985, spot prices were approaching the $10 threshold by April 1986, with real, inflation-adjusted prices in the area of $4 to $5 per barrel.[45] Iran will be hard pressed at such a low price level to meet its revenue requirements. At the same time that world oil prices are plummeting, the Islamic Republic's oil exports have been sharply curtailed by continued Iraqi assaults against Iran's oil terminals. Iran's oil price has declined from $25.50 to $8.50 a barrel in less than one year. Although exports of 2.3 mb/d in December 1985 brought in a daily income of $47 million, the same volume of oil sold in late January 1986 netted Iran only $31 million. By March 1986, the Islamic Republic's daily oil export income had fallen to only $9 million, reflecting both reduced volume and reduced prices.[46]

Faced with difficulties in maintaining both price and volume for its oil exports, the Islamic Republic has urged OPEC to curtail its exports in order to prop up world prices. In early 1986, Iran reduced its output by 300,000 b/d (barrels per day). Libya and Algeria joined Iran in urging the other producers to reduce the oil glut. Yet, most OPEC members simply cannot afford to opt for such a strategy because they need all the income they can generate in order to finance their import bills and service their debts. Most important, those within OPEC who could afford production cutbacks are unprepared to do so. During the first half of 1986, Saudi Arabia refused to curtail its exports, and, instead, continued its market-flooding strategy in the hope of forcing other producers into an agreement to stabilize world oil prices. Iran has been the big loser of this Saudi strategy: Its revenue for the first half of 1986, as compared to the first six months of the previous year, suffered a 59 percent reduction, whereas Iraqi oil income declined by only 30 percent, Saudi Arabia's by 24 percent, and Kuwait's by a negligible 8 percent. Moreover, Iraq continues to press for an increase in its OPEC production quota and once more receives "war relief" crude from Saudi Arabia and Kuwait.

Iran's Oil Pricing and Marketing Policies

Now that we have covered the major external determinants of Iran's oil policies, we shall take a closer look at how Iran's pricing and marketing policies have evolved in response to these external factors.

One of the first acts of the new government after the Revolution was the unilateral abrogation of the agreement under which the large international oil companies ("majors") had operated in Iran. The new regime was prepared to pursue its oil policies without the corporations' interference. The majors' access to Iranian crude oil was curtailed from 84.5 percent of output in 1977–1978 to about 30 percent in 1979–1980.[47] With a crude oil shortage prevailing in the world market, Iran initially had little trouble finding a wide variety of alternative buyers for its oil—even with an added surcharge. The Islamic Republic was in the forefront of the trend toward direct deals with consumer governments and national oil companies, and its success clearly encouraged other OPEC governments to follow suit. In 1980, these deals reached a peak, accounting for 37 percent of OPEC exports, while Iran sold almost all of its oil through these channels. The majority of Iran's contracts were for small amounts of oil—20,000 to 50,000 b/d—and had a duration of only 9–12 months.[48] In this period of tight supplies, Iran had no trouble curtailing its oil exports and still earning sufficient revenues. In 1979–1980, the Islamic Republic exported 46 percent less oil than in the year prior to the Revolution.

During the Bazargan government's tenure, some officials at the National Iranian Oil Company (NIOC, which is now incorporated into the Ministry of Petroleum) wanted to return to traditional marketing practices. Dealing with the majors, in their view, had the advantage of giving Iran access to sophisticated refining and distribution networks. But this position was unpalatable for the majority; in addition, the hostage crisis and the ensuing deterioration of relations with the United States precluded such a rapprochement.

During the first two years of the Islamic Republic's existence, high spot quotations made selling on this emerging market very attractive. Ranging between 5 and 10 percent of Iran's overall oil sales, spot sales were also seen as a test of what prices could be charged in term contracts. Particularly after the dismissal of NIOC's first post-revolutionary chairman, Hassan Nazih, in September 1979, Iran pursued a more aggressive pricing policy. From $13.45 per barrel (bbl) in January 1979, the price for Iranian Light was pushed up to $23.50 in October, $28.80 in December, $31.00 in February 1980, and $37.00 in April (see Table 5). Surcharges of up to $3.80/bbl were added.[49] Iranian oil was by far the most expensive of all Gulf oil.

Market Downturn

Iran's oil policy-makers failed to appreciate the underlying trends in the world oil market that initially had permitted the Islamic Republic to engage in its high-price sales policy. Global consumption was at its peak, and supplies were relatively scarce. The prevailing Western perception was one of enduring supply insecurity, and the general expectation was that prices would soon shoot through the roof. After 1979, however, a marked turnaround began that became obvious only in the years since 1981. Consumption declined precipitously in response to high prices and the global recession. At the same time, non-OPEC supplies became more bountiful, gradually "crowding out" OPEC supplies.

The Islamic Republic had little control over these changing fortunes, but its leaders were determined to retain a margin of leeway in their pricing policy. When oil prices first showed signs of weakness, Iran's oil policy-makers still believed they could stick to high prices. But slipping sales soon forced a change of mind. The Islamic Republic simply started to lack customers still willing to buy oil at the asking prices. With spot prices

Table 5 Official Iranian Oil Prices, 1978 - 1986 (in $ per barrel)

Date of Change	Iranian Light (34°)	Iranian Heavy (31°)
1978		
December	12.81	12.49
1979		
1 January	13.45	13.06
1 April	16.57	16.04
15 May	17.17	16.64
1 June	18.47	17.74
1 July	22.00	19.90
1 October	23.71	22.98
1 December	28.71	27.98
1980		
1 January	30.37	29.64
1 February	32.87	32.14
1 April	35.37	34.37
1981		
1 January	37.00	36.00
1 November	34.60	33.40
1982		
1 January	34.20	32.30
5 February	33.20	31.30
12 February	32.20	30.30
21 February	30.20	28.30
1 July	31.20	29.30
1983		
15 March	28.00	26.90
10 August	28.00	27.10
1985		
1 January	29.11	27.55
1 February	28.05	27.35
1986		
December	17.50	na

Sources: Petroleum Analysis, New York, and "Official Prices: On the Road to Extinction 1985 - 1986," Petroleum Intelligence Weekly, Special Supplement, April 7, 1986, p. 3.

dropping below official OPEC prices, consumer governments slashed their direct-supply contracts and turned to the spot market. By 1982, government-to-government deals had returned to volumes only slightly above those in 1978.

To regain the traditional markets lost after the Revolution, Iran now exhibited a stronger desire to regularize relations with major non-U.S. companies, and the Petroleum Ministry adopted a policy of relentless

TABLE 6
FLUCTUATIONS IN IRAN'S OIL PRODUCTION
(in million barrels/day)

September 1978	First Half Nov. 1978	Second Half Nov. 1978	December 1978	April 1979	January/February 1979
6.1	1.4	3.5	1.0	3.6	0.7

October 1980	First Half 1981	Second Half 1981	Early 1983	First Quarter 1984	January 1985
0.6	1.7	1.2	3.2	2.2	1.3

February 1985	First Half 1985	Third Quarter 1985
2.0	1.02	2.5

Sources: Compiled from S. Bakhash, The Politics of Oil and Revolution in Iran (Washington, D.C.: Brookings, 1982) and S. A. Schneider, The Oil Price Revolution (Baltimore, Md.: Johns Hopkins University Press, 1983).

undercutting of OPEC prices. Iran quietly reduced its prices by as much as $3 per barrel in June 1980. Critics of this new direction in oil policy were eliminated from any crucial decision-making by early 1982.[50]

The Impact of the War with Iraq

By the outbreak of the Iran-Iraq war, the flow of oil from both combatants had declined, temporarily resulting in a firming up of spot prices. But there was no respite for Iran: Growing non-OPEC and Saudi supplies soon more than made up for the temporary shortfalls, and the downward pressure on prices resumed. The initial fear in consuming countries that the war might cut them off from supplies from the Gulf subsided, and it was the oil buyers who had to be convinced that they needed Iran's oil.

The Islamic Republic thus offered price concessions and footed the bill for safeguarding oil shipments out of the war zone. During 1982, Iran cut its price to $30.20 and boosted production to 2.4 mb/d—almost double the level of 1981. A further price cut—to $28/bbl—came in March 1983. The Islamic Republic needed more revenue to finance its ambitious five-year development plan, to pay for the immense war costs, and to prolong the domestic programs essential for continued popular support. Iran never accepted OPEC's March 1982 and March 1983 production and price cutbacks. Instead, it demanded that the Saudis cut back their output to make room for expanded Iranian production.[51] Saudi Arabia's financing of Iraq's war against Tehran and the Saudis' flooding of oil markets in 1979–1981 had not only displaced Iranian oil on a massive scale (see Table 6) but also depressed prices worldwide.

Figure 1 Development of Official and Spot Prices for Iranian Light Crude Oil, January 1979 to July 1987 (in $ per barrel)

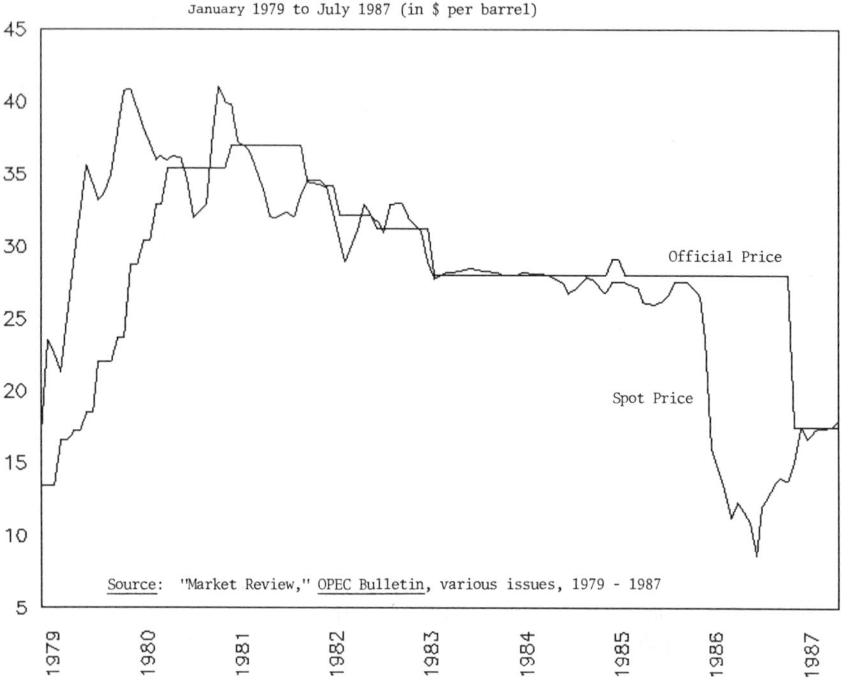

Source: "Market Review," OPEC Bulletin, various issues, 1979 - 1987

Iran has responded to the oil market's uncertainties by adopting a three-pronged sales and pricing strategy: discounts, "netback" deals, and barter sales.

Discounts

During the last 3 or 4 years, spot prices have fallen below official government prices. Oil buyers have taken advantage of this situation, putting pressure on producer nations to lower their prices. Iran repeatedly adjusted its discounts and brought its official prices more in line with spot quotations (see Figure 1). In 1984, for example, Japanese buyers (on whom Iran is particularly dependent)[52] delayed renewal of term-purchase contracts to put pressure on the Islamic Republic for increased price concessions. Oil sold under such contracts to Japanese companies declined from 490,000 b/d in mid-1983 to less than 200,000 b/d in the first quarter of 1984.[53] In response to buyers' pressure, in September 1984 Iran offered prospective buyers the opportunity to take 50 percent of the oil at official prices and 50 percent at spot rates; later, the mix was improved to 30 and 70 percent, respectively.[54] The Petroleum Ministry's current practice is to separately negotiate each deal and adjust its price once the actual offtake of oil occurs. In practice, there is thus no such thing as a fixed Iranian oil price.

"Netback" Deals

By adopting cheaply priced "netback" deals, Saudi Arabia has upped the ante in the undeclared oil price war. There is now competition within OPEC to offer prospective buyers attractive terms. Iran's terms are especially attractive in a falling market because pricing is based on spot product quotations forty-five days after loading. However, Tehran is now meeting resistance from customers in its effort to stiffen terms in negotiations to renew and expand the 600,000 b/d worth of deals started in spring 1985. The Petroleum Ministry wants to establish a price floor to prevent prices from falling below spot crude oil levels. But because customers know they have leverage over Iran—the country needs to sell more oil—they have refused to accede to the Ministry's demands.[55]

Barter Policy

Barter or countertrade exchange is now estimated to account for 10–20 percent of OPEC oil sales.[56] Iran's traditional marketing channels have been unsettled under the impact of revolutionary politics and the growth of the spot market. Iran has therefore been bartering oil for some time, but this trading method burgeoned in early 1984 after the tanker war had begun and the country's finances had deteriorated. During 1984, an estimated one-fourth of the Islamic Republic's import trade was conducted on a barter basis.[57] The partners in barter deals include a wide range of countries: the Soviet Union and other COMECON states, Yugoslavia, Turkey, Pakistan, China, the two Koreas, Taiwan, Syria, Greece, and New Zealand.

Barter transactions have helped maintain Japanese crude liftings from Iran. Japanese traders and the Iranian government have agreed that each $1 worth of goods sold to Tehran be matched by $2 in offtakes of Iranian oil.[58] Iran has stepped up the pressure on its trading partners to buy more oil in exchange for goods. It has also sought to use to its advantage the desire of foreign suppliers to maintain access to the large Iranian market. Foreign Minister Ali Akbar Velayati warned that unless its partners were willing to enter into barter deals, Iran would be forced to reassess relations with them. In particular, the Islamic Republic is seeking increased oil purchases by its largest source of imports, West Germany, perhaps under a formula similar to the one accepted by Japanese firms.[59]

Barter deals, which are often secretive and include complex arrangements, may from time to time lead to sizable oil flows beyond OPEC quota allowances. Such deals are often a smokescreen for price discounting, which in turn helped the Islamic Republic overcome a slump in oil sales in January 1985.[60] However, officials at both the Petroleum and the Foreign Trade ministries are pushing for the full official price to be charged in barter deals.[61] For want of alternative ways to sell its oil, Iran finds bartering desirable. Also, the price received is usually higher than in cash deals. However, countertrading does not yield foreign exchange, which is precisely what the country desperately needs.

Internal Disputes over Oil Policies

The barter policy has stirred up an acrimonious debate in Tehran related to overall production policies. The financial authorities view countertrade as a way to maintain the chosen economic course while protecting the country's foreign-exchange reserves. By contrast, Petroleum Ministry officials, such as former Oil Minister Mohammed Gharazi, are fiercely opposed to barter deals and would rather sell the oil for cash. Other critics within the regime say they would prefer selling the oil to state companies rather than to private firms. The latter often resell the oil to final destinations and at prices over which Iran has no control. In the view of some observers, however, the oil minister has lost virtually all of his authority over decision-making in oil matters.[62] An Oil Barter Committee with representatives from several other ministries appears to wield considerable influence over actual oil policy. The Foreign Trade Ministry continues to search ardently for customers willing to enter into barter agreements in which the full official Iranian oil price is applied.[63]

The internal debate covers not only the question of *how* to sell the oil but also *how much* to sell. The Petroleum Ministry, backed by such powerful clerics as Speaker of the Parliament Ali Akbar Hashemi Rafsanjani and Ayatollah Khomeini's son Ahmad Khomeini, has advised against a stepped-up depletion of the country's oil resources. They are opposed on this question by various fiscal and functional ministries (led by Heavy Industries Minister Behzad Nabavi), which are arguing for higher pumping rates and price cutting. No clear guidelines have been established yet, as various ministries are actually pursuing parallel, and sometimes contradictory, oil policies.[64]

Oil Operations and Investments

We have seen that the initial emphasis on drastically lower oil exports was soon modified. After the Revolution, neglected maintenance of oilfield installations (an effect of revolutionary dislocation) caused a sharp drop in sustainable oil output and, consequently, put an effective lid on production increases. This, of course, came on top of the Shah's overexploitation of the nation's oil resources, which had done great damage to the petroleum reservoirs. Initially, the Islamic Republic reduced the oil exploration budget and postponed a gas-injection program (needed to maintain oilfield pressure and production levels).[65] Nor did the revolutionary government display much interest in downstream operations.

The growing revenue needs, particularly the pressure to finance the ongoing war, made it imperative that Iran improve its capacity to pump oil. Once oil revenue maximization had again become a prime goal of the Iranian state, more funds were allocated for increased oil exploration and production. In 1983, Iran stepped up its drilling activity, raised its refining capacity, and planned to go ahead with the gas-injection scheme (this last measure will raise the extraction rate of existing oilfields from 17 to 25 percent, thus adding more than 10 billion barrels to the recoverable oil reserves).

The Petroleum Ministry's new emphasis on resource development has almost tripled offshore production to about 300,000 b/d. There are plans to develop the Nosrat field (jointly owned with Dubai) and the giant Majnoon field captured from Iraq.[66] For the first time, a comprehensive long-term plan (1983–2002) has been drawn up for the entire oil industry.[67] Refining capacity has been increased to 670,000 b/d, and construction of a sixth and seventh refinery (with 200,000 and 250,000 b/d capacities, respectively) will bring Iran's refining capacity back to prewar levels by 1989.[68]

From some of these projects, particularly the $1.6 billion reinjection plan, Iran may have to turn to foreign assistance, at least this is what a great many Western companies are hoping for. However, Iranian officials continue to pursue independence from foreign companies as a major policy goal. Shortages of foreign parts have been patched over through increased domestic manufacture.[69] Iran is trying hard to strengthen its domestic engineering base and to upgrade its capabilities in the field of petroleum technology. Successful drilling operations have proved the efficacy of these efforts.[70] The Petroleum Ministry has at times resorted to unconventional solutions when faced with technical difficulties. Iran's persistent problems—the lack of qualified and experienced technical and managerial personnel, the under-utilization of female human resources, the pressures of an endless war—may cause Iran to become more dependent on external support. The Islamic Republic's need for "hard" currency is a symptom of the country's troubles; the failure to harness its human and natural resources has forced it to rely increasingly on imports. Significant portions of the country's foreign-currency earnings are still being consumed by the purchase of goods and equipment that the government believes could be produced domestically. Under circumstances similar to those dominant in the last few years (a weak oil market, high import and revenue needs, a continued domestic deadlock, and the war with Iraq), Iran may well face increasing financial reliance on the West.

Iran and OPEC

Since 1980, the Islamic Republic frequently boosted its own oil exports by underselling OPEC. As long as OPEC was holding to official prices, Iran could rhetorically boast a "sell less, charge more" policy while offering hidden discounts and raising production. But any reductions in official prices directly affect Iran's oil strategy. An OPEC that cut its official prices would become unacceptable, because it would no longer serve as a convenient shield behind which the Islamic Republic could play its maverick role. Iran therefore vehemently denounced the organization's 1982, 1983, and 1985 price-cutting accords. In Tehran's eyes, OPEC often acted as an agency of Saudi Arabia, which the Islamic Republic sees as its enemy and archrival.

Nevertheless, it appears that as OPEC averted its own collapse, Iran grew more appreciative of the organization's value. By strengthening it, the Islamic

Republic could serve its own ends better in the long run. In February 1985, Iran therefore brought its *official* prices in line with OPEC's pricing structure; it grudgingly accepted the lower price level and consequently eliminated the wide discrepancy that had existed between it and OPEC's prices ever since March 1983.[71] Until at least May 1985 Iran was thought to be holding down production to prop up spot prices, according to a tacit understanding with the Saudis.

But this realignment did not hold. Saudi Arabia's desire to recapture lost markets and to discipline other oil producers (OPEC as well as non-OPEC) destroyed the delicate equilibrium. The Saudis' move to flood the world oil market signals another round in the ongoing struggle between Saudi Arabia and Iran to gain the upper hand in influencing OPEC policy, setting prices, and weakening the opponent. While the Saudis took advantage of revolutionary dislocation and war damages to Iran's export capability, the Islamic Revolution turned the tables on Riyadh in 1984 and 1985 by underselling its Saudi competitor. The success of Iran and other OPEC countries in expanding their exports at the expense of the Saudis in turn spurred the kingdom to rewrite the rules. Its abundant supplies and low production costs have given Saudi Arabia a big advantage in the growing confrontation with OPEC.

Since the winter of 1985–1986, official prices have become virtually meaningless. Most OPEC governments left their official prices untouched while selling their oil at the now prevalent, much lower market prices. In July 1986, international prices hit a twelve-year low of $10 per barrel and less. Iran, too, has sporadically reduced its sales, prices, and income. Of course, Iran can respond to lower oil revenues simply by printing more money. But inflation is already rampant and there are limits to mortgaging the economy. The effects of the oil price crash will translate into a further deterioration of living standards for Iranians, into less availability of already scarce food and consumer goods, into a possible collapse of the domestic economy, and, last but not least, into a sharpened struggle for power within the regime and between it and the growing popular resistance.

At OPEC meetings since the price collapse, Iran has demanded radical production cutbacks to restore prices, particularly on the part of Saudi Arabia and its Gulf allies. Yet, any serious coordination of OPEC members' policies seems elusive. OPEC (and non-OPEC) exporters, virtually all of which need to increase their revenues to pay for imports and service debts, are increasingly being locked into a massive zero-sum game that appears certain to prolong the global oil glut and depress prices.

In a move unexpected by many observers, OPEC concluded an interim agreement on a joint production ceiling and individual quotas for September and October of 1986. Iraq's insistence on being assigned a production quota equal to Iran's had been one of the major obstacles to an accord. The Islamic Republic played a pivotal role in hammering out the agreement by proposing a compromise production ceiling acceptable to both the radical and conservative wings of OPEC. That ceiling deliberately precluded the assignment of any quota to Iraq. OPEC's temporary agreement immediately lifted oil prices by 50 percent to $15 a barrel. In October, the accord was extended until the end of the year, when it was hoped that OPEC members would be able to agree to more permanent rules and guidelines.

The OPEC agreement was unexpected because it was preceded by months of internal discord. But it signals a careful and probably limited rapprochement between OPEC's leading contenders for power, Saudi Arabia and Iran. The Saudis have demonstrated their capacity to discipline "recalcitrant" members, but they could not have hoped to push those members into complete submission; the political, economic, and possibly military costs of continuing an aggressive market-flooding strategy have appeared to be too high. The stunning dismissal of Saudi Oil Minister Zaki Yamani, the principal architect of this policy, may signal a realignment within the Saudi ruling class on oil and foreign policy. Yamani had opposed not only the $18-a-barrel oil price sought by Iran but apparently also any improvement of relations with the Islamic Republic. An important factor in this policy shift may have been the threat to Saudi Arabia emanating from a widening war in the Gulf. Sharply reduced oil export volumes associated with lower prices—the result of Yamani's policies—could have driven Iran into some desperate military moves. The Iranian capture of Iraq's Fao peninsula, coinciding with the oil price collapse, produced a sense of potential events to come.

Iran has not only made overtures to Saudi Arabia (as evidenced by several spectacular visits made by Iranian officials to the Arab Gulf states), but it has also attempted generally to reduce its international isolation. These moves were motivated primarily by the Islamic Republic's desire to enhance its image abroad and to gain greater access to the international arms market. Iran has succeeded in improving relations with the Soviet Union and France, the two major suppliers of weapons to Iraq.

These diplomatic moves and OPEC's temporary accord have given Iran additional breathing space. Yet, the rapprochement with Saudi Arabia is primarily of a tactical nature. Despite the OPEC accord (under which Saudi Arabia agreed to curtail its output), rivalry between the organization's two foremost powers persists. And despite recently surfaced reports of secret Saudi supplies of fuel and arms to Iran, Riyadh's rulers remain staunch supporters of Iraq's war effort. Saudi Arabia may feel it necessary to defuse a potential direct military confrontation with the Islamic Republic, but it retains an interest in having both Iran and Iraq preoccupied with war to prevent the extension of their influence into the Gulf. To the extent that a Saudi-Iranian rapprochement within OPEC produces a stabilization of oil prices, the two belligerents will merely have sufficient resources to keep the war going. Thus, an OPEC accord, though highly desirable, cannot by itself solve the Islamic Republic's problems.

The stalemated war, the demands of oil traders and buyers for price concessions, Saudi Arabia's aggressive oil policies, and the state of the Iranian economy will continue to exert enormous pressure on the Islamic Republic's oil policies. As long as Iran remains so crucially dependent on oil—and nothing in its current policies indicates any change for the better—

it can only hope to stabilize its revenues in concert with other producers, particularly those in the Gulf region.

Summary and Conclusion

Oil continues to be the mainstay of the Iranian economy because of the Islamic Republic's failure to diversify its economy and to harness its indigenous resources for a more self-reliant course. Iran's dependence on oil has been accentuated by the endless war with Iraq. Dependence on oil revenues in turn means that Iran is vulnerable to the pressures of the world oil market. Its oil exports and the prices realized have been severely affected by the ongoing transformation of the oil industry. The Islamic Republic has ostensibly tried to reserve some leeway for itself through its increasingly pragmatic and improvisatory policies. It has also been in the forefront of the move toward direct deals, and seemingly in the lead when prices rose and again when they began to fall. But the momentum behind these policy changes has been beyond the country's reach.

Iran's desperate need for oil revenue and its decreased share of total OPEC production since the Revolution have meant that the Islamic Republic has little leverage over the organization's policies. Unlike Saudi Arabia, it cannot sustain extremely low levels of production in order to push prices up; neither could it open the tap to push prices down if it ever desired to do so. Instead, Iran has reserved for itself the option to abruptly change course when it saw fit, following closely the changing fortunes of the world market. Moreover, militant rhetoric has veiled its dependence and limited its leeway for action. But Iran could only play its maverick role behind OPEC's shield—and only as long as OPEC was a strong and viable organization. After five years of unabated crisis, OPEC's integrity has been severely undermined, and disunity among its members is clearly not helping any of them. It is only within a coherent OPEC that Iran can hope to stabilize its oil exports and revenues.

Notes

1. Exponents of the political economy school in the energy field are M. Tanzer, *The Energy Crisis: World Struggle for Power and Wealth* (New York: Monthly Review Press, 1974) and *The Race for Resources: Continuing Struggles over Minerals and Fuels* (New York: Monthly Review Press, 1980). See also M. Massarrat's *Weltenergieproduktion und Neuordnung der Weltwirtschaft* [World Energy Production and the New World Economic Order] (Frankfurt and New York: Campus, 1980). A translation of Massarrat's work appears in abridged form in P. Nore and T. Turner (eds.), *Oil and Class Struggle* (London: Zed Press, 1980).

2. Oil revenues continue to account for more than 80 percent of government income (see S. Bakhash, *The Politics of Oil and Revolution in Iran* [Washington, D.C.: Brookings Institution, 1982]) and in excess of 90 percent of foreign-exchange earnings (*OPEC Facts and Figures 1983* [Vienna: OPEC, 1983], p. 16). Accounts for 1984 indicate that oil export revenues covered a somewhat lower share of government

income—namely, 65 percent. See "Niedrige Oelpreise sind Teherans Rettungsanker," *Handelsblatt* (West Germany), December 26, 1984.

3. F. Fesharaki, *Revolution and Energy Policy in Iran* (London: Economist Intelligence Unit, 1980); Fesharaki, *Development of the Iranian Oil Industry* (New York: Praeger Publishers, 1976); and B. Mossavar-Rahmani, *Energy Policy in Iran: Domestic Choices and International Implications* (New York: Pergamon Press, 1981).

4. L. Turner and J. Bedore, *Middle East Industrialization* (New York: Praeger, 1979).

5. D. E. Long, "Oil and the Iran-Iraq War," in M. S. El-Azhari (ed.), *The Iran-Iraq War* (New York: St. Martin's Press, 1984).

6. Bakhash, op. cit.

7. Ibid., pp. 12–15; and L. Meyer, *Oelpolitik und Entwicklung im Iran* [Oil Policy and Development in Iran], (unpublished manuscript, University of Konstanz, West Germany, June 1982).

8. P. Clawson, "Iran's Economy: Between Crisis and Collapse," *MERIP Reports*, no. 98 (July/August 1981), pp. 12–13.

9. During the first two years of the Islamic Republic, capacity utilization was only about 30 percent. See L. Meyer, op. cit., p. 27, and "Ausverkauf des Schwarzen Goldes," [Sellout of the Black Gold], *Blaetter des Informationszentrums Dritte Welt* (December 1985), p. 32.

10. The amount of cultivated land has decreased substantially. While Iran's agricultural production declined, wheat imports rose almost five-fold between 1978–1979 and 1980–1981. See Clawson, op. cit., p. 11. Food imports had risen to more than $3 billion in 1982–1983 and reached $4 billion during 1983–1984. "Gulf War Drains Iran's Foreign Exchange Reserves," *Arabia*, September 1984, p. 56, and E. Hooglund, "The Gulf War and the Islamic Republic," *MERIP Reports*, no. 125–126, July–September 1984, p. 36.

11. Bakhash, op. cit., p. 31.

12. Iran also lost $6 billion in foreign exchange in 1981 when it agreed to a settlement of claims by U.S. companies against it. See ibid., p. 28.

13. Clawson, op. cit., p. 12. If the regime had not drastically cut spending in the fall of 1980, the deficit would have soared to $24 billion.

14. *Kayhan*, February 5, 1986; quoted in "Khomeini Regime's Economic Impasse" (Washington, D.C.: National Council of Resistance of Iran in the U.S.A., 1986), p. 6.

15. See "Gulf War Drains Iran's Foreign Reserves," op. cit., p. 56.

16. The accumulated balance-of-payments deficit from the Revolution until spring 1985 is on the order of $12 billion. See "Debt Burden Hits Iranian Business," *Financial Times*, August 20, 1984; and "Khomeini's Other Crisis," *Financial Times*, July 3, 1984.

17. "Iran Plays It Safe—At a Cost," *Middle East Economic Survey*, August 24, 1984, p. 17; "The Iranian Economy—Back to Essentials," and "Debt Burden Hits Iranian Business," *Financial Times*, August 20, 1984; "Niedrige Oelpreise sind Teherans Rettungsanker," op. cit.

18. Dilip Hiro, "Tehran Looks Prosperous, But Times Are Hard in Iran," *Washington Post National Weekly Edition*, January 27, 1986, p. 16.

19. *Ettela'at*, February 23, 1985; quoted in "Khomeini Regime's Economic Impasse," p. 11.

20. For example, at the same nominal price, Iran in 1982–1983 received only about 60 percent of the value of its 1977–1978 imports. See "Gulf War Drains Iran's Foreign Reserves," op. cit., p. 57. The volume of money in circulation since the

Revolution has grown nearly four-fold. See the diagram provided in "Khomeini Regime's Economic Impasse," p. 5. Inflation is estimated to be running at rates of 400 percent (ibid., p. 12).

21. "Ausverkauf des Schwarzen Goldes," op. cit., p. 32.

22. See "Iran Parliament to Propose Sweeping Budget Changes," *Financial Times*, January 18, 1985. In 1984–1985, these subsidies were budgeted at $1.2 billion. See also "Teherans Regierung Muss zum Rotstift Greifen," *Handelsblatt* (West Germany), May 7, 1984.

23. These figures are cited in "Khomeini Regime's Economic Impasse," op. cit., p. 8.

24. See "Tehran's Great Debate," *The Middle East*, April 1985, pp. 51–53. The laws stipulating nationalization of foreign trade and land reform were finally passed in April 1985.

25. According to the Iranian Plan and Budget Organization, war damages reached $163 billion in March 1983. See "PBO Estimates War Damage at $163 Billion," *Middle East Economic Survey*, July 9, 1984, p. A6. The oil industry is estimated to have suffered the most ($53.7 billion), followed by agriculture ($40.7 billion), industry ($8.2 billion), energy ($3.7 billion), and construction and housing ($2.9 billion).

26. *SIPRI Yearbook 1984: World Armaments and Disarmament* (London and Philadelphia: Taylor & Francis, 1984), p. 104.

27. Hooglund, op. cit., p. 36. About one-fourth of that amount is being spent on foreign exchange—in other words, on war-related imports. See "Khomeini's Other Crisis," op. cit. According to *Kayhan* (April 17, 1985), direct and indirect war expenditures increased from $2.1 billion in 1983 to $13 billion in 1985 (cited in "Khomeini Regime's Economic Impasse," p. 11). Alnasrawi estimates the total war cost (excluding lost oil revenue) for Iran by the end of 1985 at $220 billion. Lost oil income for the same period is estimated by the same author at $20.5 billion. The total cost to both belligerents from 1981 to 1985 is put at $416 billion. For Iran, the annual cost of the war absorbs an estimated 54 percent of the country's GNP. See A. Alnasrawi, "Economic Consequences of the Iraq-Iran War," *Third World Quarterly*, vol. 8, no. 3 (July 1986), pp. 883–886.

28. These totals were calculated from figures reported by Nicholas D. Kristof, "Assessing OPEC's Members," *New York Times*, October 29, 1984 (oil revenue), and al-Maaghi, "Of Stingers and Sams," *Arabia*, vol. 4, no. 37 (September 1984), p. 6 (military expenditures).

29. From April to June 1984, when the tanker war began in earnest, freight costs increased by $1.50/bbl (from Worldscale 31 to 70; destination Rotterdam), and $1.20 (from Worldscale 31 to 80; destination Japan), and cargo insurance rates rose by $1.20 (from 1 percent to 5 percent of cargo value) for both destinations. In January 1985, assaults against tankers pushed insurance rates from 1 percent to 6 percent of cargo value, almost quadrupling transport costs from Kharg to Europe and Japan to a prohibitive $4–5 per barrel. See *Petroleum Intelligence Weekly*, January 7, 1985, p. 6; and "Iran's Confidence Trick," *Economist*, January 26, 1985. Normal insurance rates for Gulf ports are 0.0275 percent. See "The Impact of Gulf Hostilities on Crude Oil Prices and Transport Costs," *Petroleum Intelligence Weekly*, June 11, 1984, p. 2; and "Escalating Crisis Heightening Potential for Gulf Disruption," *Petroleum Intelligence Weekly*, May 21, 1984, p. 1. Before the tanker war came into full swing, the additional costs of lifting crude from Kharg, in comparison with other Gulf ports, were only about 20–30 cents/bbl. See "Iran Takes Steps to Keep Oil Flowing Despite War Threat," *Petroleum Intelligence Weekly*, March 5, 1984, p. 2.

30. Japanese traders demanded a $4/bbl discount to cover the January 1985 surge in war-risk premiums, while Iran was prepared to give only $2/bbl. See "Iraq's Confidence Trick," *Economist*, January 26, 1985. In the wake of the May–June 1984 tanker war, traders reported an average ex-Kharg price of $21/bbl, which would have been a much deeper cut in the average official price of $26.50 than the $3.00 officially acknowledged by Iran. See "Khomeini's Other Crisis," op. cit.

31. See "Iran's New Shuttle Is Rapidly Reviving Crude Oil Exports," *Petroleum Intelligence Weekly*, February 18, 1985, p. 3; "Iran and Turkey: A Pipeline to Corner the Kurds," *Economist*, February 2, 1985; "Turkey and Iran Agree to Study Oil and Gas Pipeline," *Financial Times*, January 23, 1985; and *Petroleum Intelligence Weekly*, December 9, 1985, p. 6.

32. For policy suggestions on how to end the disastrous Iran-Iraq war, see R. C. Johansen and M. G. Renner, "Limiting Conflict in the Gulf," *Third World Quarterly*, vol. 7, no. 4 (October 1985), pp. 803–838.

33. Saudi Arabia increased its share of OPEC production from 28 percent in 1978 to 44 percent in 1981. These figures were calculated from the *BP Statistical Review of World Energy 1984*, p. 5. See Alnasrawi, op. cit., pp. 887–889. See also Table 4.

34. *OPEC Facts and Figures*, op. cit., p. 34. OPEC's current account balance was transformed from a $105 billion surplus in 1980 to a $20 billion deficit in 1983 (ibid., p. 35). See A. Al-Sowayegh, *Arab Petropolitics* (New York: St. Martin's Press, 1984), p. 47; and "Assessing OPEC's Members," op. cit. For the 1984 figure, see *Petroleum Economist*, July 1985, p. 236.

35. "Gulf War Drains Iran's Foreign Reserves," op. cit., p. 57.

36. For a detailed account of these factors and their impact on OPEC, see M. G. Renner, "Restructuring the World Energy Industry," *MERIP Reports*, no. 120 (January 1984), pp. 12–17, 25, 31; and P. Aarts and M. G. Renner, "Background to OPEC's Current Crisis," *ifda-dossier*, no. 37 (September/October 1983), pp. 67–72.

37. "Did OPEC Stumble or Was It Pushed?," *The Middle East*, December 1984, p. 30. *Petroleum Intelligence Weekly*, February 18, 1985, p. 6, including NGLs.

38. *Average world crude oil prices* are shown below (the prices represent weighted averages of 27 internationally traded crude oils based on official sales prices or estimated term contract prices; spot transactions are not included). Since 1986, elements of netback and spot-related pricing have been included in these average figures.

	12/31/78	*1/1/81*	*1/1/82*	*11/13/84*	*1/1/85*	
OPEC	13.03	34.82	34.13	28.58	28.43	
Non-OPEC	13.44	38.54	34.35	28.18	28.16	
World	13.08	35.49	34.18	28.43	28.33	
	3/26/85	*9/17/85*	*10/15/85*	*11/15/85*	*12/13/85*	
OPEC	27.99	27.92	27.88	27.79	27.81	
Non-OPEC	27.86	26.30	26.73	27.39	26.60	
World	27.94	27.24	27.41	27.63	27.31	
	2/28/86	*3/7/86*	*4/11/86*	*5/9/86*	*6/13/86*	*7/18/86*
OPEC	26.88	15.65	13.03	13.48	11.94	9.70
non-OPEC	18.73	15.56	13.44	12.72	12.02	9.49
World	23.73	15.61	13.08	13.21	11.97	9.62

Source: Compiled from *Petroleum Economist*, various issues (1984–1986).

39. "Why This Oil Glut Could Spill into the 21st Century," *Business Week*, November 12, 1984, p. 37.

40. "Spot Prices for 45 Percent of Oil," *New York Times*, July 3, 1984; and *Petroleum Economist*, January 1984, p. 9.

41. Futures contracts are used to hedge against losses in oil trading, particularly on the spot market. On the New York Mercantile Exchange (the largest futures trading arena), quantities equaling one-sixth of the crude oil production and 60 percent of the oil products consumption of the capitalist world changed hands in 1984—on paper. In reality, less than 2 percent of the volumes traded are actually being delivered. However, futures quotations are instantly made known via computer around the world.

42. *Petroleum Intelligence Weekly*, February 11, 1985, p. 4.

43. "OPEC Seeks Plan to Monitor Output," *New York Times*, December 21, 1984.

44. Under "netback" deals, the prices of crude oil are linked to the actual market value of the crude's refined products. At present, this means that netback deals constitute a veiled discount of $2–3 per barrel. Saudi Arabia is selling more than half of its oil exports on a netback basis. See "Saudis Adopt New Oil Price Formula," *Financial Times*, November 26, 1985.

45. See "Price Crash Impact Magnified by Its Effect on U.S. Dollar," *Petroleum Intelligence Weekly*, May 12, 1986, p. 1.

46. Figures are taken from "Khomeini Regime's Economic Impasse," pp. 4–5.

47. Meyer, op. cit., p. 24.

48. Bakhash, op. cit., p. 10.

49. See ibid., pp. 15–16; and S. A. Schneider, *The Oil Price Revolution* (Baltimore, Md.: Johns Hopkins University Press, 1983), p. 440.

50. See Bakhash's account in Bakhash, op. cit., pp. 31–36.

51. Schneider, op. cit., pp. 450–455.

52. Japan is Iran's top oil customer, importing $4.2 billion worth of oil from the Islamic Republic in 1983. See "Arabs Woo Japan for Support Against Iran," *Financial Times*, May 9, 1984.

53. *Petroleum Intelligence Weekly*, April 9, 1984, p. 7; and "Much Ado About Something," *Economist*, May 26, 1984.

54. *Petroleum Intelligence Weekly*, September 24, 1984.

55. Iran's Petroleum Ministry is negotiating with Shell, BP, Agip, and other companies for deals of about 700,000 b/d. See "Buyers Seek to Tie New Term Contracts to Netback Pricing," *Petroleum Intelligence Weekly*, December 23, 1985, pp. 1–2.

56. Syria, Algeria, Libya, Iraq, and Nigeria are among the most active countertraders aside from Iran. See *Financial Times*, December 13, 1985.

57. "The Iranian Economy—Back to Essentials," *Middle East Economic Digest*, April 6, 1984, p. 21; and "Exports Maintained Despite Difficulties," *Financial Times*, April 1, 1985, Iran Supplement, p. 12.

58. "Iran Boosts Crude Oil Sales," *Middle East Economic Survey*, November 26, 1984, p. A1.

59. "Iran May Force Trade Partners to Buy Oil," *Financial Times*, February 11, 1985. Usually, Iran is asking its partner to buy at least 30 to 50 percent more oil than the value of the countertraded good involved would suggest.

60. "Oil Price Erosion Evident in Anatomy of a Barter Deal," *Petroleum Intelligence Weekly*, August 13, 1984, p. 1. Oil purchased under barter deals is usually priced at a level reflecting both official and spot values. Although the terms may vary,

frequently a mix of 70:30 (official:spot) is being adopted. See "Tehran Steps Up Drive to Barter Crude for Goods," *Financial Times*, February 25, 1985.

61. "Exports Maintained Despite Difficulties," *Financial Times*, April 1, 1985 (Iran Supplement), p. 12.

62. It is too early to tell whether Iran's new petroleum minister, Gholamreza Aghazadeh (who succeeded Mohammed Gharazi in late 1985), will retain greater decision-making power.

63. "Tehran Steps Up Drive to Barter Crude for Goods," op. cit.; "Exports Maintained Despite Difficulties," op. cit.

64. J. Clad, "The Oil Sales Slide Is Iran's Unending Bad Dream," *Far Eastern Economic Review*, July 4, 1985, pp. 26–27.

65. Schneider, op. cit., p. 480.

66. See *Petroleum Intelligence Weekly*, May 23, 1983, p. 7, and October 8, 1984, p. 7; and "Iranian Oil Cited in Price Downturn," *New York Times*, November 26, 1984. Although the Islamic Republic had vowed to withdraw from foreign oil operations, it is still considering participation in the development of a North Sea oil field jointly owned with BP. See "Iran and BP Consider North Sea Development," *Financial Times*, November 26, 1984. Iran is also maintaining an investment made by the Shah in an oil refinery in Madras, India, but it has sold off a 40 percent stake in another refinery in South Korea. See J. Clad, "Teheran's Asian Links: Pragmatism Prevails," *Far Eastern Economic Review*, July 4, 1985, pp. 26–28.

67. See "Focus on OPEC Oil Companies—IR Iran: NIOC," *OPEC Bulletin*, April 1985, p. 24.

68. *Petroleum Intelligence Weekly*, May 23, 1983, p. 7, and December 10, 1984, p. 10.

69. Clawson, op. cit., p. 13.

70. "Focus on OPEC Oil Companies," op. cit., p. 24.

71. "Iran Raises Oil Prices to OPEC Levels," *Financial Times*, January 9, 1985; "Iran May Force Trade Partners to Buy Oil," op. cit.; "Iran Claims OPEC Clearance to Discount Prices," *Financial Times*, November 3, 1984.

12

U.S.-Iranian Trade Relations After the Revolution

Mehrdad Valibeigi

The American interest in Iran is a vital one. Iran represents strategically, both in an economic and political sense, a vital cog in the system. Therefore, we have a considerable stake in the peaceful management of Iranian modernization.

—Zbigniew Brzezinski*

Introduction

In an attempt to uncover the realities behind the rhetoric of hostility between Iran and the United States, this chapter gives an overall view of the dynamics of post-revolutionary trade relations between the two countries. As of 1983, the volume of trade between the two countries has grown significantly. It is hypothesized here that expansion of trade relations has been the logical outgrowth of (1) Iran's crisis of foreign-exchange earnings in 1982 due to its costly war with Iraq, and (2) the country's technical dependence on U.S. capital and military goods. Iran's strategic economic and political significance as a major supplier of oil and as a significant military force in the Gulf region is argued to be the main reason behind the United States' intention to revitalize its economic relations with Iran.

Historical Background

The origins of economic relations between the United States and Iran can be traced back to the turn of this century. However, such relations became significant only in the post–World War II era. After the CIA-sponsored coup of 1953 against nationalist Prime Minister Mohamad Mossadeq, the

---

*U.S. Congress, House of Representatives Committee on Foreign Affairs, Subcommittee in Europe and the Middle East Hearing, "U.S. Policy Toward Iran," January 1979, pp. 1, 3.

The author would like to extend his appreciation to Hooshang Amirahmadi and Carol Grabauskas for their careful reading and constructive criticisms of earlier drafts of this chapter.

Shah rewarded five U.S. oil companies with a 40 percent share of Iranian oil production.[1] Then, on March 5, 1959, the two countries signed a bilateral economic and military agreement in which the United States regarded the preservation of the "independence and integrity" of Iran as "vital to its national interest and world peace." Between 1953 and 1961, during what is called the "Mutual Security Act" period, the United States provided Iran with loans and grants totaling $548.1 million for economic development and $500.6 million for military purposes.[2] In 1962, under pressure from the Kennedy administration, the Shah carried out a set of fundamental reforms that paved the way for further economic cooperation between the two countries. Such reforms, known as the "White Revolution," were considered necessary by the United States if its economic assistance was to contribute to a major economic mobilization and to the expansion of industry and markets in Iran. Economic and military assistance continued well into the early 1970s, until the unprecedented increase in Iranian oil revenues rendered such financial assistance unnecessary. U.S. military assistance to Iran in the period from 1962–1975 reached $844.7 million, whereas economic assistance fell from $548.1 million to $186.5 million in the same period.[3]

Nixon's visit to Iran in May of 1972 resulted in far closer political and economic ties between the two countries. In light of the newly articulated Guam (later Nixon) Doctrine, which recommended less U.S. direct involvement and greater responsibility by U.S. allies for their own defense and that of their regions, Iran was to receive military assistance to the point where, in harmony with the United States, it could ensure the free flow of oil from the Gulf region. Subsequently, the United States began supplying Iran with a substantial amount of sophisticated military equipment.

The 1972–1978 period can be regarded as the peak of U.S.-Iran economic and military cooperation. In 1976, the two countries signed an agreement that projected an annual nonoil, nonmilitary trade of $15 billion by 1981, almost all of it in the form of U.S. exports to Iran. In 1978, the United States became Iran's second largest supplier of nonmilitary goods (after West Germany), exporting $12.7 billion worth of such goods. During the same year, Iran's military purchases from the United States reached $12 billion.[4] Total capital exposure by U.S. banks in Iran rose to $2.2 billion by 1979, while direct investment by about 500 U.S. companies amounted to a total of $6.82 billion. The number of American citizens working in Iran reached 50,000. In the same period (1972–1978), the United States became a major customer for Iranian oil, buying up to 15.9 percent of Iran's produced oil, which was equivalent to 5.6 percent of the United States' total supply of oil.[5]

The Immediate Effects of the Revolution

After two years of revolutionary turmoil, the Shah departed Iran on January 16, 1979, and the cabinet of Shahpour Bakhtiar was replaced by the provisional government of Mehdi Bazargan on February 4, 1979. As a liberal politician and moderate Muslim with a Western education, Bazargan was favorably received by the United States as a better alternative to the more radical factions of the revolutionary regime. Indeed, during Bazargan's tenure, the partial control by liberal elements over the revolutionary government prevented the sudden disruption of economic ties between the two countries.

Bazargan's government was immediately recognized by the United States. General Valiollah Gharani, then chief of the armed forces, expressed the government's intentions to continue Iran's purchase of military spare parts in August 1979. Subsequently, the United States resumed export of $300 million in military supplies for the F-4 and F-5 fighter planes.[6] In addition, it reached an agreement with Iran to buy back $765 million worth of military equipment.

Among the most important immediate economic effects of this period was the cancellation of $12.46 billion in contractual orders for U.S. weapons, the largest of which entailed $5.7 billion for 300 F-16 fighters and $1.75 billion for an advanced air-defense system based on 7 E-3A Airborne Warning and Control System (AWACS) aircraft. A $20 billion order for the purchase of eight nuclear reactors from Westinghouse and General Electric was also recalled as a result of the revolutionary disturbances (see Table 1).[7]

The Revolution also had a substantial impact on the volume of trade between the two countries, particularly on U.S. exports to Iran. During 1979, the value of U.S. exports to Iran dropped by 72 percent, from a pre-revolutionary high of $3.678 billion in 1978 to $1.02 billion. In 1979, a 75 percent reduction in U.S. exports of capital goods and machinery to Iran far exceeded the 12 percent reduction in the export of food.[8] The negative rate of capital formation in Iran explains this sharp decline in imports of capital goods from the industrial countries, including the United States.

While U.S. exports to Iran declined rather sharply during 1979, U.S. imports from Iran remained close to the pre-revolutionary level. They dropped only 3 percent, from $2.87 billion to $2.78 billion, of which $2.59 billion was in oil and the rest was in major nonoil export items such as caviar, carpets, animal skins, and pistachios. Indeed, in this year, Iranian nonoil exports to the United States actually increased by 57 percent for food items and by 65 percent for carpets.[9]

As stated in the Joint Economic Committee Report to the U.S. Congress on November 4, 1979, the primary impact of the Revolution on U.S.-Iran economic relations was neither reduction of the volume of trade nor the magnitude of financial transactions between the two countries but, rather, the "creation of uncertainty."[10] In such relations, what came about as a result of the hostage crisis rendered the Joint Economic Committee's fears about the element of "uncertainty" quite relevant. On November 2, 1979, a group of Iranian oil workers threatened to boycott the supply of oil to the United States. This was only one day after a meeting between Bazargan and U.S. National Security Advisor Zbigniew Brzezinski in Algeria, which allegedly had not been authorized by Ayatollah Khomeini. On November 4,

TABLE 1
CANCELLED ORDERS FOR MILITARY EQUIPMENT

	Equipment	Manufacturer	Quantity	Price ($billions)
1.	F-16 Fighters	General Dynamics	300	5.700
2.	F-4E Fighter-Bombers	McDonnell Douglas	31	0.350
3.	Shrike Air-to-Surface Missiles	Texas Instruments	1,000	0.105
4.	F-14 Fighters	Grumman	70	1.750
5.	Airborne Warning and Command System	Boeing	7	1.200
6.	Spruance Class Destroyers	Litton Industries	2	0.800
7.	Helicopter Production Plant	Trextron, Inc.	1	0.575
8.	Phoenix Air-to-Air Missiles	Hughes Aircraft	400	0.100
9.	RF4E Reconnaissance Planes	McDonnell Douglas	16	0.219
10.	M48M Tank Reconstruction Plant	Harso	1	0.080
11.	Misc. Missiles, Other Weaponry and Training	Different Companies	---	0.752
12.	Misc. Naval Weaponry	Different Companies	---	0.350
13.	Naval Construction Project	Planning Research	1	0.030
14.	Construction Project	Harris Corporation	1	0.065
15.	747 Military Transport	Boeing	4-5	0.200
		TOTAL:		12.476

Source: Khosrow Fatemi. "The Iranian Revolution: Its Impact on Economic Relations with the United States," International Journal of Middle East Studies, vol. 12 (November 1980): 307. Reprinted with the permission of Cambridge University Press.

1979, a group of students supported by the radical fundamentalist faction of the regime took over the U.S. Embassy, holding fifty-eight Americans hostage. By rallying popular masses by means of anti-U.S. rhetoric, the radical faction successfully out-maneuvered the liberals in power and gained control of the state political power. Shortly after Bazargan resigned on November 6, the transitional period came to an end. Thus began a drastically different period in the two countries' history of economic and political relations.

Hostage Crisis: The Settlement of U.S. Claims

The interruption of economic relations between the United States and Iran after the Revolution was completed following the seizure of the U.S. Embassy by student followers of Ayatollah Khomeini. It was 444 days, from November 4, 1979, until January 20, 1981, before the hostages were released, following an agreement signed by the two countries in Algiers, Algeria, on January 19, 1981.

According to the Algiers agreement, the United States rescinded the freeze on Iranian government assets in U.S. banks, totaling $7.977 billion. This amount broke down as follows: $5.5 billion in Iranian deposits in foreign branches of American banks, $1.4 billion in Iranian deposits with the Federal Reserve System, $940 million worth of Iranian gold, and $137 million in miscellaneous Iranian assets (such as the Iranian military trust fund) which were immediately deliverable (i.e., not tied up in lawsuits).[11]

Following the agreement, the assets were deposited in an escrow account, known as Account Number Two, held by the Central Bank of Algeria in the Bank of England.[12] Out of this escrow account, two immediate payouts were made: $2.85 billion to the Central Bank of Iran and $3.7 billion to a group of American and non-American banks that had made syndicated loans to the Shah's regime. Among this group were the Bank of America, Chase Manhattan, Citicorp, Manufacturers Hanover, Morgan Guaranty Trust, and the First National Bank of Chicago. Regarding repayment of the syndicated loans, *The Economist* reported that "the banks are getting back 100 cents on the dollar—a wonderful deal considering that Chrysler is offering only 15 cents on the dollar."[13]

The remaining $1.427 billion of the original $7.977 billion in frozen Iranian assets remained in the escrow account. Decisions concerning disbursement of this amount were left to the discretion of a nine-member international arbitration commission composed of three Americans, three Iranians, and three members from Third World countries.

Aside from the $7.977 billion originally frozen, there was an estimated $2.2 billion worth of Iranian assets that were not immediately transferable. Under the Algiers agreement, the U.S. government terminated all lawsuits against these assets, ordering the banks to transfer the funds to the Algerian accounts.

Of this $2.2 billion, $1.2 billion went to the Central Bank of Iran, making the Iranian share of the original $10.177 billion equal to $4.05 billion. The remaining $1 billion was deposited in De Nederlandsche Bank in an escrow account known as Number Three. Escrow Account Number One, amounting to $300 million, was held in the U.S. Federal Reserve Bank.

Originally, 2,800 corporate and individual claims were filed against the assets. Five hundred companies had claims of more than $250,000. The total value of American claims amounted to more than $10 billion, against which Iran had $35 billion worth of claims (including funds allegedly misappropriated by the Shah's family) and $12 billion of undelivered military equipment.[14]

TABLE 2
COMPENSATION TO U. S. COMPANIES UNTIL NOVEMBER 1984

Company	$ Thousands
B.F. Goodrich	182
Air La Carte (ARA)	416
Singer Company	281
International School Service	81
Danial Man Johnson Mendenhall	420
Honeywell Information Systems	700
Granite	369
Sperry Univac	2,800

Source: Compiled from data given by various issues of the Middle East Economic Digest, 1982-1984.

The first hearing of the arbitration tribunal took place in the summer of 1982. The first U.S. company to receive compensation awarded by the tribunal committee was the B. F. Goodrich Tire Company, which, on May 8, 1982, received $182,250 of the $351,280 originally claimed.[15] Since then, various U.S. companies and banks have received more than $350 million in compensation (see Table 2).

On December 22, 1983, the Bank of America received $472 million in repayment of nonsyndicated loans, from which it returned $289.1 million to the Central Bank of Iran. This agreement initiated a whole new round of large sum compensation payments to U.S. banks. The total amount of unpaid nonsyndicated loans is estimated to be nearly $1 billion.[16]

The final outcome of the hostage crisis and the settlement of U.S. claims can be argued to have been a significant victory for the American companies and banks. These parties, which would not have received a single cent as compensation under a different scenario of political developments in Iran, could now revitalize millions of dollars invested in, or lent to, Iran.

After the Hostage Crisis: Revolutionary Rhetoric Versus Economic Realities

Political and diplomatic relations between the United States and Iran since the hostage crisis have been dominated by an attitude of hostility, intimidation, and occasional direct confrontation, as in the bombing of the U.S. Embassy and Marine barracks in Lebanon by an Islamic fundamentalist group allegedly supported by the Iranian government. However, the economic relations between the two countries have not entirely mirrored the level of political hostility between them.

TABLE 3
U. S.--IRAN TRADE ($ MILLIONS)

Year	U. S. Export		U. S. Import		Volume of Trade	
	Value	% Growth	Value	% Growth	Value	% Growth
1978	3678	+ 35	2877	+ 3	6555	+ 19
1979	1019	- 72	2783	- 3	3802	+ 42
1980	23	- 98	338	- 88	361	+ 5
1981	300	-120	63	- 81	363	+ 1
1982	121	- 59	124	+ 97	245	- 5
1983	190	+ 57	1112	+797	1302	+ 42

Source: Compiled from two sources: U. S. Bureau of the Census, U. S. Exports Schedule E: World Area by Commodity Grouping, Annual (F.T. 455), and U. S. Imports (F.T. 155).

In November 1979, President Carter placed a trade embargo on Iran as a reaction to the hostage crisis. The result was an abrupt reduction in the volume of trade to the historically low level of $361 million. U.S. exports fell by almost 98 percent, from $1.019 billion to $23 million, during 1980 (see Table 3). However, as the trade ban was lifted by President Reagan on January 19, 1982, and as Iran ran into serious balance-of-payment problems in 1981–1982, the volume of trade began to rise. The United States' purchase of Iranian oil accounted for most of this—an increase of 431 percent between 1982 and 1983.

Continuation of trade relations, and its gradual increase from 1983 onward, can be explained by two factors: (1) Iran's dependence on oil income, which constituted about 75 percent of government revenues, and its technical dependence on imports of certain U.S.-manufactured military and nonmilitary goods and spare parts (both were aspects of a more deeply rooted structural dependence of the country on Western economies); and (2) the United States' desire to keep the doors open for possible future normalization of relations.

U.S. Oil Purchases from Iran

The United States resumed purchases of Iranian oil in April 1982. Although the Iranian oil minister categorically denied the existence of direct sales of Iranian oil to the United States, the U.S. Department of Defense announced that "it [had] recently bought 1.8 million from a Geneva-based trading company, Gatoil International."[17] The purchase was approved by the State Department. U.S. officials further noted that "the sale was purely commercial and should not be seen as signalling better relations with Iran."[18] However, the act was perceived by U.S. oil companies as "obviously a clear signal

TABLE 4
U. S. IMPORT OF IRANIAN OIL IN 1983/84 ($ MILLIONS) (BBC)

Month	Current Month Net Quantity	Current Month Custom Value	Cumulative Custom Value
1983			
January	3,064,781	96	96
February	2,290,268	71	167
March	---	--	167
April	---	--	167
May	1,585,173	45	212
June	1,370,511	39	251
July	512,759	15	266
August	9,795,606	283	549
September	6,442,237	184	733
October	4,969,442	140	873
November	4,177,710	120	993
December	2,297,662	65	1058
1984			
January	829,889	24	24
February	1,736,338	49	73
March	1,900,690	54	127
April	519,709	15	142
May	---	--	142
June	---	--	142
July	4,147,063	116	258
August	1,795,396	50	308

Source: U. S. Bureau of the Census, U. S. General Imports and Imports for Consumption (F.T. 135), 1983, 1984.

from the U.S. government that buying Iranian oil is not only legal but moral,"[19] in the words of one American oil company executive. Consequently, the importation of Iranian oil in large quantities was resumed after January 1983. The volume of imported oil from Iran reached its peak in August 1983, when the United States purchased almost the same amount of oil from Iran as it did from Saudi Arabia. In this month, the United States imported 9,795,606 barrels of Iranian oil valued at $283 million; at $28.9 per barrel, this price was 11 cents less than Saudi Arabia's oil price in the same month. On average, the United States imported more than 100,000 barrels a day from Iran, and the total bill amounted to $1,057 billion during 1983.[20] The importation of Iranian oil continued during 1984. Its total value for the first eight months of the year amounted to $308 million.[21] Yet, despite such large transactions, the United States purchases of Iranian oil are not shown in official Iranian statistics (Table 4).

A strong case may be made for the proposition that the increased volume of trade between the two countries was caused by the financial crisis faced

TABLE 5
IRAN'S CRUDE OIL PRODUCTION AND EXPORTS 1978--1983
(in thousand barrels/day)

	1978/79	1979/80	1980/81	1981/82	1982/83
Total Production	4,252	3,433	1,476	1,441	2,679
Total Crude Exports	3,455	2,632	770	791	1,997

Source: Vahe Petrossian, "Iran: Special Report," Middle East Economic Digest, November 8, 1984.

by the Iranian government during the 1981–1982 period. The eruption of the war with Iraq and the toll this took on the Iranian economy abruptly increased the import bill both for military and consumer goods, and thus exerted substantial pressure on the country's foreign-exchange reserves. Iran's total imports increased by $2.67 billion (14 percent) from $10.84 billion in 1980 to $13.51 billion in 1981. In 1982, the growth of Iranian imports declined. However, unofficial estimates by foreign observers, which are often more reliable, indicated that in 1983 the import bill increased astronomically to a historic high of $21.5 billion (almost 50 percent higher than the highest pre-revolutionary level during 1978).[22] Incidentally, it was in 1983 that the United States resumed large-scale purchases of Iranian oil and the Iranian government launched a comprehensive campaign to overcome the deficit in its balance of payments, which amounted to more than $2 billion for the year. The effort was overwhelmingly successful, with the negative balance becoming a positive one by the end of 1983. This outcome would not have been achieved if OPEC had not expanded the oil market by selling $4 billion above its assigned quota and made indirect sales of oil to the United States that amounted to over $1 billion in 1983. It is worthwhile to note that Iran has increasingly been selling oil on the spot market. Prior to the recent oil glut, spot prices were usually higher than those associated with long-term contractual sales; but after the glut, the spot prices tended to be lower. As Table 5 indicates, Iranian oil production for export increased by 1.525 billion barrels a day from 791 million to 1.997 billion barrels a day.

The other strain on foreign-exchange earnings during 1982–1983 resulted from the reduction of official OPEC oil prices. By the end of 1982, the world oil and energy situation had changed profoundly. A sustained decline in energy use per unit of output, in addition to low levels of economic activity, brought about a steep decline in the total consumption of energy. On March 14, 1983, the members of OPEC decided to lower the benchmark price of crude oil from $34 per barrel to $29 per barrel—a 15 percent reduction that later became a 17 percent reduction as oil prices fell to $28 per barrel in 1984.[23]

The Composition and Terms of Trade

Historically, oil has been the main component of Iran's exports to the United States and other industrial countries. In this regard, no change has come about as a result of the Revolution. Oil still constitutes more than 90 percent of U.S. imports from Iran. Carpets, pistachios, dates, animal skins, and caviar account for most of the rest.

With the exception of caviar, all major Iranian nonoil exports have lost a significant share of their U.S. market to the competition. For example, in 1978 Iran exported $22.5 million worth of Persian carpets to the United States. In 1979 only $57.4 million worth were exported. This figure was reduced to the negligible amount of $1.4 million in 1982.[24] Competitors from India, Pakistan, and the People's Republic of China have been able to fill the gap created by the interruption of trade with Iran. The same applies to the market for Iranian pistachios, which has been hurt by the introduction of California pistachios to the American market. In 1978, $21.8 million worth of Iranian pistachios were exported to the United States. This figure declined to $8.3 million in 1984.[25] The Iranian exports that have suffered the most are goat and sheep skins. Iran was formerly a major supplier of these products to the United States, with a pre-revolutionary level of exports amounting to $26 million; but in 1982, exports of animal skins from Iran to the United States totaled only $0.4 million.[26]

The interruption of trade during the hostage crisis, the low level of internal production, the confusion and barriers created by the Iranian government's effort to nationalize foreign trade (legislation that has been approved by the Council of Guardians), and, most important, the dual-system exchange rate (consisting of both the official and the free, or black, markets) are among the most important factors responsible for the loss of Iran's export markets.

While the composition of U.S. imports from Iran has not significantly changed, there has been a considerable change in the composition of U.S. exports to Iran. The available data indicate that the relative share of capital goods and machinery exports has increased substantially, from 39 percent of the total U.S. exports to Iran in 1978 to 81 percent in 1983.[27] In absolute terms, however, the level of capital goods and machinery imports from the United States in 1983 was 88 percent lower than the level in 1978 ($0.16 billion in 1983 compared to $1.44 billion in 1978). Whereas the relative share of capital goods imports from the United States has increased, the relative share of food imports has declined substantially. Until 1981, the United States was the main supplier of grains, primarily wheat and rice, to Iran. After 1981, Iran shifted its purchases of wheat to Argentina and rice to Thailand, India, and Pakistan. In 1983, the relative share of food in total U.S. exports to Iran dropped to less than 1 percent.

Although until 1980 the magnitude of U.S. exports to Iran was greatly reduced, the volume as of 1981 has increased at the surprising rate of 125 percent, with the export of capital goods accounting for most of the increase.[28] Such a rate of growth, which was not welcomed by the Iranian government, led to the enforcement of new guidelines, according to which purchases from U.S. firms were allowed "only when the goods [could not be] obtained elsewhere."[29] However, as mentioned earlier, Iran's technical dependence on U.S. capital goods has not yet allowed the enforcement of such guidelines in practice. Indeed, the volume of U.S. exports of capital goods to Iran remained high. This was admitted by the Iranian minister of heavy industry in an interview.[30]

The other major Iranian import from the United States has continued to be U.S. munitions. This is the case despite the United States' ban on the sale of military equipment to Iran. Official data concerning the volume of transactions do not exist, but military intelligence agencies, such as the Stockholm International Peace Research Institute (SIPRI), have documented the transfer of arms from the United States to Iran. In an attempt to verify the validity of various reports concerning such transactions, *Time* magazine conducted a comprehensive investigation of the matter. According to its findings, the Islamic Republic had indeed been buying U.S. munitions and parts through international arms dealers. Carlos Vieira DeMello, a Brazilian arms dealer, has disclosed the facts for the press in the following words: "After subcontractors sold parts to us two or three times, knowing they were being shipped to Iran, and saw that no one had been arrested, they began dealing directly themselves and cut us out."[31] SIPRI brings up the same issue in its 1984 report as follows:

> The United States and the Soviet Union have both declared their neutrality in the war [between Iran and Iraq], they both envisage unpredictable advantages or losses from the war, and they have both, directly or indirectly, supplied both belligerents with weapons during the course of the war.[32]

The terms of trade between the two countries has deteriorated against Iran in the post-revolutionary period—this despite the sharp increase in oil prices from $14 in 1979 to $35 in 1982.[33] However, it was during the same period that the United States did not purchase any Iranian oil.

Oil is not the only Iranian commodity that has been reduced in price. The prices of other Iranian exports to the United States (with the exception of caviar) have also been reduced. For example, Iranian pistachios, which were sold for the average price of $2.98 per pound in 1978, were priced at $1.88 six years later in 1984.[34] As one U.S. observer of Iranian trade believes, such price reductions are a premium paid by the Iranians to compensate for factors such as political and economic instability and other forces that pose barriers to smooth trade between the parties involved.[35]

The declining price of oil and other export goods is not the only factor responsible for the deterioration of the terms of trade for Iran in world markets. The declining value of the rial versus the dollar is also a major factor. In 1978, the exchange rate was 70.44 rials per dollar; currently this figure is about 80 rials per dollar (the free market rate in 1987 was about

950 rials per dollar). According to a study by the International Monetary Fund, the external purchasing power of oil-producing export earnings of the oil countries, including Iran, is estimated to have returned in 1983 to its 1978 level. This means that Iran experienced a 44 percent decline in its oil export receipts over the 1978–1983 period.[36]

Conclusion

It can be argued that the Islamic Republic's original attempt to put an end to all economic ties between Iran and the United States has not been fully successful. Despite a significant reduction of economic relations between the two countries, there are forces at work that necessitate continued trade relations. As demonstrated in this chapter, the financial needs of the Iranian regime and its heavy reliance on oil revenues have been the most important factors responsible for this failure. Secondary to its financial needs is the country's technical dependence, both in industry and in the military, on U.S.-made products. One could argue that as long as the Iranian economy remains dependent on oil revenues and the United States regards the region as strategically important to its interests, direct or indirect economic relations between the two countries will continue regardless of the political differences that divide them. These are the material realities reflected in economic activities that have finally overcome the ideals of the revolutionary practitioners.

Notes

1. The five American oil companies were Exxon, Mobil, Texaco, Standard Oil of California, and Gulf.
2. U.S. Congress, Joint Economic Committee, "The United States and Iran: An Overview," by Bernard Reich, in *Consequence of the Revolution in Iran: A Compendium of Papers Submitted to the Joint Economic Committee*, 1979, p. 7.
3. Ibid., p. 18.
4. *Wall Street Journal*, February 9, 1979.
5. Khosrow Fatemi, "The Iranian Revolution: Its Impact on Economic Relations with the United States," *International Journal of Middle East Studies,* vol. 12, November 1980, p. 1.
6. *Middle East Economic Digest*, August 1979.
7. "Danger Looms in Industrial Contracts," *The Economist*, February 10, 1979.
8. U.S. Bureau of the Census, Department of Commerce, *U.S. Exports, World Area by Schedule E Commodity Grouping* (Foreign Trade 455), 1979.
9. Ibid.
10. U.S. Congress, Joint Economic Committee, op. cit., p. 8.
11. "Bully for Banks, Messy for the Rest," *The Economist*, January 24, 1981, p. 20.
12. Ibid., p. 20.
13. "Bully for Banks Messy for the Rest," op. cit., p. 20.
14. *Middle East Economic Digest*, January 22, 1982, p. 12.
15. *Middle East Economic Digest*, May 14, 1982.

16. Vahe Petrossian, "Iran: Special Report," *Middle East Economic Digest*, November 8, 1984.

17. *Middle East Economic Digest*, April 30, 1982, p. 8.

18. Ibid.

19. Ibid.

20. U.S. Bureau of the Census, *U.S. General Import: World Area by Commodity Grouping* (Foreign Trade 155), 1983.

21. Ibid., 1984.

22. Petrossian, op. cit., p. 8.

23. For details on developments in the oil markets and on prices in 1985 and 1986, see Chapter 11 in this book.

24. U.S. Bureau of the Census, *Highlights of U.S. Exports and Imports Trade* (Foreign Trade 990), 1982.

25. U.S. Bureau of the Census, *U.S. General Import: World Area by Commodity Grouping*, op. cit., 1983, 1984.

26. Ibid.

27. U.S. Bureau of the Census, Department of Commerce, *U.S. Exports-Schedule E Commodities–World Areas by Commodity* (Foreign Trade 455), 1984.

28. Ibid.

29. *Middle East Economic Digest*, September 2, 1983.

30. *Iran Times*, July 7, 1984.

31. Ed Magnuson, *Time*, July 25, 1983.

32. SIPRI, *1984 Yearbook* (London: Taylor & Francis, 1984), p. 197.

33. World Bank, *World Development Report*, 1984.

34. *U.S. General Imports* (New York: Oxford University Press, 1983.)

35. Interview with James Parker, Deputy Assistant Administrator, Commodity and Marketing Programs, Foreign Agricultural Service, U.S. Department of Agriculture, Washington, D.C., October 20, 1984.

36. International Monetary Fund, *World Economic Outlook*, April 1984, p. 56.

PART FOUR

Conclusions

13

Middle-Class Revolutions in the Third World

Hooshang Amirahmadi

Introduction

Third World revolutions, whether socialist or middle class, reflect the failure of dependent capitalism as a model for balanced development, a nationalistic reaction to dependency on imperialism and to underdevelopment, a popular desire for political participation and social justice, and a strong desire to return to the native culture and way of life. Where capitalism has lost its legitimacy and socialist forces have been unable to offer a viable alternative, middle-class revolutions have become increasingly attractive. These revolutions are made by a broad coalition of popular forces under the leadership of the middle-class intelligentsia; such revolutions often adopt an indigenous ideology and are predominantly nationalistic in nature.

The Iranian Revolution is a case in point. Implementation of the capitalist growth model between the 1950s and 1970s generated poverty, income and spatial concentration, uneven sectoral development, dependency, cultural destruction, denationalization, and dictatorship.[1] In conjunction with memories of the Shah's illegitimate return to power with the help of the CIA in 1953 and his despotic methods of governing for more than thirty years, the problems led to the speedy loss of the legitimacy of the *status quo* for the majority. Coupled with a complex of other historical, sociocultural, economic, and political factors (particularly the long and continued legacy of revolutionary political activism), the system's illegitimacy fueled the revolutionary movement that began in 1978.[2]

Among the contending forces, the middle class was most prepared to lead the Iranian Revolution: It had not only quantitative superiority but also qualitative advantage over both the upper and the lower classes. An absolute majority of the Iranian intelligentsia critical of the Shah's policies were among the middle class. A good number of intellectuals among them subscribed to socialist ideals, but many more (both religious and secular) were nationalistic and/or reform-minded.[3] It was natural for a revolution that sought to dispel foreign influences to rely upon a native ideology such as Shi'ah Islam.

In addition to satisfying the nationalistic/progressive ideals of the protesting people, Shi'ah Islam promised a regeneration of the lost cultural/ideological identity. The cross-class and universal character of the ideology made it particularly attractive to the crowd in the streets, who needed national unity above all. The distance between choosing Islam and accepting the leadership of the charismatic Ayatollah Khomeini was only a short one. Ayatollah Khomeini had remained uncompromising to the Shah and was able to articulate the many ideals of the people both in his speeches and through the practical leadership of the Iranian Revolution.[4] Nothing significant in the historical memories of the Iranian people had suggested that the Islamic leadership might break its promise to realize the revolutionary demands of social justice, democracy, and national independence. It is thus not surprising that Islam captured the spirit of the Iranian Revolution and became hegemonic in a very short time.

Imperialism and Third World Revolutions

The primary purposes of imperialism in its struggle against middle-class revolutions are to moderate their leaders, direct them toward accepting existing international arrangements, and prevent them from making policy changes that would undermine capitalist forces at home or the interests of imperialism worldwide. Imperialism also tries to nurture anti-communism in the post-revolutionary societies and puts increasing pressure on the middle-class leadership to adapt an anti-Soviet international policy. Finally, imperialism attempts to prevent middle-class revolutions from supporting revolutionary movements elsewhere in the world. Instead, it expects the leadership to cooperate with the movements against Third World revolutions.

Imperialism uses a variety of methods and means, violent and peaceful, covert and overt, to achieve its goals. Armed aggressions, direct and/or indirect (acting through the domestic "fifth column," exiled oppositions, and/or friendly states in the region), are usually used when all other methods have failed to produce the intended results.[5] Destabilizing campaigns, on the other hand, tend to begin immediately after the middle class seizes state power. Money, organization, moral support, and intrigues are used to exploit ethnic, racial, religious, ideological, and political differences in the country; diplomatic pressures and disinformation campaigns are applied to isolate the revolution and inflict damage on its credibility in the international community; and material sabotage—including destruction of production and infrastructural facilities, trade sanctions, and financial restrictions—is employed to exacerbate existing socioeconomic problems, thereby creating dissatisfaction among the population and stirring riots.

Economic pressure is particularly damaging to post-revolutionary Third World societies, especially the ones led by the middle class. Long after their revolutions, these societies continue to remain dependent on the capitalist world economy for the volume, flow, and prices of their exports, foreign exchange, industrial inputs, technology, finance, and food items. Most of these and other resources, including means of mass communication and cultural domination, are in the monopoly of a few transnational corporations antagonistic to Third World revolutions of any kind. Moreover, most Third World countries depend on a single export commodity, such as oil, coffee, and certain minerals, for their foreign-exchange earnings, and, therefore, are particularly vulnerable to the whims of the international economy.[6]

Thus, for the Third World, many of the key parameters for changing the logic of the post-revolutionary economy, from one based on accumulation for profit to one directed toward the basic needs of the population, are determined externally—in particular, by hostile transnational firms. Most multilateral agencies, including the World Bank and the International Monetary Fund, also follow the dictates of imperialism, making any economic pressure imposed against post-revolutionary societies even more damaging.[7] If dependency on the world economy is the major cause underlying Third World articulation in the capitalist world economy, the reverse dependency of the latter on the former has largely diminished the chances for their immediate or easy disarticulation. Thus, while an anti-capitalist and self-reliant development strategy would become extremely hard to manage, the success of the alternative "open policy" would largely depend on the leadership's attitude toward imperialism.

Third World middle-class revolutions also have friends outside their borders. The socialist bloc is supportive, although it remains uncommitted to the survival of these revolutions. Progressive forces within imperialist countries and national liberation movements are important sources of strength for middle-class revolutions. Such revolutions might attain additional benefits by exploiting the power politics in imperialist countries (e.g., those between the conservatives and the liberals) whose leaders must operate within the constitutional limits imposed on the executive branch. Middle-class revolutions might also take advantage of the competition between capitalism and socialism and of intra-imperialist rivalry. Various regional and commodity integration schemes (e.g., OPEC) might equally be used to further strengthen the revolution in question. The United Nations might also be able to help in special circumstances. Imperialism, however, attempts to neutralize or weaken these sources of strength whenever and wherever possible in order to increase its control over the post-revolutionary period.

The consequences of imperialism's armed aggression and/or destabilizing campaigns for middle-class revolutions and post-revolutionary societies are tremendous, in both their positive and negative manifestations. The transfer of scarce resources, including that of energetic and productive young people from the generally underdeveloped basic industries to the defense sector, significantly reduces the economic production of the post-revolutionary society and undermines the state's social programs. The export sector usually suffers the most, thereby exacerbating the foreign-exchange crisis and creating repercussions for the dependent industries and food imports.

These problems are further aggravated by the imposition of economic sanctions and other international restrictions.

Coupled with war destruction and other types of damage, declines in the supply of resources and production lead to unemployment, inflationary pressure, and reduction in the living standard of the majority. Rationing and price control become logical solutions to hyper-inflation and declining real income, but they also become sources of dissatisfaction among people inasmuch as the policies produce black markets and lead to uneven distribution of available consumption items. Among the negative consequences of armed aggression and destabilizing campaigns by imperialism are reduction in information flow and curtailment of democratic freedoms.

The middle class may also experience positive effects: The revolution may become consolidated as its military strength increases; continuing ideological mobilization may lead to the alienation of opposing ideologies; and the society may gradually become disentangled from the capitalist world economy as it is forced to find innovative ways to deal with its enormous problems. The overall effect of imperialism, however, is generally negative.

In the specific case of Iran, many of the above-mentioned methods have yielded mixed results for imperialism (i.e., in terms of the achievement of its objectives), but with devastating consequences for the Iranian economy and the people.[8] Destabilizing campaigns against the Islamic Republic began when the Islamic leadership made a shift to radical politics in order to drive the "liberals" out of the government. This move coincided with the hostage crisis (which lasted from November 4, 1979, to January 20, 1981) and the increasing hostility of the Islamic Republic toward imperialism. The Iran-Iraq War, which began in September 1980 at the peak of the hostage crisis, cannot be reduced in essence to a simple imperialistic plot. But it also cannot be understood in isolation from the overall strategy of imperialism toward the Iranian Revolution and, more generally, in the Middle East. While Saddam Hussein had his own reasons for invading Iran (e.g., so that he could become the new regional power after the downfall of the Shah), the U.S. government's tacit approval of the aggression was probably based on its intention both to punish Iran for taking American hostages and to moderate the Islamic leadership. Aggression and destabilizing campaigns against the Islamic Republic were exemplified to an equal degree by a few unsuccessful military coups, the most ambitious of which was centered in the Nuzheh air base near Hamadan in July 1980; by the CIA-funded activities of the Iranian exile contras, such as the Tribal Alliance of Iran; by periodic economic sanctions, the last of which was announced in October 1987; by continuous diplomatic pressures on the leadership through friendly individuals and states, as well as through the United Nations; by covert initiatives such as the one that culminated in the so-called Irangate scandal; and by the recent U.S. attacks on Iranian targets in the Gulf.

In retrospect, every armed aggression seems to have followed a period of intense but unsuccessful diplomatic initiatives and economic pressures. Insofar as imperialism remains unhappy with the policies of the Islamic

Republic, and to the extent that the Islamic leadership remains distrustful of the real intentions of imperialism and considers it an illegitimate, domineering player in world politics, the negotiation-cum-aggression cycle will continue. In other words, the Islamic Republic, distrusting socialism and under the pressure created by enormous problems, will continue to regulate its relationship with imperialism; at the same time, its hatred for imperialism will prevent it from changing its attitude, thus inviting pressure and aggression against itself.

The war and many destabilizing campaigns may not have changed the attitude of the Islamic leadership toward imperialism, but they have certainly had a tremendous impact on the society of post-revolutionary Iran.[9] Economic production—particularly by the oil-export sector—has declined significantly, with devastating effects on Iranian foreign-exchange earnings and, consequently, on its dependent industries. Economic decline has also translated into cuts in social and developmental programs, high unemployment and inflation, and reduction in the real income of the majority of Iranians. The government's rationing and price-control policies, in the absence of an effective distributive policy, have led to the emergence of black markets and to a shortage of consumption items in controlled markets.[10] In the meantime, however, the Islamic Republic has used the war and the destabilizing campaigns to consolidate its newly created institutions (including military and para-military forces),[11] curtail information flow to the public, restrict democratic measures, and eliminate domestic organized oppositions. On balance, therefore, the impact of imperialism has been unquestionably negative for the Iranian Revolution.

Models of Development and the Middle Class

Current middle-class revolutions are occurring largely in reaction to the consequences of the capitalist growth model (or strategy) for development. This model is dismissed by the middle-class leadership as inappropriate for post-revolutionary transformations. It is considered too economistic and efficiency oriented for post-revolutionary societies, in which the existing political structures and ideology would have to be transformed and in which demands for equity and social services run high.[12]

The growth-with-equity strategy of capitalist development has also been dismissed as inappropriate. Although this model seeks to mitigate socioeconomic imbalances by means of certain reforms (e.g., in land tenure and education) and through reorientation of priorities (e.g., toward increased investments in agriculture, rural development, intermediate technologies, basic needs, and social services), it fails to tackle the larger problems of underdevelopment and dependency primarily because of its neo-Malthusian view of limits to growth and anti-industrialism. The middle-class leadership also criticizes the model for both its acceptance of capitalist institutions and its call for a reformed version of existing international arrangements under the banner of the New International Economic Order. Finally, assumptions of rational economic behavior and political stability underlying the growth and growth-with-equity capitalist development models make them significantly less applicable to the situations of rapid change and violent politics found in most post-revolutionary societies.

The middle-class leadership is equally nonsympathetic to socialist models of development, including the Soviet and Chinese models and the "non-capitalist way of development."[13] These models are dismissed for radically different reasons than those cited for rejections of the capitalist models. Specifically, they require large-scale nationalization of major means of production and services, extensive public management, central planning, and a radical redistributive policy. But these measures do not fit the popular (i.e., middle-class) vision of the desired post-revolutionary society. Their implementation also goes beyond the skills and technologies available to the leadership, particularly inasmuch as many technocrats of the old system tend to leave the country after a revolution. Undue emphasis on equality and on anti-entrepreneurship also leads to economic inefficiency and tends to kill individual initiative. Moreover, the models are disliked for their partisanship, ideological loads, political radicalism, and tendency to create and maintain inefficient large bureaucracies. Finally, the allegation has been made that socialism seeks a material society in which spiritual motivations and family ties are significantly undermined.

The middle class's rejection of both the capitalist and socialist models of development is not grounded only or even largely on their policy prescriptions or outcomes. Indeed, the so-called "third way" of development that is sought or implemented by most middle-class revolutions includes elements from both models. The lack of affinity with the models also, and perhaps mainly, emanates from the middle class's fear of dependency on the superpowers; from its deep sense of nationalism, which is generated in response to the models' lack of sensitivity to local history, culture, and way of life; and from its fear of losing newly acquired economic privileges and political power to either the lower or the upper class. The political prestige and propaganda advantages gained by rejecting the "non-native" models and the intellectual/psychological satisfaction associated with searching for an alternative in the wake of post-revolutionary enthusiasm are additional sources of motivation for dismissing the capitalist and socialist models of development.

It is thus natural that most middle-class revolutions in search of an alternative road to development should adopt or attempt to initiate models deeply rooted in native cultures, national characters, and religious ideals. Examples include Peronism in Argentina, Nasserism in Egypt, the Arab nationalism promulgated by the Ba'th parties in Iraq and Syria, African socialism (including Arusha Declaration in Tanzania and the Algerian national liberation revolution), Islamic radicalism in Libya and Iran, and numerous populist movements around the world.[14] Despite many differences, these experiences have one major characteristic in common: After an initial ideological period, they tend to submit to the tension between the middle-class utopia and the mandates of the real world. A frequent result is the emergence of an eclectic pragmatic approach as various pieces from different strategies are juxtaposed to arrive at a workable model. The emergent model is initially progressive; however, as pragmatism dominates the mentality of the agencies making policy decisions, ideology loses its potency and the revolution begins to slip toward moderation and reformism.[15] What imperialism is not able to achieve on its own can thus be accomplished by the collective forces of objective conditions in the post-revolutionary society.

The search for a third way has also occupied the ideologues and policy-makers of the Islamic Republic since the Revolution in 1979.[16] They dismissed the existing socialist and capitalist models for almost the same reasons as those already discussed—citing, above all, the specificities of Islam and of Iranian traditions and culture. The ensuing debates as to what constitutes these specificities and how they should be incorporated into a development strategy for the new Republic have been presented to the public in many forms, but they have also been withheld from the people for political reasons. In fact, a body of experts has been appointed to define the many elements of an ideal Islamic society. The earliest comprehensive delineation of that society was given in the Islamic Constitution, which characterizes the economy as comprising three sectors (public, private, and cooperative) and specifies national independence, social justice, and democracy as the three fundamental goals of the Islamic Republic.[17] Of particular emphasis is the cultural transformation of the post-revolutionary society on the basis not only of these goals but also of Islamic values and national traditions. However, subsequent attempts to formulate a coherent and consistent development strategy on the basis of the Constitution have generated many ideological debates, political conflicts, and practical difficulties.

Hence, despite the apparent shift from strictly ideological considerations toward a more pragmatic policy in recent years, a unified position on many fundamental development issues has not yet emerged.[18] These issues include the extent to which the private sector should be allowed to accumulate wealth and to engage in the management of the society, self-sufficiency versus integration into the world economy, the proper mix of modernity and tradition in culture and the use of technology, the conflict between economic growth and social justice in a declining war economy, the place of regional development in national economic planning, state-society relations with respect to decentralization and public participation, organization of the masses in sectoral and spatial councils, the place of cooperatives in the economy, and, above all, the multidisciplinary problems that possible introduction of democracy would create. Factors influencing the lack of consensus on these and other development issues include the tension between Islam as a cross-class ideology and middle-class interest (or, more precisely, the vision of these interest held by key leaders and ideologues), the war with Iraq, factional politics, enormous domestic problems, and external constraints.

Nevertheless, the mix of ideological and pragmatic debates along with attempts to cope with a dependent war economy have led to the accumulation of considerable knowledge about the development needs and obstacles, available resources, and required means of obtaining those resources, in post-revolutionary Iran. In addition, scores of massive and important legal and policy documents have been produced. Although many of these have not been implemented, they can be taken as crude indications of the type of pragmatic (i.e., less ideological) development strategy that might yet emerge in the Islamic Republic.

In brief, the Islamic development strategy will most likely resemble a mixed market/planning framework incorporating elements of capitalist and socialist strategies as well as certain fundamental aspects of Islam and the national traditions. Specifically, the public, private, and cooperative sectors will coexist in continuous competition, with the former sector dominating industrial production, banking, infrastructures, and social services, and the latter two sectors handling agriculture, small-scale productive activities, and consumption/distribution services. The impact of Islam and the national traditions would be felt particularly at the level of sociocultural and ideological relations between the state and the society, among the people, and within the family institution. Education and the judiciary would probably become the most Islamicized.

Post-Revolutionary Transformation

A political revolution can claim the status of a social revolution only if it successfully transforms the old society into a new one. Among the critical elements of the old society to be transformed are ideology (including culture), politics, and economics (including social sectors). These structures should be changed not only at the national level but also at the levels of international relations and local communities. The transformation should begin immediately following the capture of the political power in question but must proceed gradually and with utmost tolerance for inherited structures. The art of transformation should involve the integration of indispensable old structure and emerging new structures at all societal levels. The transformation should also exhibit a clear sense of the intended ends and targets as well as of the means and methods required. Transformation of the post-revolutionary society thus demands a deep theoretical understanding of the old and the new society in addition to a well-conceived and coherent development strategy.

Post-revolutionary transformations are faced with both opportunities and constraints. The impacts of adversaries and friends abroad have been detailed earlier. The extreme sensitivity of imperialist forces to policies and actions designed to change the old system emanates from their fear of the radicalism of middle-class revolutions as well as from their geostrategic concerns. In attempting to block post-revolutionary transformations, imperialism is assisted by enormous domestic constraints. These include problems inherited from the old system and difficulties created by the revolution itself. Influences from the nature of the old system, the tactics of the movement, and the composition of the opposition and the leadership are also powerful. The resiliency to change of an old system that works, at least for a minority, and the extremist politics of the opposition and the leadership are particularly damaging to revolutionary goals. Additional difficulties emanate from institutional constraints, material shortages and external dependency, lack of adequate managerial and technical skills (a situation worsened in the short run by the departure of educated people from the country), in-fighting within the state, and the absence of a coherent development strategy.

These international and domestic constraints are only partly neutralized by limited support from friends abroad (e.g., socialist countries) and the domestic opportunities generated by the revolution itself. Specifically, middle-class revolutions liberate the majority from the yoke of the minority and transform the mostly passive pre-revolutionary crowd into a highly motivated, conscientious, creative, and energetic group. The liberation of these new hands and minds also generates massive energies, enthusiasm, innovative ideas, new organizations, and fresh means of social transformation.

Ideology

The ideological transformation of the post-revolutionary society is particularly problematic.[19] The middle class has many ideas but no ideology of its own. It makes its revolution against the dominant ideology (usually dependent capitalism) by means of a borrowed ideology (usually nationalism or the native religion). The old dominant ideology is generally conservative and tends to fix or otherwise distort the real essence of the existing social order. Thus, the new dominant ideology must not only offer a true analysis of reality but must also call for change. In addition, it must be able to wed theory with practice, make agents of change fully aware of the implications of their practice, and develop an understanding of capitalist imperialism as a global economic-military complex. Dogmatism is the number-one enemy of such an ideology; the new ideology must be open and critical.

The ideological transformation faces two parallel processes: delegitimization of the old dominant ideology and adaptation of the borrowed hegemonic (cross-class) ideology to the specific needs and interests of the middle class. In the case of Iran, borrowed hegemonic ideology was Islam, the native universal religion.[20] Although Islam had won the competition for the capture of the majority even before the victory of the political revolution in 1979, the struggle for its adaptation as the ideology of the post-revolutionary state began almost immediately.[21] Despite a loss of legitimacy, the old dominant dependent capitalist ideology was retained by upper-class Iranians, the inherited socioeconomic and political structures, and various public and private institutions. Its further delegitimization took the form of denouncement of dependency, dictatorship, and the injustices of capitalism; it also took the form of attacks on any signs of westernization. Both religious and secular forces (the Left and the "liberal" nationalists) participated in the crusade against the ideology of the Pahlavi state.[22]

Soon, however, hegemonic Islam turned against the other competing ideologies (including socialism, nationalism, liberalism, Left, Islamism, and regionalism) in order to firmly establish its dominance.[23] This process, which was both peaceful and violent, led to the propagation of alternatives for the post-revolutionary society. The alternative of hegemonic Islam is spelled out in the Constitution of the Islamic Republic and was accepted in entirety by the majority, despite disagreements over certain details. The subsequent Islamization of the state, particularly in the areas of law, justice, and education, has had a profound impact on Iranian society.[24] Hegemonic Islam is cross-class in nature, however, hence its interests extend beyond the interests of the middle class. As the middle class itself also encompasses several factions (each with distinct interests), the use of Islam as the class ideology has become even more problematic. Thus, the adaptation of hegemonic Islam as the new state's ideology (i.e., as the ideology of a dominant faction of the middle class) resulted unavoidably in inter-class and intra-class struggles. These initially intense conflicts have become more moderate over time as hegemonic Islam has eliminated many rivals and allowed for a more liberal and pragmatic interpretation of its tenets.

Politics

The political transformation of the post-revolutionary society is even more formidable.[25] The middle class has no clear political stance and is constantly vacillating between extremism and moderation. Its leadership, too, faces difficulties inherited from the previous regime, including impaired political independence, dictatorship and repression, centralism, bureaucratism of governance and decision-making, and corruption. It is not surprising that middle-class revolutions should make national independence, democracy, and popular participation central to their revolutionary demands. Of these, the first demand is usually achieved despite continued economic dependence on the capitalist world market. Most post-revolutionary states assume a non-aligned position in world politics at least in the early revolutionary years. However, the realization of the other two demands—particularly democracy—faces considerable odds.

The Islamic Republic is politically independent and perhaps one of the best examples of nonaligned countries in the world.[26] Its famous "No East, No West" slogan seems deeply genuine despite the Republic's continued economic dependency on the capitalist world market. It has been trying hard to project its ideology to the Third World as a real alternative to the ideologies of capitalism and socialism. However, implementation of other political goals of the Revolution, particularly popular participation in the management of the post-revolutionary society, has not been equally successful.[27] Although the Iranian Revolution generated considerable mass participation, its formal institutionalization remains largely limited to a few "Revolutionary Institutions" (*Nihadha-ye Enghelabi*). At present, participation in the governance of the state, decision-making, planning, and policy-setting range from inadequate at the lower and intermediate levels to completely absent at the higher echelons of the bureaucratic hierarchy. Despite attempts to decentralize certain state functions, centralism persists in the Islamic Republic. The failure to decentralize is partly due to the fact that the old unitary (as opposed to federal) and sectoral (as opposed to regional) structure of the state remains largely intact. The ongoing war with Iraq, conflict with the Kurds, attempts to cope with destabilizing forces, and expansion of the public sector of the economy are among the other factors contributing to continued centralism under the Islamic Republic.

The most pressing political problem of the Republic, however, is the lack of democracy, particularly where the dissidents and political opposition are concerned. The Constitution recognizes representative democracy, allows dissent, and guarantees considerable democratic rights for individuals and institutions, especially in the realms of basic needs, social justice, speech, ideology, the private press, organization, and participation in the politics of society. It also delineates the various means for implementation, including consultation (e.g., through Parliament and through the sectoral and spatial councils), free and open elections, establishment of the necessary mediating institutions, and political appointments. In practice, however, democracy remains an abstraction. Many observers of Iranian politics have tried to explain the country's lack of democracy in terms of the restrictive nature of Islam as a religion of obedient followers and the Supreme Will.[28] But this argument fails to acknowledge that Shi'ah Islam also encourages self-esteem and liberty as well as bravery and rebellion.[29]

The major factor contributing to the lack of democracy in the Islamic Republic is political instability (both real and perceived), caused by the war with Iraq, the destabilizing campaign being waged by imperialist forces, the extremist politics of the Left and the Right, the Kurdish autonomy movement, and the autonomous activities of many grass-roots organizations within a state that is still in its formative stage. Democracy in Iran also suffers from the legacy of the Shah's dictatorship, centralist orientation, and disregard for human rights.[30] In addition, the lack of a democratic tradition in Iran reflects the country's extremely low tolerance for criticism and opposing views, the absence of a decentralized decision-making system, and the lack of institutions designed to mediate political differences (including grass-roots organizations and trained personnel). Not only are these obstructive factors still in place, but the Islamic Republic has created additional barriers in the course of its struggle against the destabilizing forces. Examples of these new obstructions include the imposition of Islamic codes on individuals (particularly women) and on family life as well as behavioral and cultural restrictions. Finally, democracy in Iran suffers from the lack of legality, security, and a theory of dissent. While the state is unable to incorporate the opposition as a legitimizing force, the opposition is completely confused about the limits of its legal rights.

Economics

The economic transformation of the post-revolutionary society constitutes the most difficult task facing the middle-class leadership. On the one hand, revolution imposes demands for economic sovereignty and social justice. On the other hand, many of the key parameters (e.g., prices, technology, finance) for achieving these goals are externally determined. Added to the problem of external dependency are the economic and extra-economic difficulties that imperialism creates for radical middle-class revolutions. The inability of the middle class to formulate a coherent development strategy further complicates the task of economic transformation. Additional problems arise from the shortage of resources, including skilled personnel, material and institutional bottlenecks, and the smallness of the market. Yet the leadership continues its considerable efforts to transform the post-revolutionary economy, according to the demands of the middle class, to create a largely independent, equitable, and mixed economy.[31] The efforts are, however, only partially successful. The initial self-reliant strategy is changed to a policy of diversifying the sources of dependency, the concern for equity is balanced with a similar concern for efficiency, and the private sector is gradually expanded at the expense of the public sector in the mixed economy.

Despite such unique factors as a long and destructive war, the dominance of the oil sector in the economy, and the hegemonic role of Islam in the Revolution, the Iranian experience closely confirms the lesson of economic transformation under middle-class leadership in post-revolutionary Third World societies.[32] Specifically, the Islamic Constitution incorporates the goals of economic sovereignty, social justice, and a mixed economy. These were to be achieved by means of a strategy emphasizing self-reliance, contentment, social reforms, asset redistribution, expansion of the public sector, and structural changes in sectoral/spatial dimensions of the economy. Planning was to guide the market forces. After some initial efforts and under mounting international and domestic problems, the state had to revise its policies, including the call for an Islamic economic system, in favor of a more pragmatic approach focusing on the maximum utilization of the existing productive capacities, stimulation of the export sector, and diversification of sources of dependency.

Economic sovereignty was to be achieved by means of a self-reliant strategy. Even before the war destroyed the Iranian oil installations, oil production had been cut back substantially from the pre-revolutionary period in an attempt to reduce the dependency of the economy on this single export commodity and, consequently, on the capitalist world market.[33] Many of the large-scale industries had been closed, and others were working with substantially reduced capacity because of labor-management disputes and/or the lack of inputs for which they were more than 55 percent dependent on the world market. Except for a few strategic units, the state made only limited efforts to revive these industries, out of a fear of perpetuating dependency. Instead, its attempts focused on reviving agriculture and promoting small-scale productive units by means of various credit and price-support policies. A parallel policy of import-substitution industrialization and protectionism was also followed in the hope of stimulating domestic production of certain durable and nondurable consumer products. Most new industrial investments went to production units that used more local inputs. These and other similar policies were complemented by a policy of encouraging contentment on the part of the population. The mass media was used to convince the people that national independence could not be achieved without an acceptance of hardship in the short run and, in particular, that sacrifices had to be made in the standard of living. It also denounced the "Western pattern of consumption" as non-Islamic and harmful to the goal of self-sufficiency.[34]

The goal of social justice was to be achieved by means of certain reforms and changes in national priorities. A Seven-Member Council was formed to look into the land question and the Land Reform Bill, and several measures were adopted.[35] A Housing Foundation was created to provide housing for the poor, particularly in urban areas.[36] The Ministry of Plan and Budget was directed to allocate national resources more equitably throughout the provinces. The Reconstruction Crusade (now a ministry) was established to provide rural areas with electricity, water, feeder roads, schools, health clinics, and housing among other social and infrastructural services. Legislation was passed to reduce the gap among wage rates, resulting in a 60 percent boost to workers' wages. A policy of price support in the form of subsidies for basic-need items was instituted to protect the poorer groups from the rampant inflation that had followed the economic decline during the Revolution. Finally, modifications were proposed in the tax system both to make it more progressive and to prevent excessive concentration of wealth in the hands of a few. Nationalization of major industries, banks, insurance companies, and foreign trade weakened further prospects of emerging large-scale private accumulation. The Constitution had already made nationalization mandatory, along with the provision of jobs and affordable social services for every citizen of the nation.

The mixed-economy objective was to be achieved through the creation of a leading state sector, a subordinate private sector, and a balancing cooperative sector. The economy was to be planned and publicly managed, with market mechanisms and policy tools to be used in conjunction with private and collective management. The state decided early in the post-revolutionary period that the share of the oil sector would decline as a portion of the gross national product but that agricultural and industrial shares would increase. The service sector was to gain little or nothing at all. The policy aimed at a more productive economy. Although both large- and small-scale production units were supported, the latter were favored and received more direct public support for the first time since the 1950s. The technology policy followed a similar pattern: Capital-intensive technologies were to continue while labor-intensive techniques using local resources were highly encouraged in the hope of reducing technological dependency on the West and of generating jobs for the growing unemployed population.

Most of these policies, which were attempted at different times during the post-revolutionary period up to the end of 1982, were subsequently suspended, reversed, or modified under enormous domestic and international pressure.[37] Even before the war began, politics had become polarized as the leadership moved to monopolize power and the opposition responded. At one and the same time, a radical shift of the state's policies toward imperialism manifested itself in the hostage crisis (November 1974–January 1981) and a call for export of the Revolution. Imperialism responded with diplomatic pressure, economic sanctions, and destabilizing campaigns. Then came the Iran-Iraq war in September 1980, less than two years after the victory of the Revolution. The political polarization had already crippled the state's attempts to formulate a coherent development strategy. The First Social, Economic, and Cultural Development Plan of the Islamic Republic (1983–1988) had to be shelved because of factional politics within the state.[38] Conflicts within the power bloc had also encouraged the intensification of the extra-legal activities of the poor peasants to obtain land, the workers to obtain control and management of large industrial units, the urban poor to obtain housing, and the national minorities to obtain a degree of autonomy. The added pressure from imperialism and the war only worsened the significant decline that the economy had been experiencing since the start of the Revolution in late 1977.[39]

The oil sector, on which the country depended for more than 95 percent of its foreign-exchange earnings, was the main and most immediate casualty of the war.[40] Its production declined to well below the desired level. Soon after, many of the remaining Iranian dependent industries, which were still operational, had to be shut down or operated at significantly reduced capacity. Further decline in the supply of goods and services exacerbated the already double-digit inflation and unemployment rates. Propagation of the ideology of contentment became hard to justify as hardship became a fact of life for the majority in the country. The war continued to create additional human, material, and financial problems while usurping more than one-third of the state budget. It also generated additional needs for foreign exchange at a time when oil production was not picking up and oil prices were in general decline.

Pressure began building up for revisions in the policies of self-reliance, social justice, and a balanced mixed economy in the beginning of 1983. This pressure took many forms. Support for agriculture, rural and regional development, small-scale productive units, labor-intensive techniques, major economic reforms, and social services was reduced. Wages and employment were frozen in the state sector, but price subsidies for basic consumption items continued. Taxes were increased in an attempt to reduce dependency on oil, but also to boost the public budget. Under the new policy, deficit spending became acceptable to the government, and a more active role was given to the private sector and to market mechanisms. A number of nationalized industries were sold to the public or returned to their original owners, and the role of the cooperative sector in the economy remained weak and ambiguous. Modern technology again became acceptable to planners and policy-makers.[41]

The money saved was not, however, put to use in building new industrial capacities. Rather, it went partly to the war effort, in payment of operating expenses and as investments for restructuring certain industries in the direction of defense production. Of the remaining part, a sizable portion was directed toward the completion of ongoing projects and the improvement of existing capacities in the oil and large-scale industrial sectors. To maximize the utilization rate of the existing industries, the government began removing obstacles in the areas of infrastructure and management in particular. In the meantime, a policy of diversifying the sources of dependency on exports and imports was pursued and barter trades were expanded with the socialist nations. The hope was that these changes would generate the needed foreign exchange, that dependency would remain under control, and that economic growth would be stimulated to make continuation of the war possible. The new policies also meant to improve management of the creeping inflation and unemployment and of the declining real income of the majority.[42]

Although they initially looked feasible, the new policies soon ran into domestic and international difficulties similar to those afflicting the previous self-reliant/equity-based policies. The state was again unable to develop a strategy that would systematically apply and coordinate the policies, and the lack of logical relations among various state actions made intra-governmental cooperation for removing obstacles to industrial growth extremely difficult. Despite a reduction in social and development programs, the additional money generated by increased taxation could not be earmarked for growth purposes; war activities had to be expanded. More important, the policy of diversifying the sources of dependency for exports and imports was only marginally successful. The price of oil continued to be determined within the capitalist world market, where the bulk of Iranian foreign trade was carried out—regardless of the West's periodic economic sanctions against the Islamic Republic.[43] The trade with socialist and Third World countries, except for Turkey and Pakistan, did not expand to any significant degree despite frequent policy pronouncements to the contrary. With the failure of the new policies and worsening economic problems, the state turned to an Emergency Plan in 1986 and has since been trying to find a more feasible alternative to the strategies implemented thus far.

Conclusions

A host of socioeconomic, political, cultural, and historical factors, including undesirable living conditions under dependent capitalism in the Third World, often leads to the system's illegitimacy for the majority and fuels the middle-class or socialist revolutions. Third World revolutions achieve political independence in the form of a nonaligned international policy and create enormous possibilities for a new social organization of post-revolutionary societies. They generate massive energies and enthusiasm, new and creative ideas, innovative means of social transformations, high-powered expectations, and friends throughout the world. But before these potentials could be translated into a purposeful practice for the creation of a new middle-class society, equally powerful constraints begin to develop, some by the actions of the leadership itself and others by various hostile domestic and international forces.

The most important factors preventing middle-class revolutions in the Third World from realizing their visionary society include the capitalist world economy on which the post-revolutionary societies continue to depend, various imperialist destabilizing campaigns, polarized domestic politics, the inability of the middle-class leadership to advance its version of a coherent development strategy, institutional obstacles, and the lack of needed material, managerial, and/or financial resources. The middle-class leadership, however, will continue to struggle against all these and other odds until it is convinced that its utopia cannot be realized without serious compromises and that moderation is the only hope for survival or peaceful coexistence in a largely hostile world. Historical experiences indicate that if these revolutions are not overthrown by a bourgeois counterrevolution, they gradually develop into a reformist state capitalism with a more or less native cultural identity and tightly controlled politics. In the meantime, these revolutions hang on the opposite poles of borrowed ideology and pragmatism, conflicting policy pronouncements, and contradictory actions. Algeria and Tanzania are examples. Whether the Islamic Republic will also develop in this direction remains to be seen. Clearly, the Islamic ideology and the specificities of Iranian culture would have significant impact on the teleology of the Islamic Republic. Yet there are indications that the Iranian experience will correspond to those of other Third World middle-class revolutions.

Still, my conclusion concerning the limits of Third World middle-class revolutions is a conditional one: These revolutions will continue to occur regardless of the results so long as the demands for national independence, social justice, and democracy remain legitimate. Motivation can also be drawn from tensions between socialism and capitalism and among various domestic interest groups. Moreover, if the present trends are any indication, the forces constraining middle-class revolutions in the Third World are in gradual decline, whereas opportunities for their success are widening. The future of imperialism is hardly bright, given its foreign-policy failures and its recurrent internal crises. In sharp contrast, Third World middle-class revolutions are increasing in strength. The aspirations prompting these revolutions are derived from socialism, from supportive progressive forces around the world, and from the revived ideologies of Islam in the Middle East and the liberation theology in Latin America.[44] In the final analysis, the desire for political independence, social justice, national dignity, and cultural revival will remain among the strongest motivating factors behind most Third World revolutions, middle-class or socialist.

Notes

1. Hooshang Amirahmadi, "Regional Planning in Iran: A Survey of Problems and Policies," *The Journal of Developing Areas*, vol. 20, no. 4 (July 1986), pp. 501–530; Hooshang Amirahmadi and Farhad Atash, "Dynamics of Provincial Development and Disparity in Iran, 1956–1984," *Third World Planning Review*, vol. 9, no. 2 (May

1987), pp. 155–185; Robert Looney, *Economic Origins of the Iranian Revolution* (New York: Pergamon Press, 1982); Thomas Walton, "Economic Development and Revolutionary Upheavals in Iran," *Cambridge Journal of Economics*, no. 4 (1980), pp. 271–292; Farhad Kazemi, *Poverty and Revolution in Iran* (New York: New York University Press, 1980); Homa Katouzian, *Political Economy of Modern Iran, 1926–1979* (New York: New York University Press, 1981); Ervand Abrahamian, *Iran Between Two Revolutions* (Princeton, N.J.: Princeton University Press, 1982); Nikki Keddie, *Roots of Revolution* (New Haven, Conn.: Yale University Press, 1981); Robert Graham, *Iran: The Illusion of Power* (New York: St. Martin's Press, 1979); Hossain Razavi and Firouz Vakil, *The Political Environment of Economic Planning in Iran, 1971–1983* (Boulder, Colo.: Westview Press, 1984); M.M.H. Malek, *The Political Economy of Iran Under the Shah* (London: Croom Helms, 1986); and Eric J. Hooglund, *Land and Revolution in Iran, 1960–1980* (Austin, Tex.: University of Texas Press, 1982).

2. *Iranian Revolution in Perspective*, a special issue of the journal of *Iranian Studies*, vol. 13, nos. 1–4 (1980). See here pp. 369–390 for a bibliographical survey of the Iranian Revolution. See also William H. Forbis, *Fall of the Peacock Throne: The Story of Iran* (New York: McGraw-Hill, 1981); Amin Saikal, *The Rise and Fall of the Shah* (Princeton, N.J.: Princeton University Press, 1980); Graham, op. cit.; Abrahamian, op. cit.; Richard Cottam, "Goodby to America's Shah," *Foreign Policy*, no. 34 (Spring 1979), pp. 3–14; James Bill, "Iran and the Crisis of 1978," *Foreign Affairs*, no. 57 (Winter 1978–1979), pp. 323–342; Mansour Farhang, "The Revolution in Iran," *Inquiry* (April 1979), pp. 13–16; Fred Halliday, *Iran: Dictatorship and Development* (New York: Penguin Books, 1979); Ahmad Jabbari and Robert Olson (eds.), *Iran: Essays on a Revolution in the Making* (Lexington, Ky.: Mazda Publishers, 1981); Ahmad Ashraf and Ali Banuazizi, "The State, Classes and Modes of Mobilization in the Iranian Revolution," *State, Culture and Society*, vol. 1, no. 3 (Spring 1985), pp. 3–40; Theda Skocpol, "Rentier State and Shi'ah Islam in the Iranian Revolution," *Theory and Society*, vol. 11, no. 3 (May 1982), pp. 265–283; Richard Cottam, *Nationalism in Iran* (Pittsburgh, Penn.: University of Pittsburgh Press, 1979); Barry Rubin, *Paved With Good Intentions: The American Experience and Iran* (New York: Oxford University Press, 1980); and Michael Fischer, *Iran: From Religious Dispute to Revolution* (Cambridge, Mass.: Harvard University Press, 1980).

3. Hossein Bashiriyeh, *The State and Revolution in Iran* (London: Croom Helms, 1986); H. Adibi, *Tabaqah-e Moutavaset-e Jadid Dar Iran* [New Middle Class in Iran] (Tehran: Jame'ah Publications, 1979); Graham, op. cit., Chapter 12; Abrahamian, op. cit.; and Keddie, op. cit.

4. Abrahamian, op. cit., pp. 530–535.

5. Roger Burbach, "The Conflict at Home and Abroad: U.S. Imperialism vs. the New Revolutionary Societies," in Richard Fagen et al. (eds.), *Transition and Development: Problems of Third World Socialism* (New York: Monthly Review Press, 1986), pp. 79–96.

6. Michael Conroy, "External Dependence, External Assistance, and Economic Aggression against Nicaragua," *Latin American Perspectives*, vol. 12, no. 2 (1985).

7. M. Manley, *Jamaica: Struggle in a Periphery* (London: Writers and Readers Publishing Cooperative Society, 1982); J. R. Mandel, "Jamaican Democratic Socialism and the Strike of Capital," in C. K. Chase-Dunn (ed.), *Socialist States in the World-System* (Beverly Hills, Calif.: Sage Publications, 1982); Agit Singh, *Tanzania and the International Monetary Fund* (Cambridge, Mass.: Dept. of Applied Economics, Harvard University, 1983); and Cheryl Payer, *Tanzania and the World Bank* (Bergen, Norway: Christian Michelsen Institute, 1982).

8. Kuross Samii, *Involvement by Invitation: American Strategies of Containment in Iran* (University Park, Penn.: Pennsylvania State University Press, 1987); Jonathan

Marshall, Peter Dale Scott and Jane Hunter, *The Iran-Contra Connection: Secret Teams and Covert Operations in the Reagan Era* (Boston, Mass.: South End Press, 1987); Dilip Hiro, *Iran Under the Ayatollahs* (London: Routledge & Kegan Paul, 1985), pp. 317–331; and Richard Feinberg, *The Intemperate Zones: The Third World Challenge to U.S. Foreign Policy* (New York: W. W. Norton, 1983).

9. Hooshang Amirahmadi, "Destruction and Reconstruction: A Strategy for the War-Damaged Areas of Iran," *Disasters: The International Journal of Disaster Studies and Practice*, vol. 11, no. 2 (1987), pp. 134–147. See also Chapters 8 and 11 in this volume.

10. Hooshang Amirahmadi, "Economic Operations in Post-Revolutionary Iran: Major Impacts, Problems and Policy Directions," paper presented at the 20th Annual Meeting of the Middle East Studies Association of North America, Boston, November 20–23, 1986.

11. See Chapter 5 in this volume.

12. Tamas Szentes, *The Political Economy of Underdevelopment* (Budapest, Hungary: Academia Kiado, 1976); and J. Weaver and K. O. Jameson, *Economic Development: Competing Paradigms* (Washington, D.C.: University Press of America, 1981).

13. Hooshang Amirahmadi, "The Non-Capitalist Way of Development," *Review of Radical Political Economics*, vol. 19, no. 1 (Spring 1987), pp. 24–46.

14. Jose Luis Romero, *A History of Argentine Political Thought* (Stanford, Calif.: Stanford University Press , 1963); John Waterbury, *The Egypt of Nasser and Sadat* (Princeton, N.J.: Princeton University Press, 1983); Dean McHenry, *Tanzania's Ujamaa Villages: The Implementation of a Rural Development Strategy* (Berkeley, Calif.: University of California Press, 1979); and C. Young, "The Populist Socialist Pathway" in C. Young (ed.), *Ideology and Development in Africa* (New Haven, Conn.: Yale University Press, 1982). See also *World Development*, vol. 9, nos. 9–10 (1981) on Syria, Iraq, Burma, Angola, Guinea-Bissau, and Mozambique.

15. Jean Leca, "Algerian Socialism: Nationalism, Industrialization and State Building," in Helen Defosses and Jacques Levesque (eds.), *Socialism in the Third World* (New York: Praeger, 1982); T. A. Kofi, "Prospects and Problems of the Transition from Agrarianism to Socialism: The Case of Angola, Guinea-Bissau, and Mozambique," *World Development*, vol. 9, no. 9 (1981); A. F. Lowenthal, *The Peruvian Experience* (Princeton, N.J.: Princeton University Press, 1975); A Fenichel and A. Khan, "The Burmese Way to Socialism," *World Development*, vol. 9, nos. 9-10 (1981); Fouad Ajami, "Egypt's Retreat from Economic Nationalism," in G. Abdel-Khalek and R. Tignor (eds.) *The Political Economy of Income Distribution in Egypt* (New York: Holmes & Meier, 1982); and Alfred Stepan, *The State and Society: Peru in Comparative Perspective* (Princeton, N.J.: Princeton University Press, 1978).

16. Ruhullah Khomeini, *Islam and Revolution: Writings and Declarations of Imam Khomeini*. Translated and annotated by Hamid Algar (Berkeley, Calif.: Mizan Press, 1981); Albolhassan Banisadr, *The Fundamental Principles and Precepts of Islamic Government*. Translated from Persian by Mohammad R. Ghanooparvar (Lexington, Ky.: Mazda Publishers, 1981); Murtaza Mutahhari, *Fundamentals of Islamic Thought: God, Man and the Universe*. Translated from Persian by R. Campbell (Berkeley, Calif.: Mizan Press, 1985); Mahmud Taleghani, *Society and Economics in Islam*. Translated by R. Campbell (Berkeley, Calif.: Mizan Press, 1982); Mahmud Taleghani, *Islam and Ownership*. Translated from Persian by Ahmad Jabbari and Farhang Rajaee (Lexington, Ky.: Mazda Publishers, 1983); Ali Tehrani, *Eqtesad-e Islami* [The Islamic Economics]. In Persian (Mashhad: The Khorrasan Publishing House, 1974); Mohammad Baqir Sadr, *Islam Va Maktabha-ye Eqtesadi* [Islam and Schools of Economic Thought].

Translated from Arabic into Persian by Mohamad Nabi Zadeh (Qum: Mehr Publications, 1976). An English translation is available through the Muslim Students Association, North America; Ali Shari'ati, *On Sociology of Islam: Lectures.* Translated by Hamid Algar (Berkeley, Calif.: Mizan Press, 1982).

17. *Constitution of the Islamic Republic of Iran.* Translated by Hamid Algar (Berkeley, Calif.: Mizan Press, 1980).

18. Ministry of Plan and Budget, *Gouzaresh-e Eqtesadi-ye Sal-e 1363* [Economic Report of the Year 1984], in two volumes (Tehran: Ministry of Plan and Budget, 1985). See also Chapters 7 and 8 in this volume.

19. June Nash, Juan Corradi, and Hobart Spalding, Jr. (eds.), *Ideology and Social Change in Latin America* (New York: Gordon and Breach Science Publishers, 1977).

20. Shahrough Akhavi, *Religion and Politics in Contemporary Iran* (Albany, N.Y.: State University of New York Press, 1980); Said Amir Arjomand (ed.), *From Nationalism to Revolutionary Islam* (Albany, N.Y.: State University of New York Press, 1984), particularly Chapters 9 and 10; Hamid Algar, *The Roots of the Islamic Revolution* (London: The Open Press, 1983), pp. 71–98; Bashiriyeh, op. cit., pp. 53–83; and Chapter 1 in this volume.

21. Mansour Farhang, "How the Clergy Gained Power in Iran," in Barbara Freyer Stowasser (ed.), *The Islamic Impulse* (London: Croom Helm, 1987); and Bashiriyeh, op. cit., pp. 125–165.

22. Shaul Bakhash, *The Reign of the Ayatollahs: Iran and the Islamic Revolution* (New York: Basic Books, 1984); Abrahamian, op. cit.; and Bashiriyeh, op. cit. See also Chapter 3 in this volume.

23. Bashiriyeh, op. cit., pp. 125–165; Bakhash, op. cit., pp. 71–165; and Farhang, op. cit., pp. 157–174.

24. Cheryl Benard and Zalmay Khalilzad, *"The Government of God": Iran's Islamic Republic* (New York: Columbia University Press, 1984); and Hiro, op. cit., pp. 250–263. See also Chapter 9 in this volume.

25. Amit Bhaduri and M. A. Rahman (eds.), *Studies in Rural Participation* (New Delhi: Oxford Publication Co., 1982); and Richard Fagen et al., op. cit.

26. Benard and Khalilzad, op. cit., pp. 150–153; and Hiro, op. cit. See also Chapter 6 in this volume.

27. See Chapters 3 and 4 in this volume.

28. Sepehr Zabih, *Iran Since the Revolution* (Baltimore, Md.: Johns Hopkins University Press, 1982); Bernard and Khalilzad, op. cit.; and John D. Stempel, *Inside the Iranian Revolution* (Bloomington, Ind.: Indiana University Pres, 1981). See also Chapters 3 and 4 in this volume.

29. Roy P. Mottahedeh, *The Mantel of the Prophet* (New York: Simon and Schuster, 1985).

30. Abrahamian, op. cit.; Katouzian, op. cit.; Graham, op. cit.; and Halliday, op. cit.

31. Mahmoud Abdel-Fadil, *The Political Economy of Nasserism* (Cambridge: Cambridge University Press, 1980); Ciaes Brundenrus, *Revolutionary Cuba: The Challenge of Economic Growth with Equity* (Boulder, Colo.: Westview Press, 1983); Edmund W. Clark, *Socialist Development and Public Investment in Tanzania* (Toronto: University of Toronto Press, 1978); Lowenthal, op. cit.; James Mittelman, *Underdevelopment and the Transition to Socialism: Mozambique and Tanzania* (New York: Academic Press, 1981); and Andrew Coulson, *Tanzania: A Political Economy* (Oxford: Clarendon Press, 1982).

32. *Gouzaresh-e Eqtesadi-ye Sal-e 1363* [Economic Report of the Year 1984] (Tehran: Ministry of Plan and Budget, 1984), in two volumes; Bakhash, op. cit., pp.

166–239; and Amirahmadi, "Economic Operations," op. cit. See also Chapters 7, 8, and 11 in this volume.

33. Fereidun Fesharaki, *Revolution and Energy Policy in Iran* (London: Economist Intelligence Unit, 1980). See also Chapter 11 in this volume.

34. *Barnameh-e Avval-e Tous'ah Eqtesadi-Ejtema'i-Farhangi-ye Joumhouri-ye Islami-ye Iran, 1362–1366, Geld-e Avval: Hadafha Va Siasatha* [The First Economic-Social-Cultural Development Plan of the Islamic Republic, 1983–1988, volume one: Objectives and Policies] (Tehran: Ministry of Plan and Budget, 1983); *Gouzaresh-e Eqtesadi*, op. cit.; Razavi and Vakil, op. cit.; and Amirahmadi, "Economic Operations," op. cit. See also Chapter 7 in this volume.

35. Bakhash, op. cit., pp. 201–206; and Bashiriyeh, op. cit., pp. 140–143. See also Chapter 10 in this volume.

36. Bakhash, op. cit., pp. 185–190.

37. Ibid., pp. 189, 209, and 214.

38. See Chapter 7 in this volume.

39. Amirahmadi, "Economic Operations," op.cit.

40. See Chapter 8 in this volume.

41. These policy revisions are indicated in many official documents but most notably in the Annual Budget Laws, the Revised First Plan, and Annual Reports by the Central Bank. See also *Kayhan-e Hava'i*, June 25, 1986; January 7, 1987; April 8, 1987; September 3, 1986; January 22, 1986; July 2, 1986; June 25, 1986; March 18, 1987; August 31, 1983; November 6, 1985; and November 5, 1985; *Ettela'at* 7 Azar 1363 [1984]; *Iran Times*, June 20, 1986; January 24, 1986; June 6, 1986; *Ettela'at-e Siasi Va Eqtesadi*, nos. 1-9 (1986–1987); and *Economic Bulletin* (Tehran: Iran Press Digest, Echo of Iran), various issues.

42. *Gouzaresh-e Eqtesadi*, op. cit.; and Amirahmadi, "Economic Operations," op. cit.

43. See Chapter 12 in this volume.

44. Thomas Dean, *Post-Theistic Thinking: The Marxist-Christian Dialogue in Radical Perspective* (Philadelphia, Penn.: Temple University Press, 1975); Said Amir Arjomand, op. cit.

About the Contributors

Hooshang Amirahmadi holds a Ph.D. in city and regional planning from Cornell University and is an assistant professor in the Department of Urban Planning and Policy Development and director of Middle Eastern Studies at Rutgers University. He helped found the Center for Iranian Research and Analysis (CIRA) and is its current executive secretary. He has taught at Cornell University and Wells College. Dr. Amirahmadi's articles have appeared in the *Journal of Asia-Pacific and World Perspective, African Urban Quarterly, Journal of Planning Education and Research, Journal of Developing Areas, Review of Radical Political Economics, Third World Planning Review, Disasters: International Journal of Disaster Studies and Practice, Regional Development Dialogue*, and *Ethnic and Racial Studies*, among others. He is the editor (with W. W. Goldsmith) of "Third World Cities: Problems and Prospects," for the *Journal of Planning Education and Research*. Professor Amirahmadi has also authored several literary and social-scientific publications in Persian.

Manoucher Parvin holds a Ph.D. in economics from Columbia University. He is a professor of economics at the University of Akron and previously taught at Columbia University, Fordham University, and the City University of New York. Professor Parvin is currently president of the Middle East Economic Association and was a founder of the Society for Iranian Studies. He has served on the editorial and advising board of the *Journal of International Affairs*. His numerous articles have appeared in such publications as the *Journal of Economic Literature, Journal of Environmental Economics and Management, Journal of Management Science, Journal of Energy and Development, Orient, International Journal of Policy Analysis, Journal of American Economist, Journal of International Affairs, Journal of Energy, Journal of Conflict Resolution, Middle East Journal, International Journal of Middle East Studies*, and *Iranian Studies*, among others. Professor Parvin is also the author of a recent historical-political novel, *Cry for My Revolution, Iran*; he has written (in Persian) on chess, engineering, and social science.

Akbar Aghajanian holds a Ph.D. in sociology from Duke University and is an associate professor at Shiraz University, Iran. His articles have appeared in the *Journal of Comparative Family Studies, Journal of South Asian and Middle Eastern Studies, Journal of Marriage and the Family, International Journal of Middle East Studies, Genus*, and *Bio-Social Science*. He has written widely on the demography of Iran and has several publications in Persian.

Assef Bayat holds a Ph.D. from the University of Kent at Canterbury, England. He was a visiting research associate at the University of California, Berkeley, during 1985–1986 and is currently assistant professor of sociology at the American University in Cairo, Egypt. He is author of *Workers and Revolution in Iran: A Third World Experience of Workers' Control* and is currently editing *The Political Economy of Workers' Participation in the Third World.* He has also published in *MERIP Middle East Report.*

Sohrab Behdad holds a Ph.D. in economics from Michigan State University and was a member of the faculty of economics at Tehran University from 1973 to 1983. He is currently an assistant professor of economics at Denison University, Ohio. His articles have appeared in *Iranian Studies*, and one is forthcoming in the *International Journal of Middle East Studies.* Many of his works have been published in Iran.

Hamid Dabashi holds a Ph.D. in sociology from the University of Pennsylvania and is currently with the Middle East Center of the University of Texas, Austin. He has published in *Iranian Studies* and *Islamic Quarterly*, and has contributed writings to Thomas Robins and Ronald Robertson's book *Church-State Relations: Tensions and Transition*, and to *Contemporary Sociology*. His book *Shi'ism: Origins, Tradition, Present Realities*, co-edited with S. H. Nasr, is forthcoming.

Nader Entessar holds a Ph.D. from St. Louis University and is an associate professor and chairman of the Social Science Division at Spring Hill College, Mobile, Alabama. He has also served as a research associate at the Institute for International Political and Economic Studies in Tehran. His publications include *A Study on Chinese Foreign Policy* (in Persian and English), *Middle East Politics: A Developmental Approach* (in Persian), *Political Development in Chile: From Democratic Socialism to Dictatorship,* and several articles in such journals as *Third World Quarterly*, *Journal of South Asia and Middle East Studies*, and *Conflict Quarterly.*

Val Moghadam holds a Ph.D. in sociology from The American University and is a lecturer at New York University, Department of Sociology. Her articles have appered in such publications as *Monthly Review*, *The Review of Radical Political Economics*, *Iranian Studies*, and *International Sociology.* She has also contributed essays to two edited books.

Ali Mohammadi holds a Ph.D. from Teachers College, Columbia University. He has taught at Tehran University and the National University of Iran and now lectures in communications at Hunter College, City University of New York. With A. Sreberny-Mohammadi, he is currently working on an analysis of the political communication of Iranian exiles. He has published in *Third World Quarterly.*

Michael G. Renner holds a master's degree in international relations from the University of Amsterdam, the Netherlands. He is a member of Middle East Research Associates and was employed as a senior research associate at the World Policy Institute in New York. He is currently a research fellow with World Watch Institute in Washington, D.C. His articles have appeared in *Third World Quarterly* and *World Policy Journal.*

Annabelle Sreberny-Mohammadi holds a Ph.D. from Columbia University and is presently the coordinator of the Graduate Program in Media Studies at Queens College, City University of New York. She is founding editor of *Communications and Development Review* at the Iran Communications and Development Office in Tehran. She has published in the *Journal of Communication, The Guardian, MERIP Middle East Reports*, and *Third World Quarterly* and has edited a monograph on international news flow for UNESCO.

Majid Taghavi was awarded a Ph.D. from the University of Exeter in 1984. He has taught at Exeter and other universities in the United Kingdom.

Mehrdad Valibeigi holds an M.A. in sociology from George Washington University and is a Ph.D. candidate in economics at The American University in Washington, D.C.

Index